HALLOWED GROUND

REDISCOVERING OUR SPIRITUAL ROOTS

HALLOWED GROUND

REDISCOVERING OUR SPIRITUAL ROOTS

STEPHEN BURGARD

FOREWORD BY
BENJAMIN J. HUBBARD, PH.D.

 **INSIGHT BOOKS**

PLENUM PRESS · NEW YORK AND LONDON

Library of Congress Cataloging in Publication Data

Burgard, Stephen.
    Hallowed ground: rediscovering our spiritual roots / Stephen Burgard;
foreword by Benjamin J. Hubbard.
        p. cm.
    Includes bibliographical references and index.
    ISBN 0-306-45568-4
    1. Democracy—Religious aspects.   2. United States—History—Religious
aspects.   3. United States—Moral conditions.   4. United States—Politics and
government—1993–   I. Title.
BL2525.B86   1997   96-39457
291.1'7 '0973—dc21   CIP

ISBN 0-306-45568-4

© 1997 Stephen Burgard
Insight Books is a Division of Plenum Publishing Corporation
233 Spring Street, New York, N.Y. 10013-1578
http://www.plenum.com

An Insight Book

10 9 8 7 6 5 4 3 2 1

Printed in the United States of America

For Swami Sarvagatananda

For many years he has worked in and around the
university communities of Boston, Cambridge, and
Providence to advance the idea of the
harmony of religions.

Foreword

Steve Burgard's *Hallowed Ground: Rediscovering Our Spiritual Roots* is the right book to advocate for religion's importance to public life, just as Stephen Carter's *The Culture of Disbelief* was the right book a few years back. Where Carter argued against the marginalization of religion in public life primarily by citing court cases, Burgard does so by describing grassroots situations. Drawing mainly on examples from southern California, Burgard shows how religious groups from various points on the political and theological spectrum have been able to cooperate on a variety of issues—for example, gang violence, drug abuse, and ethnic and religious tensions—for the common good (and, Burgard would argue, for the common God!).

Burgard is convinced that religious people can disagree on matters theological and moral, yet agree that there are common problems of great magnitude that must be addressed by the religious community acting in concert. This variegated ensemble stretches on the Christian side from Methodists to Mormons, on the Jewish side from the ultra-Orthodox to the ultraliberal, on the Buddhist side from Sri Lankan–American conservative Theravadans to Japanese-American Mahayana liberals, and so on.

These groups can meet on the "hallowed ground" of spirituality—the common property of religion and of humankind in general. Burgard argues eloquently that no one religious tradition has a corner on the spirituality market. He is convinced that there is a "common core," a perennial philosophy behind the many traditions that make up the nation's religious landscape. In so doing, he echoes the work of philosopher of religion Huston Smith, whose 1995 conversations with Bill Moyers became the fine PBS series *The Wisdom of Faith with Huston Smith*.

Burgard's common-core theological approach will not be met with favor from religious conservatives, including the religious right. However, I would invite them to consider the following: Conservative Christians, Jews, and Muslims in America have more in common with liberal religionists than they realize—including support of the First Amendment guarantee of religious freedom, the core moral values they share (no one, for example, is pro-drugs, pro-gang violence, or pro-hate crimes!), and the virtue of tolerance (only the KKK and its cousin, the so-called Identity Church, would balk at tolerance, I presume).

Another example of how the diverse religious community can cooperate is through grassroots healthcare at the church–synagogue–mosque–temple level. As former president Jimmy Carter notes in an essay in the October 21, 1996 issue of *Time* magazine, 7000 religious congregations in the United States currently have trained healthcare personnel or "parish nurses" engaged in neighborhood work with the sick and elderly. What a wonderful way to serve the physical and spiritual needs of the sick! And few would argue that their faith has a corner on the compassion market. All the world's religions practice it in various ways, and everyone needs it when they are ill. Having recently experienced a serious illness, I can personally attest to the importance of having compassionate people around to help you heal.

Burgard is no doctrinaire liberal, either. For instance, on the matter of a moment of silence at the beginning of a public school day, he notes that it is hard to see how "a moment of calm and quiet in a world travelling at top speed" would not be "a useful statement about getting control over our collective lives" (p. 172). He further argues that the moment of silence is surely preferable to mandatory prayer (which would result in the cheapening of all religion, in my view).

Burgard also makes a call for overcoming the religious illiteracy so common in America. Most people know something about the theology, history, and traditions of their own faith but almost nothing about their coreligionists in this the most religiously diverse nation on earth. For example, there are 350 Buddhist temples in southern California alone, 4 million Muslims in a nation where they outnumber Methodists in Chicago, and one-half million Hindus nationwide. To heal the nation, we must become better informed about "the other" in our midst. If we do so, we will shatter stereotypes and build bridges of tolerance, understanding, and—as Burgard argues so well—cooperation.

In sum, Steve Burgard has done a real service to an American public tired of "culture wars." He has described the kinds of grassroots work that can go on between people with very different theologies but a core of common goals. His "moral middle" is where most Americans are and where society-changing work can happen.

BENJAMIN J. HUBBARD, PH.D.

Professor and Chair
Department of Religious Studies
California State University, Fullerton,
Fullerton, California

Preface

The idea for this book grew out of some editorial writing I did in the early 1990s for *The Los Angeles Times* in two general areas: the search for meaningful and constitutional ways of expressing religious values in our national life and the activities of faith-based activists to reinforce the viability of troubled local communities.

Also, although based in Orange County, I was working in downtown Los Angeles during the days immediately following the rioting in 1992. Witnessing the Rev. Cecil Murray and others work quickly to minister to the city's spirit, while there were troops in the streets, left an impression on me.

For a journalist, exploring the collective spiritual aspirations of Americans for a better society is a challenge. The press has been criticized for focusing too much on conflict in religion coverage and for missing the things that are important to ordinary Americans because it does much of its work among movers and shakers in a world driven by secular concerns and attitudes and dramatic developments. I'm convinced after more than 20 years on deadline, handling all sorts of news, that reporting on the current crisis of values involves paying attention not only to the larger boisterous conflict and to the search for personal meaning in individual lives, but also to community building at the local level.

This layered complexity is one reason it is so difficult to get the story right. The public is overwhelmed with data about our moral crisis, but there is little out there to "connect the dots" to help people understand the whole of our search for some spiritual bearings as a nation. I wrote this book because it is clear to me that a nation on the verge of a new century needs fresh, clear, and forward-looking thinking about the role of spiritual values in the new "public square"—that is, our shared experience in modern democracy.

I agree with the conclusion of one of our leading journalists, Bill Moyers, who said in a 1995 public television series entitled *On Values* that the search for spiritual significance in modern America was a crucial story in our time. Moyers has said he learned much about democracy from his boyhood at a small Texas church; likewise, my own preparation for writing about the country's spiritual dynamics began long before reporting on communities trying to cope with their problems.

As a boy, I served Mass and recited the liturgy in Latin alongside young friends whose Portuguese families on Cape Cod were making their way in American life in the manner of the apostles, as fishermen. Later, I was part of a small group of Brown University students who studied Indian philosophy, with some attention to the broad modern teachings of the nineteenth-century saint Ramakrishna and his emissary to the West, Swami Vivekananda.

Many of the ideas in this book have been bubbling for some time; in some cases, since before I took up journalism. Others, like the concept of the "moral middle," evolved as the 1990s unfolded. In the case of the latter idea, I became intrigued when the cable television industry's public affairs network, C-SPAN, opened the call-in lines at the 1992 Republican National Convention in Houston, and callers expressed their displeasure with what they were seeing. This random group of Americans, which seemed to be thoroughly mainstream in its general outlook, was appalled at the intolerance that was on display from the podium.

Finally, after working in newsrooms on both coasts, after witnessing firsthand the struggle of communities large and small to cope with their problems and to lift their vision, I have assembled some of my reporting and observations in this book about our "hallowed ground"—the place in the hopes and aspirations of a multiethnic nation where faith, democracy, and the future intersect.

Contents

PART III. L.A. STORY:
HOW THE RIOTS GOT PEOPLE THINKING

PART IV. CULTIVATING THE "MORAL MIDDLE"
FOR OUR FUTURE

Introduction

The dissonance in our politics over "family values," the struggle to rescue troubled communities, and the nation's fledgling attempts to reckon with conflicting perspectives over race, religion, and ethnicity are all signs of seismic shifts in American life as the country approaches a new millennium. Almost every pundit feels the earth creaking and has an explanation.

America seems to be struggling to identify a fresh set of principles around which to organize its common experience at a time that so many are alarmed about the moral direction of the society. This book explores some of that effort and goes on to suggest how the country might frame a new "spiritual style" to make religious values a more meaningful force in our common life. We hear a lot about relying on churches and religiously motivated individuals to do more in an era of limited government and emphasis on "personal responsibility." There has been very little written to explore or clarify exactly what that will have to be all about in a new multiethnic society.

In a nation of many perspectives, religion offers modern democracy its services as the one reliable unifier. The lesson is coming home that our professed allegiance to democratic values and privileges may not be enough by itself to see us through times of conflict and division. Democracy tells us that we all share the same hopes and the same constitution with its vitally important separation of church and state. The free exercise of religion supports and sustains this democratic experience and suggests that there are avenues of bringing Americans together in ways that go deeper than allegiance to the political system.

The good news is that the nation is slowly developing a reservoir of shared spiritual resources. Evidence of this is reported here, offering some prospects for overcoming the crisis of values that has attended the deterioration of life in our communities and for getting beyond racial and ethnic divisions. But there is much to do.

Much of the important work of finding common spiritual ground in a multiethnic society is in its infancy. That realization ought to sober us. The first two-thirds of this book deal with two aspects of this condition. In Part I, we shall see America in ideological conflict, a nation too far apart over the proper role of religious values in American life. In Parts II and III, we explore the work of some of the pioneers who are acting as transitional figures for a country trying to find its spiritual bearings. The conclusion points the way to a new accommodation for religious values in a multiethnic society.

The book finishes with a challenge that the country does not seem to be willing to heed just yet. We know that religion is a powerful current in American life, but that alone may not be enough to do us sufficient good. We need to make religion the unifier it can and must be. That means we and future generations will have to be less wedded to religious dogmas, hierarchies, and traditions, at least to the extent that they make exclusive claims on their followers. That will not be easy for many to do. Even some of the forward-looking participants on the interfaith front seem at times tentative in their acknowledgment that others also are proud possessors of windows on ultimate truth, or God.

If we cannot respect and accept others on the level of their core beliefs, our restive society always will stand on shaky ground. In the future, Americans will have to be more willing to regard the messengers and messages of all faiths as assets belonging to all people. This may require rethinking some cherished parochial beliefs.

Along that rocky road to a meaningful accommodation, however, we will learn something in the middle part of this book that should cheer us on. Sheer pragmatism, a quality of American life that saw us through depression and war in the twentieth century, is very much in evidence on the spiritual front lines today, where people are trying to make sense of religious, ethnic, and racial divisions. Already it has gathered groups otherwise opposed on ideological grounds with the larger objective of saving communities from destruction.

This book's most sobering conclusion is that we remain far from where we will need to be in the future to avoid being locked in recurring conflict over such explosive issues as race, ethnicity, and sexuality. As it now stands, some of the people who have identified a moral crisis in the country from religious platforms are the very instigators plunging the society deeper into division. We should not underestimate the potential harm that will result from having the custodians of values be the ones to drive wedges between us.

The polarized national discourse over values contrasts with more quiet work being done by ordinary citizens and clergy who believe that the nation needs a stronger role for religious impulses in American life. The latter are faith activists who are more broad-minded and moderate than some of the cultural and religious conservatives who are getting so much notice as the so-called "religious right." They are the ones transforming rigid institutions into responsive and even radical forces for the betterment of society.

The hour is late, and their voices are not loud. We are not anywhere near as far along the road as we need to be in developing and acting on a set of universal spiritual principles to inform our common life in an unwieldy democracy.

The religious conservatives who are politically active have been basking in the attention and influence derived from their social and cultural agendas. They have enjoyed considerable clout, especially within the Republican Party, where their power to shape a party platform was evident in San Diego in 1996. But this book will suggest, among other things, that while the religious right has been successful in identifying concerns that are out there and in getting the attention of politicians, its gains in the sphere of public policy may prove to be relatively short term. Its impact is being felt, and it is likely to be a force for a long time. However, it may not be able to sustain the influence in the policy realm its supporters would like, and it need not pose the threat its detractors fear.

One reason for this is that while the religious right derives ideology and enthusiasm from the political right, its clout at any time is a reflection of the concerns of the political and moral *center*. Again, good old-fashioned American pragmatism is a constructive asset in our national moral arsenal for combating extremism. The country has a practical but increasingly concerned and in some cases engaged middle ground of religiously motivated Americans of good will. To a point, they share with religious conservatives a potent set of values-based concerns about the challenges to the family and the moral direction of the country.

Americans regularly demonstrate a facility for separating messages with which they agree from objectionable messengers who may affix themselves to them. For example, there were African Americans who managed to support the constructive themes of the Million Man March in the fall of 1995 even as they sought to transcend the controversy over Minister Louis Farrakhan.

Can the nation do this on a sustained basis to help us all pull together? Being hopeful about the future of democracy likely means having faith in the power in this group in the center. The politicians certainly recognize a need to address these concerns. It was the prospect of turning off the center that prompted the Republicans of San Diego in 1996 to present a different message from the podium than was contained in the platform. Alternatively, the movement to the center of Democrats under Bill Clinton after 1994, and on to the Chicago convention of 1996, was in part an acknowledgment of the moral preoccupations of a great group of Americans in the middle.

There may be a temptation to overstate the influence of the most extreme politically active religious conservatives. Some of the very Americans who are put off by Pat Robertson and others also happen to agree that there needs to be a much fuller play of religious ideas and values in American society. But they are shrewd enough to size things up for themselves. Their response to the perceived crisis of spirit in America is informed more by common sense and toleration than is evident in the pronouncements of some political activists. They also are put off by a perceived indifference to religious concerns that they see on the left.

For the long term, this group has more clout than perhaps it realizes, both for keeping democracy on keel and for answering basic questions about what our society will be like. The greatest danger is not that these people will be swayed by extremists, but that they will do nothing. If this group fails to step up to the challenge of finding innovative ways of bringing their spiritual values into the public square, the extreme wing of the religious right and others misusing religious themes will be only too eager to speak on behalf of everybody else.

Today, the nation is struggling with bringing faith more actively and openly into its common life. How might this be done if it is acceptable to do so? It is one thing to say, as some are, that we should embrace religious values and not drive them from the public square. If we can manage this without violating the separation of church and state, well and good. It is a more dubious proposition to suggest, as others are, that particular policy positions, say, vouchers for school choice or amending the constitution to have a balanced budget, are the solutions that must be derived from religious principles. The Christian Coalition's "Contract with the American Family," issued in the spring of 1995, demonstrated the conceit of turning God's will into a position paper.

In considering the free exercise of religion, our great national charter under the First Amendment, we find ourselves asking with increasing regularity how we feel about the fact that people are bringing religious perspectives into the fray at all—and how we feel about the specific answers they are offering. We are, in fact, in the midst of a national reassessment of the character of religion in our common life. This is true not just over policy matters but also over the actual content of religious ideas.

The argument for a fuller role for religious values, advanced mostly but not exclusively by conservative intellectuals, usually has come around in a fairly limited circle. To date, it has focused largely on the perspectives of Christians and Jews, the traditional mainline groups in the country's history. This book will argue that a broader transformation of the religion-based values landscape is already underway. It has powerful implications for how the country will succeed in living up to its highest ideals in the new century unfolding before us.

Today, there are important things going on outside the traditional mainstream faiths. Our new diversity, brought on by recent immigration, inevitably is changing some of the country's spiritual focus, but it is also bringing the possibility of new answers to our problems.

On the national scene today, the people who inhabit the intangible moral center of the country seem willing to experiment with fresh approaches to our problems, while to the left and right, others are operating from rigid positions about what God and country should and should not mean. Whatever our point of view, the role of religion concerns our deepest aspirations. My hope is that this book will shed light on the discussion and help people think in broad and less predictable new ways about religious values in our shared democratic experience.

Part I

America Is Divided
Where It Ought to Be United

Chapter One

The Language of "Values" Is Doing Us In

Three broad spiritual arenas exist in America as it stands at the close of a century. At the national level, a fractious debate over the proper role of religious values in our common life is being conducted. At the same time, a moral and spiritual dialogue is evolving at the grassroots level in neighborhoods, between congregations, and even between members of the religious community and local government. The third area encompasses the individual and the search for "meaning" that finds expression in both traditional and new and unconventional forms of piety.

We seem to be doing reasonably well as a nation in the second and third of these areas. The print and electronic press are full of accounts of burgeoning religiosity, both traditional and New Age, and public concern with values necessarily draws religious perspectives into discussions of right and wrong. Public opinion polls reveal an abiding concern in the general population with the fabric of society.

However, the first of these arenas—religion in our common life—finds the nation on ground that is much less firm. On the face of it, it would seem that it ought to be easy enough to frame a kind of accommodation in which public religiosity does not rip the country asunder, strain the line of church and state, and make people feel that religious expression in just another form of bigotry. In fact, we are not having an easy time of it. Much of the discussion about the place of religious values in what is called "the public square"—that is, our shared democratic experience—is being either clouded by politics or conducted by those who tend to hold the most extreme views on both the left and the right. The public, meanwhile, seems to be of a somewhat uncertain mind.

A poll by *U.S. News & World Report* conducted in 1994 found a paradox: 65 percent of Americans believed that religion was losing its influence on American life, yet 62 percent said that religion was increasing in importance to them personally. A full 78 percent were looking to a constitutional office, the presidency, for moral and spiritual leadership, and three decades after the U.S. Supreme Court ruled prayer in public schools unconstitutional, nearly 65 percent would approve if the court now found a moment of silent prayer acceptable.[1]

Meanwhile, politically active religious conservatives, "the religious right," have been having a field day, but not without taking some lumps along the way. In 1994, they exercised unprecedented influence in national politics, building on success in local and state campaigns in earlier years to help Republicans win many races across the country. Millions of dollars were spent on voter education campaigns; *Time* magazine reported that the Christian Coalition, the most important and influential of these groups, spent $2 million distributing 33 million voter guides to 60,000 churches nationally.[2] The coalition, for one, was not bashful about laying claim to influence in House and gubernatorial races, even though a *Wall Street Journal*/NBC poll found that 12 percent of those who voted said a religious right endorsement mattered, 35 percent said the opposite.[3]

By the presidential election year of 1996, religious conservatives even were viewing confidently their differences over Republican candidates as a sign of maturity and clout.[4] At the Republican National Convention in San Diego in 1996, the party overall made a conscious effort to put on a moderate face, but the considerable influence of religious conservatives was abundantly clear in the party platform. They also were poised to fight another day; Gary Bauer, president of the Family Research Center, told partygoers under a tent at Sea World that their celebration would take place inside the party's convention hall, rather than outside, in the year 2000.[5]

Their influence over their party's agenda was so complete that during the final months of the 1996 presidential campaign, the Christian Coalition was denouncing the incumbent Democratic president on character grounds at its annual convention, and its executive director, Ralph Reed, was complaining aloud that the Republican candidate, Bob Dole, was not doing enough in this area. This was so even as President Clinton appeared to be running well in the polls with evangelical Christians and other voters concerned with traditional social values.[6]

In Washington, the House Republican leadership long since had been sufficiently impressed to promise a vote after the 1994 election on a prayer amendment in the schools, a pledge that later evolved into the aim of having a religious freedom bill or even a new "Religious Equality Amendment." In May 1995, the Christian Coalition presented its "Contract with the American Family," which was modeled on the GOP's "Contract with America," and issued it at a Washington press conference attended by House Speaker Newt Gingrich (R-Georgia), and U.S. Senator Phil Gramm (R-Texas). The contract included the amendment as well as a number of specific public policy positions, including tax cuts, local control of education, and new restrictions on abortion.

This political activism in recent years raised concerns on the left about separation of church and state and questions on the right as old as the political ideal of having freedom of religion about whether political involvement corrupts the purity of vision of the faithful.

This also has contributed to the uneasiness in the nation on the moral and spiritual front and to a two-track discussion in the public sphere about values. On the national stage, there has been a bitter political debate between the left and the right about the proper role of moral and religion-based values in the realm of public policy. The contentiousness has been carried on amid a fundamental area of agreement, namely the importance of these values to ordinary Americans. The content of the political conventions of 1996 demonstrated the degree to which concern with social issues such as the welfare of children and family have become common currency in the nation's political discourse. At the local level, there has been, as we shall see in Parts II and III of this book, a more quiet exploration of areas of agreement for addressing some of these social and family concerns.

RELIGIOUS VALUES AND PUBLIC DISCORD

The most obvious answer to the question about what might be achievable is that there is no good reason why we can't have fuller play for a religious sensibility in public life provided that it is constitutional. We know from our own history the founders' religious concerns even as they established a secular government. Today, we have ample evidence of interfaith efforts in various communities. Yet on the national stage, mobilizing "values" has often meant political warfare.

Why this is so may have something to do with the nature of public conversation in an unwieldy and fractious society. It may also be that important big themes have a way of getting reduced to quibbling over gray areas in the warfare over agendas on the national stage. For example, there obviously is a serious church–state separation question raised if groups funded by the government were to engage in proselytizing. However, would it really be so harmful to poor people—that is, would it subject them to undue influence—if they happened to see religious symbols on the walls of a church facility where they went to receive social services? This narrow question was debated in Washington during the wrangling in 1996 over changes in the welfare system.

Violence in the neighborhood, by contrast, has a way of focusing the mind rather quickly on the big picture of community survival and sustenance. Having children and families at peril on the front lines of society certainly puts things into perspective. In the Beltway, talk is plentiful currency, and indeed an industry unto itself, on radio and television, in political campaigns, and among special interest groups, congressional leaders, and opinion leaders.

Ideological warfare has marked the pursuit of political objectives on the stage of contemporary culture. Religious conservatives certainly have done this in pursuing their agenda. They complain about being unfairly criticized "for having imported the contaminating elements of religion into the pure air of politics," as the conservative intellectual Irving Kristol put it in a *Wall Street Journal* op-ed article.[7] But they cannot dismiss so easily the church–state separation concerns of liberals. This is so although religious conservatives make a compelling case for not excluding religious sentiment from the public square and, as Kristol did, deplore a prevailing secularism in American life since 1950.

One of the most illustrative instances of this problem, and indeed, one of the most decisive moments in the 1992 presidential campaign, came when the conservative columnist Pat Buchanan took the podium at the Republican National Convention and proclaimed, "There is a religious war going on for the soul of America." The remarks set an unpleasant tone for the entire convention and proved to be a benchmark in the developing rancor over what otherwise ought to be an area of agreement: the pervasive dissatisfaction that many Americans feel about the nation's moral and religious climate. The remarks became fodder for columnists deploring the divisive politics of the moment and so profoundly influenced the general perception of the 1992 Houston gathering that they contributed to shaping the moderate convention strategy of Republicans four years later in San Diego.

The current round of political activism of Christian fundamentalists that preceded that moment had roots during the Carter administration. During battles over the Equal Rights Amendment, gay rights, abortion, and other issues, morality became the stuff of polemics. By 1980, Jerry Falwell's Moral Majority had met privately with Republican presidential candidate Ronald Reagan and was active in influencing the party's convention platform. Reagan, the political figure who successfully bonded various political elements in the conservative movement, courted religious fundamentalists during his presidency but also kept them discretely at bay. It was significant that, as his party's elder statesman, and somewhat liberated by having his campaigns behind him, Reagan delivered a speech at the 1992 Republican convention that sharply contrasted with Buchanan's in tone and spirit. He said, "I see possibilities as vast and diverse as the American family itself."

By this time, however, the battle had been joined fully on religious territory for the moral high ground in America. Politically active fundamentalists had, like Buchanan, mobilized language in a cause to rescue America from moral decline.

Others who did not share their vision saw this attempt to influence public policy through the political process as an outright assault on pluralism and the separation of church and state. The apparent public rejection of the strident political messages of that convention, which became more apparent with the passage of time, suggested that many who may have shared the fundamentalists' concerns about the moral fabric were at the same time uncomfortable with their tone and rhetoric.

That did not stop the politically active fundamentalists from speaking as if they were the custodians of the nation's morality. Nor did steady public concern about a crisis in American life abate. The years immediately after the 1992 convention produced a series of skirmishes between liberals and religious conservatives over the very meaning of values in modern America. In one classic collision of perspectives on values, voters in Vista, California, recalled several religious conservatives from the school board who were pursuing a narrow ideological agenda. This reversal was in a sense a recognition by a sufficient portion of the local electorate that language with which they initially agreed in principle had been misappropriated.

It was evident in the early going of the 1996 presidential election year that some of the partisans continued to believe that they had the exclusive claim on the language of morality and family. For example, Ralph Reed, the executive director of the Christian Coalition, suggested at one point early on that the departure of former vice president Dan Quayle from the field meant that the "family values" mantle was up for grabs. The Republican Party for months thereafter jockeyed for positioning on candidates acceptable to social conservatives, absurd as it might be to suggest that one group or candidate could make exclusive claims.

WHOSE "FAMILY VALUES" ARE BEST?

By contrast, perspectives on the "family values" debate have a way of being more pragmatic down on the ground in communities affected directly by problems like gang violence that tear at the sense of civic well-being.

The Rev. Stephen Mather of the First Presbyterian Church in Anaheim, California, is a thoughtful frontline activist who we will get to know more about later through his work with an interfaith group working to shore up the community. Through his work while he was chairman of Planned Parenthood in conservative Orange County and as a target of Operation Rescue protests, he also knows something about the divisive power of social issues. He believes that in the national debate over morality, "The key is how different groups make the best use of language. That's what the next few years will determine." Mather, in the thick of his own community's unique experiment in faith activism, says that many mainstream people of moral and religious persuasion are reluctant "to put their feet in the water" when they look around them and see the intensity and unpleasantness of the nation's discourse over values. He asserts that many adults "are looking at the same data and coming to radically different conclusions."[8]

Indeed, at the national level as the Christian Coalition was about to unveil its "Contract with the American Family," a group of ecumenical Christian leaders responded in an entirely different way to their own perceived concerns, suggesting the alternative morality-based views that are out there in America. They readied a statement saying that the nation was caught in a spiritual crisis aggravated by the mobilization of churches to advance politicized agendas. "The Cry for Renewal: Let Other Voices Be Heard" warned of the identification of the "religious right" with the Republican congressional majority in Washington, and it criticized religious liberals for being so closely identified with the Democrats.[9]

The identification of Christian fundamentalists and their political suitors with the term "family values," often to the exclusion of other perspectives, is itself an illustration of the inflamed rhetoric that has clouded shared concerns about the moral health of the nation. The fact is, Americans all across the political spectrum—and across ethnic and religious lines—have come to be deeply concerned with the fate of the family unit, in whatever size or shape it may come nowadays. Also, newer Americans who are Muslims, Hindus, and Sikhs have drawn their own conclusions that are based much more on their own experiences and perceptions of threats to quality of life than on the politics of left and right.

In this fluid battle over language, mainstream churches can have leverage if they recognize an inherent asset simply in having been around awhile in a changing society and in being, as Mather puts it, "here to stay," with all that it suggests about constancy, about having facilities such as schools and meeting places available, and about long-term commitment to individual communities. He believes that if ordinary people acting out of religious and moral motivation can learn to operate within the give-and-take of the political process, the model of activism "may change the larger perception that politics is dirty and cynical."[10] In other words, the old-line churches, which are perceived by some to have been declining in influence, need not be out of the loop in the current debate over values and need not be excluded from partnerships with some of the newer religious groups. Nor do they have to cede the language of "values" and "family" to others who have made claims to it.

THE CLEVER MANIPULATION OF LANGUAGE

In the meantime, the language of family and values has been mobilized brazenly by religious conservatives as a wedge to advance particular political perspectives or policy positions, as if God himself had relayed the right position on welfare reform or fiscal policy. For example, in an article written for *The Wall Street Journal* claiming "unity on the right," Reed of the Christian Coalition marshaled the language of religious values to argue that concerns about government's effect on business and those of religious conservatives went hand in hand. The conclusion drawn was that there was no place for government as a solution to America's problems and that "traditionalist ends can be advanced through libertarian means."[11]

Many readers in the audience of elite business leaders no doubt would agree with the recitation of failed government initiatives in the face of a declining moral climate that Reed recited. But did that mean that government should be dismantled entirely? Reed wrapped this position cleverly in an observation that might enlist the agreement of a much broader group of Americans: "too often, a scowling intolerance greets those who bring their faith to bear in the public square." On closer examination, however, it turned out that even that observation had its own particular policy aim, Reed's call for "a religious liberty statute and constitutional amendment."[12]

In 1995, some Christian leaders issued a statement challenging the religious right in an attempt to reclaim Christianity from the partisan political sphere and to restore its true spiritual meaning. The Rev. Jim Wallis, a leader of a coalition of evangelical, mainline Protestant, Catholic, Greek Orthodox, and African-American church members named Call to Renewal, lamented that religion had become mobilized for partisan purposes. He said, "Even the word 'Christian' has become associated with a particular brand of very conservative Republican politics."[13] Wallis, editor of *Sojourners* magazine, later met with his group in Washington at the same time the Christian Coalition was meeting for its 1996 convention, and warned that if the Republicans were defeated at the polls, "the religious right is going to be left holding the bag" for having pushed that party's agenda so far to the right.[14]

There have been other strong reactions, some at the local level, from groups like the southern California-based Progressive Religious Alliance, whose leadership included Unitarians, Jews, Episcopalians, Methodists, and Seventh-day Adventists. In 1996, in response to perceived divisiveness caused by religious conservatives, it sought to emphasize abortion rights, equal rights for homosexuals, immigrants' rights, and separation of church and state. For example, among those supporting its emphasis on diversity was the Rev. Nancy Wilson, of the Metropolitan Community Church of Los Angeles, which has a large gay and lesbian congregation.[15]

Moreover, there were Republican women who felt increasingly uncomfortable with the rightward drift of their party as a result of the activism of religious conservatives. For example, Eileen Padberg, a political consultant in California, told *The Los Angeles Times* as the 1996 presidential campaign unfolded that her party was pushing women out and that, "Religious and family values should be defined by individuals and not by government. It's gone too far."[16]

Reed, however, turns out to be a complicated figure, adaptable and capable of articulating a broad moral vision. On another occasion, when *People* magazine profiled him, he said, "We want to include our black and brown and yellow brothers and sisters. That will help our coalition have a friendlier face."[17] In April 1995, when relations between the Christian Coalition and the Anti-Defamation League of B'nai B'rith had become especially chilly, he deplored anti-Semitism, said it was wrong for the religious right to talk about the United States as a "Christian nation," and pledged to inform members of his 1.5 million member coalition of the history of the persecution of Jews.[18]

In the middle of the Republican Party's preconvention angst over platform language in 1996, Reed's book *Active Faith* raised the question of whether Christian conservatives would be marginalizing themselves by insisting on a constitutional amendment to ban abortion.[19] The failure of that view to prevail during the Republican platform debate in 1996 was a significant indication that as a political movement, the Christian Coalition was at a crossroads that tested its very maturity; that is, it faced a choice between pursuing the uncompromising objectives of its most hard-line members or joining the mainstream of coalition politics.

In his earlier book, *Politically Incorrect*, Reed seemed to recognize that achieving his objectives could be facilitated by broadening the base of his organization to include minorities who feel morally disenfranchised by the Democratic Party.[20] Were the Christian Coalition called something else, were it more broad-based in its religious inclusion, and were it not tinkering with specific policy, it might be a lot more formidable than it is. Those are big ifs, and then there is the matter of Reed's boss, Pat Robertson.

In a remarkable book, *The Religious Right: The Assault on Tolerance & Pluralism in America*, the Anti-Defamation League charts Robertson's statements as a figure who has far more on his mind than wishing that religious values had a better standing in a materialistic society. In 1992, for example, he suggested in a newsletter that the 1990s would be a period of potentially bloody confrontations over institutions. He likened Christians in "liberal America" to Jews in Nazi Germany, suggested that the idea of separation of church and state was a Soviet concept, and made anti-Jewish pronouncements. His 1991 book, *The New World Order*, envisioned a godless world brought into being by a cabal under the direction of Lucifer.[21]

New York Times columnist Frank Rich suggested at the time that the kinder, gentler rhetoric of Reed was no accident; it was a deliberate effort to put a more reassuring figure than Robertson out front to soothe and deceive mainstream Republicans. He wrote, "In a country with so short a memory, many have forgotten that if you buy Reed, you're buying Robertson—that the former works for the latter, not the other way around."[22] Whatever the strategy of the Christian Coalition brain trust, Robertson in 1995 was under sufficient fire that he was forced to defend a 4-year-old book after a critical review in the *New York Review of Books*. He denied his book had any intention of being anti-Semitic and said he had actively lobbied for Israel and had many friends and allies among Jews.[23] With Robertson vigorously asserting his sympathy with Jewish causes, the lesson of the need for inclusiveness in any movement claiming to be based in moral and religious values was coming home to the Christian Coalition—or at least to Reed—

after a period of capitalizing on the power of moral language with which many Americans no doubt agreed.

PUBLIC MORALITY AND BROAD COALITIONS

The Christian Coalition, through Reed's attempts, seemed to be recognizing the need to engage in outreach efforts and that there was a more tolerant moral mainstream out there to be mined. The people who could be attracted by the coalition's larger message of a nation at moral risk were not necessarily those with uncompromising positions on the social issues with which the coalition became associated as Republicans were figuring out who to put up against Bill Clinton.

But a fundamental problem presented itself to Reed and company at the Republican National Convention in 1996; his call for focusing on strategies that would reduce the number of abortions seemed to get lost in the resolve of hard-liners to amend the constitution to ban them outright. The difficulty the country has been having in conducting a discussion on abortion without getting derailed by platform language, court cases, and constitutional strategies is itself a striking testimony to the polarization in our politics.

The middle ground is in fact peopled with religiously motivated Americans who may hold complex and varying positions on matters not easily summarized in the "family values" sound bite. For example, there are those who may want to see the number of abortions conducted annually reduced, but who still want them kept safe and legal.

Or, to cite another example, there are those who may find homosexuality an anathema or at least a puzzle, but who believe that gays should be treated with dignity. Indeed, in spite of the hostility of some religious conservatives, many gays and lesbians like those involved in the Los Angeles coalition that aimed to present an alternative viewpoint are deeply concerned with questions related to family and religion. In 1995, the half-sister of

House Speaker Newt Gingrich (R-Georgia) demonstrated the complexity of the entire "family values" debate by traveling around the country to such places as conservative Orange County, California, reminding Americans that gays and lesbians are "part of America and American families. We don't come from dysfunctional or strange or odd families."[24]

The language of morality exists in a real world where, as in all things political, it may be necessary to build broad coalitions that are sustained by compromise. Depending on who is doing the talking, the language of public morality can be affected by a host of political, ethnic, and religious considerations.

It is easy for moderates in the current national atmosphere to fall behind or be shouted down. It is safer for many of those who are churchgoers or religiously inclined who believe in putting their shoulders to the wheel to do their work out of the line of fire at the local level. Or, as the journalist Bill Moyers suggested in more general terms in an interview on the PBS series *On Values*, there are people who are tuning out the noise they hear in favor of pursuing more personal moral and religious objectives.

A contributing factor to the polarization at the national level is that the people most likely to directly challenge religious conservatives for time at the national microphone likely are those who want to see religion entirely kept out of the public square and practiced almost entirely in private. Their statements can appear extreme in contrast to the nation's moral and religious center, and they make targets for ideologues on the right. Many Americans who are less vocal generally agree that the nation needs to make room for the play of religious values in a society that doesn't seem to them to be doing all that well as a moral enterprise.

One significant suggestion on bridging the nation's divisions without the explicit help of religion was floated by National Endowment for the Humanities leader Sheldon Hackney, who said in 1994 that the nation needed to conduct "a national debate" on values. It was a worthwhile idea, but if discussion of values in an entirely secular setting is useful, it may fall short for the many Americans whose morality is inspired by religious conviction.

After all, for most religious people, values and moral conduct are informed by a religious base; without the latter, normative behavior may seem optional or give way to self-interest.

Many conservatives, by the way, are acutely aware of the power of religious sentiment beyond simply the expression of support for "values." The emphasis they place on the uniqueness of religion-based values turns up in another context: their argument that introducing sanitized prayer for common consumption into the public schools does nobody any good and could strip religion of its force.

Since some the national polling of the early 1990s suggests that many Americans who describe themselves as religious do in fact agree with the fundamental premise of Reed and others about a moral crisis, broad attacks on the religious right can be interpreted as efforts by liberals to impose their secular values on a majority motivated and inspired by faith, not as defenses of pluralism.

In the political war of words, there is high risk for Democrats like Representative Vic Fazio, a Californian who as chairman of the Democratic Congressional Campaign Committee lashed out at what he termed the "Christian radical right." Indeed, it was precisely this kind of sentiment that Reed was claiming victory over in his *Wall Street Journal* article.[25] John C. Green, a political science professor at the University of Akron, has summarized the dilemma facing the secular critics of religious conservatives: "This business of bashing the religious right inspires a certain fear in people. What if it's interpreted as bashing religious people?"[26]

The answer in part may be that those who openly contest the religious right's vision of America have not done anywhere near as much to neutralize their impact as the religious right has done itself. It is through their own limited vision of the ideas behind language that, on its face, is broad and spiritually meaningful that politically active fundamentalists have distracted others from the real work of bringing Americans of spiritual good will together. Without a fuller participation of America's many religious and ethnic groups, the debate over values looks more like a last stand for those who refuse to recognize that the country has changed.

The Christian Coalition has sensed the need to include minorities in its moral initiatives, but except for its defensive overtures to the Jewish community, it is far from reckoning with the true religious pluralism of the country.

THE MODERATES ARE MISSING

There are, in fact, far more strident voices on the religious right than the Christian Coalition and groups like the Family Research Center, whose leader talked in San Diego of better days to come. The cumulative result is that rather than arriving at a consensus over a remedial course of action for the nation, we have become a society whose intellectual leadership is essentially polarized on the very question of values that many hope might help the nation deal with its problems. Many people's response to this "noise" is to simply back away and pursue their own private moral and spiritual endeavors.

Trying to conduct urgent national business on the poles is not restricted to the values arena these days. The political writer David Broder, for example, has noted that there are fewer moderates in political parties at the national level. It may be that it is becoming more difficult for people of good intention to occupy middle ground on either politics or religion, and that this is so at precisely the time that consensus is most needed. By early 1995, there was a sense on the part of analysts like Martin P. Wattenberg, a political scientist at the University of California, Irvine, that "The middle is not being occupied, and that's where most of the people are."[27]

A seminal survey conducted by the Times Mirror Center for the People and the Press before the important 1994 election found Americans "angry, self-absorbed, and politically unanchored." The polling uncovered divisions within the Republican and Democratic parties and an appeal for "some alternative to the traditional two-party system." The survey found polarization on social policy and cultural issues and that the public was "two-minded about social change. While the vast majority feels that women should not return to their traditional role in society, eight in ten say they have old-fashioned values about family and marriage, and three in four think that too many children are sent to day care."[28]

Polarization at the national level had become so extreme by 1995 that some were wondering about basic civility in the society at large and a disconnection of that debate from the concerns of ordinary people. Senator Bill Bradley (D-New Jersey), whose announcement in the summer of 1995 that he would not seek reelection caused a stir in presidential politics, was one of the people to address the topic in a speech given earlier that year at the National Press Club. He cast the debate in terms of fixed political ideology:

> Crudely put, government action versus the free market utterly dominate our sense of the possible, or sense of what is relevant in and meaningful in public affairs. Yet the issues that most concern Americans today seem to have little direct connection with either the market or government. Consider the plague of violence, guns, and drugs; the racial tensions that afflict so many communities; the turmoil in public education; the deterioration of American families.[29]

Ironically, the national discussion over "family values" ought to be something we could be energized by, or maybe even feel good about. Instead, it is a battle that has been joined with the volume turned up loud.

Chapter Two

Strutting the Politics of Virtue

As suggested at the end of the preceding chapter, the polarization of our national dialogue over political philosophy and public policy provides a framework for understanding why the narrower discussion over "family values" and the role of religion in society is also so conflicted.

Ronald Brownstein, a *Los Angeles Times* political writer, has observed that in the policy area,

> It remains uncertain that the political system can deliver change that reflects the broad consensus in public opinion.... On issues from health care to deficit reduction to crime, polarization has appeared to be the oxygen of the political system, equally indispensable as an organizing tool for liberals and conservatives alike.[1]

This dynamic applies also to the debate over values, even in the midst of shared perceptions that the nation's backbone needs shoring up. The revival of modern Protestant fundamentalism in the 1970s as a political force that found expression in the Moral Majority was a reaction to a perception that a liberal and secular culture was coming unraveled.[2]

The sense that public morality was in decline, the dissatisfaction over the Supreme Court's pronouncements on prayer in the public schools, the civil rights movement, and the explosion of demands from new and different interest groups in a complex society drove religious conservatives out of the gate in their political activism. Recent news has only reinforced perceptions of a moral crisis: for example, concerns that surfaced during the 1996 presidential election about increased drug use among teenagers and discouraging revelations about children having children.

While the religious right since has cemented its identification with a particular set of positions on social issues, its core concerns about the fabric of society are now shared by a much broader group of Americans. However, even as this has happened, the debate on the national stage has been conducted in extremes.

Our diversity is our strength, but we must live with the fact that national consensus is going to be elusive in a nation that consciously separates church and state, renounces the establishment of an official religion, and promotes religious pluralism. People can talk about the same democratic values but bring very different perspectives to the table.

The national welfare debate provides a parallel in the policy area to this division. It is an area where, as in the case of "family values," many on both sides of the political debate by the mid-1990s agreed that improvement was needed. But there was still deep division over exactly what to do, and this division was fueled by the political components of decisions having to do with what it is that a society considers important. Even with a growing consensus that more "personal responsibility" was needed, by 1994 there was an inability to translate a widespread belief that the welfare system was terribly wrong into some kind of remedial plan that everyone could agree on. Sweeping changes were made in the welfare system during the political season of 1996, but the fact that Democrats were divided over President Clinton's decision to sign legislation indicated that polarization remained.

PUBLIC ARGUMENT IN A DEMOCRACY

The perceived crisis of spiritual values in America is a broader and more elusive subject than any particular policy debate about which politicians and the public might be reaching conclusions. James Davison Hunter, a professor of sociology and religious studies at the University of Virginia, has labeled the polemics over values "a culture war," and he says that this war ranges from the nature and structure of the family, to concepts of race and justice, and on through the familiar list of controversies over abortion, gays in the military, sexual harassment, church–state issues, and more. He argues, "Cumulatively, these disputes amount to a fundamental struggle over the 'first principles' of how we will order our life together. It is through these seemingly disparate issues that we struggle to define ourselves as Americans and the kind of communities we will build and sustain."[3]

Hunter concludes that there is no easy way through these conflicts other than to argue them out, and, interestingly, he regards the very grassroots institutions we shall see at work in this book as the "institutions of civil society" and, accordingly, the proper places to try and resolve these conflicts.

While the nation awaited the successful mediation of these issues through local institutions, the war continued on the national stage. A good example was the sharp response drawn when Representative Vic Fazio, chairman of the Democratic Congressional Campaign Committee in 1994, warned that religious views were spilling over into the act of legislating. John J. Pitney, Jr., a professor of government at Claremont McKenna College, wrote, "Whether through calculation or mere insensitivity, such attacks are profoundly offensive and utterly inconsistent with the spirit of tolerance that liberalism professes to."[4]

In one of his articles, the journalist Ronald Brownstein described the Fazio remarks as part of a "hothouse holy war" that raised a question on the other side of the aisle about whether the Republican Party would be able to represent a larger national interest when its agenda was pulled to the right by a powerful special interest group. He argued that "a party can only articulate the national interest when it is willing to temper the demands of its supporters, not just the groups allied with its rival."[5] This question continued to have relevance once the Republican Party gained the majority in Congress after the 1994 election.

By 1996, it was clear that while there were widespread concerns about the direction of the country, the so-called "gender gap" and concerns about immigrants were also important factors in the national debate. When a *Los Angeles Times* poll conducted in the spring of 1996 found that 70 percent of women respondents thought the country was "seriously off on the wrong track," the newspaper followed up and found some interesting results. Celia Cruz, a graduate student at Carnegie Mellon University in Pittsburgh, described herself as "conservative in many ways" but said she was put off by Republican hard-line positions on immigrants. Madeline Stoner, an associated professor at the University of Southern California's School of Social Work, observed that women had unique clear economic and social perspectives and that Republicans, despite their talk about family values, were not connecting adequately with women's core concerns about children and the future.[6]

The Democrats, at their Chicago convention in 1996, leaned heavily on emotion and empathy, but they obviously were mindful of the advantages of playing to their strengths with women and minorities in the values arena. They seemed to answer successfully the Republican barbs at the Democratic theme, "it takes a village," by suggesting that the successful nurturing of children was not only a familial task but a communal one, too.

The journalist and commentator Michael Kinsley has pointed out that both liberals and members of the religious right have engaged freely in hardball in the political arena, and then complain when they are attacked, saying that they are victims of religious prejudice. But, he observes correctly, they can't have it both ways. He noted the process of marginalization on both sides of the debate, where, for example, a Democratic presidential candidate's patriotism was questioned in 1988.[7]

In one sense, Pat Buchanan was right: By 1992 the country was polarized in its moral discourse, and much of the dispute was based in religious perceptions. But Buchanan as a convention speaker was what he had been as a columnist, trafficking in the extreme portrayal. Where he proved to be short-sighted was not in the perception of moral distress in the country, but in the appeal of a narrow perspective. Getting the moral crisis message right has proved to be difficult for politicians across the spectrum.

By 1994, the wedge that Buchanan's convention remarks drove was sufficiently evident that many mainstream Americans, and even religious conservatives, were being turned off by the harsh rhetoric. When the Christian Coalition met that year in Washington to consider its political agenda, a number of religious conservative candidates had fared well in organizational struggles within the Republican Party, but were failing to appeal to a wider electorate, even within that party.[8]

REPUBLICANS, DEMOCRATS, AND VALUES

The new Republican party of the 1990s was in fact made up of both the social conservatives who were driven to work hard in grassroots campaigning and the more traditional members of the party whose concerns centered on economic and, from Cold War days, defense issues. Meanwhile, the party's intellectual vanguard seemed to have perceived a potential advantage in connecting the approaches to budgets, size of government, and the political system with underlying core values that provide a springboard to these and other areas of public policy. But there has been risk in trying to construct a values-based tent.

In February 1995, Ralph Reed, executive director of the Christian Coalition, which had worked hard for Republican candidates in 1994, fired a warning shot in a speech, saying that Republicans should not try to put anybody with abortion rights inclinations on the 1996 presidential ticket; abortion continued to be a problematic issue under the Republican "big tent" throughout the election cycle. By that time the larger political polarization on values was clear. President Clinton and former Vice President Dan Quayle had made appeals to morality, family, work, and taking care of children the same month as the Christian Coalition meeting. Quayle later dropped out of consideration, but by that time the American political system was fully engaged.

With almost everybody in politics reaching for the mantle of "family values," nobody has had a corner on it. The relationship of the major political parties to spiritually based themes is actually a complex and fascinating subject. Each has argued public policy from assumptions about "social justice" or "personal responsibility," the very things we hear from the pulpit. But ultimately the political process comes down to a battle over the allocation of limited resources, so the extension of religious or ethical concepts to what kind of government we will have or what kind of incentives we will provide is always tricky business.

A good example of this dilemma is contained within all the complexity of the issue of giving people public money in the form of state vouchers to attend religious schools. It turns out to be a classic test of true priorities—and of commitment to principle—when the question of "family values" is addressed by both liberals and conservatives. Those who oppose vouchers, even for families who long to have them, are actually in the position of arguing that there is something uniquely harmful about a moral and religious education in a country that purports to foster the free exercise of religion and in which many agree there is a moral crisis. Likewise, those who vigorously advocate vouchers as an alternative to exclusively private funding of efforts to assist low-income students are caught in a dilemma of reconciling conservative opposition to other worthy investments of public funds in the shoring up of the social fabric.

The Democrats have been hobbled by an unrelenting full-court press from Republicans on the "family values" theme and have not always been able to score significant points with the electorate even when their ideas about values are good. The political writer E. J. Dionne, Jr., for example, observed about the time of "the hothouse holy war" that liberals in fact had come to accept a point made by Senator Daniel Patrick Moynihan (D-New York) as a maverick nearly 30 years earlier: that the rise in families where children were being raised without fathers was having devastating effects. Dionne suggested that Democrats were being portrayed unfairly since they had reached a point where they had begun to see the government's role not as fixer of everybody's problems but as an enabler for stronger family and neighborhood units. It was, he said, time to "stop pretending that our political opponents are sinners, knaves or freaks."[9]

At the same time, there was liberal critique of the "return to values" themes espoused by such Republican insiders as former speech writer for Presidents Reagan and Bush Peggy Noonan and conservative syndicated columnist Arianna Stassinopoulos Huffington. James Wolcott, *The New Yorker*'s caustic TV critic, issued a bill of particulars when he suggested that the conservatives' approach to values was too fuzzy and soporific and that it somehow constituted a rejection of modernity in favor of nostalgia.[10] Noonan's public television series, *On Values*, was better than the criticism suggested and more favorably received by others, but the complaint was somewhere in the ballpark on a larger point of where and how conservatives can fly off track. The Republicans' reading on the modern values dilemma in general has been conspicuously silent on diversity of religious perspectives. They have had the "family values" ball in their court, but at times they seem almost intent on fumbling it by leaving out many outside the loop of Christians and making others feel that they need not apply or that their perspectives somehow are being overlooked by design.

The Democrats, on the other hand, intuitively grasp a connection between the nation's new diversity and the larger picture of a nation's moral well-being because women and minority groups are now a large part of their core constituency. In 1996, they shrewdly focused on concerns about children. But Democrats in general can't always seem to get a handle on what to do or say about the politics of God and country. If they were not being given sufficient credit for recognizing the value of values, it was because they were making such a point of secular liberalism on cultural issues that they had contributed significantly themselves to the divisiveness of the national debate. Writing in the Catholic magazine *Commonweal*, David R. Carlin, Jr., suggested, for example, that much of Bill Clinton's problem during the first years of his presidency resulted largely from the unacknowledged importance of "cultural issues," which meant that the President too often hitched his wagon with the liberal wing of his party. Democrats, he wrote, had allied themselves with a "religion of cultural liberalism," and accordingly, "… the public is convinced, and is becoming more convinced daily, that liberals are wrong on cultural issues: wrong on morality, wrong on religion, wrong on family, wrong on sex, wrong on education, wrong on crime, wrong on the underclass, and perhaps even wrong on race."[11]

ENTITLEMENTS, COMPASSION, AND RESPONSIBILITY

The Democrats' frustration has arisen in part from an inability to find the right tone and voice on the religious values question and to satisfactorily address the criticism of conservatives like Heather R. Higgins of the Council on Culture and Community that liberals have redefined rights to mean "rights-as-entitlements."[12] By late 1994, they were talking more about the need for responsibility. But oddly, the virtues of self-discipline, work ethic, and sacrifice had become a political problem, because as the Republicans shrewdly calculated in the battle over affirmative action, the Democrats' fragile coalition of different interest groups could be shaken if constituencies were pitted against each other over who was doing the sacrificing and who was on the receiving end.

If the Republicans had staked out the territory of "family values," the Democrats cornered the "compassion" market. This trump card, which was successfully exploited in the public debate over school lunches for poor children in 1995, was on full display in a heartfelt *Los Angeles Times* op-ed article written by a longtime Democratic activist, calling on President Clinton to let someone else be the party's standard bearer in 1996. Paul Lewis, a professor of English at Boston College, a Jesuit school in the Democratic base of Massachusetts, wrote a progressive's lament, deploring "a rich nation's tolerance for poverty and despair" and for having "interests of corporations advanced at the expense of basic decency."[13]

A problem for the Democrats is that the Republicans have scored points with the idea that it is more "compassionate" to get people thinking about what they need to do to help themselves rather than doing for them. Moreover, to whatever degree the Democrats' progressive ideals arise out of true spiritual concerns, noble sentiments may be doomed to orbit in abstraction until the party can find a way to regroup for the long haul on programs, policies, and a core mission statement.

Certainly the centrist and conservative Democrats have something to build on in their idea that government assistance for people who are going to produce jobs and other good things for the society at large has social value for all, including those who most need help. The Democrats also remain positioned philosophically to benefit whenever Republicans seem to favor the rich to the detriment of others. Still, the most powerful spiritual themes running through American political life in the 1990s were centered in notions of individual responsibility and empowerment. This was so as the larger society increasingly seemed uncomfortable with social and legislative engineering.

The Democrats did manage to retain credibility as advocates of the middle class and as proponents of that elusive concept, "economic fairness." As noted, they were well ahead of the Republicans in coming to terms with the realities of diversity and tolerance in outlook in a multiethnic society. Moreover, the Republican zeal for fixing America their way always runs the risk that "family values" might be obstructed or retarded by trimming the slack in the safety net too tightly. Nevertheless, some of the party's intellectuals have compelling ideas that have been showcased on the op-ed page of *The Wall Street Journal*. Critics like Higgins have talked about the capacity of humans for both good and evil, which provides a powerful base, and one rooted strongly in religious perspectives, for the rejection of the welfare state.

To the extent that there is a spiritual basis from which partisan policy arises on the left and right, our politics tells us much about what we consider important as a society and who we are as a people. The American experience is very much about enlightened self-interest, whatever our political point of view. Religion is an important underlying component of democratic aspirations, but it also serves as a check on what happens when self-interest crosses the line into selfishness.

It should be no surprise that neither major party seems to have been able to marry all the virtues sought by liberals and conservatives in the political struggle to be standard-bearer for a range of clamoring interest groups. Their hopes drowned in partisan noise, and many citizens seem to have decided that much of the nation's political discourse is irrelevant to the search for spiritual meaning for them as individuals, just as they have become turned off to politics in general. By 1995, for example, some evangelicals were complaining openly that politically active Christian conservative groups like the Christian Coalition were becoming too wrapped up in party and policy matters in a way that compromised the purity of religion.[14]

What we have as a result is a kind of trickle-down seriousness of purpose. The scut work of bringing moral and religious values to bear on troubled communities is left largely to those at ground level. Some national politicians have sensed that their debate is being carried on somewhere other than where the people are. There have been calls within the Republican camp for more moderation, and in the centrist group, the Democratic Leadership Council stirred after the casualties of the midterm elections of 1994. However, the political debate over values still generally has seemed removed from the lives of many Americans.

Chapter Three

Why Some Opinion Leaders Are Far Apart

The debate over values has been taking place not only between partisan players in the political process but also between other interest groups. Specifically, it has been going on between liberal and conservative elites, and ultimately, it has played out in the courts. It has covered differing points of view over the proper place of moral and spiritual concerns in a democratic society. What is most significant is that any moderate positions on the national stage that might combine the best of the concerns of both left and right have tended to be overshadowed by the rhetoric on the poles.

In 1993, the Americans United for Separation of Church and State, a group that advocates what its title suggests, reported a growing number of church–state conflicts at state and local levels. In ominous language, it said that, "Separation of church and state faces at least two serious challenges that could undermine its ultimate survival." It went on to say that the evidence was the religious right's advocacy of a return to state-sponsored prayer in public schools and the effort to implement voucher plans for state aid to sectarian schools. The group also cited attitudes of many Americans who supported the concept of separation but who also favored both a school prayer amendment and aid to religion or display of religious symbols by the government.[1]

In a society of competing perspectives on values, one person's serious challenge is another's beachhead. At the same time, a ruling by a federal appeals court that student-initiated prayer was permissible in Texas led to a national campaign by Pat Robertson's American Center for Law and Justice to assert in national mailings that students had a "free speech" right to have prayer at school events.[2] The action prompted the American Civil Liberties Union to wage a vigorous countercampaign, a battle that put school officials in the middle. This quarreling has put the public education system on the spot, and it is among the democratic institutions often cited as crucial places to work out divisions in American society.

The courts still are trying to sort out all of this; after 30 years of Supreme Court decisions banning official school prayers, now public high schools are open to prayer and bible reading. On one extreme are those who fear that nonbelievers will be forced to hear religious messages or that the government will be advancing the interests and beliefs of particular groups over others. On the other are those who worry that the educational system and society in general will permit a societal drift toward secularism, draining spiritual content from American life.

The Supreme Court has taken on a difficult assignment by holding as a standard in church–state conflicts the idea that government must be "neutral" toward religion, neither promoting nor inhibiting it. This is the so-called "Lemon test" arising from the 1971 case *Lemon v. Kurtzman*. In fact, what we have since the court's 1962 ban on organized school prayer is a bouillabaisse of decisions on what is permissible. In 1995, the American Jewish Congress performed a service by issuing a "Joint Statement of Current Law" on religion in the public schools, but what was most remarkable about this effort to inform bewildered parties about the state of the art on student prayer, baccalaureates, teaching about religion, and more was that its many signatories were agreeing on something. What was that achievement? It was that the document was simply an accurate statement of what the law currently was.[3]

While much has been written about the Lemon standard, the balancing act for the courts suggests the larger dilemma arising from a reliance on judicial review as a last resort in determining how a society accommodates spiritual principles in the life of the nation. One of the contributions of Yale Law School professor Stephen L. Carter's book *The Culture of Disbelief* was to point out how awkward or illogical it can be when legal arguments turn on whether or not religious motivation is at the source of encounters between religion and government.

The standard sounds fair, but in practice government can appear to oppose religion-based activity in the public arena, while promoting or funding it for other groups. This standard may be among the best we can hope to construct, but by holding to it the court effectively has left some Americans to see government as hostile to religious interests and as encouraging secularism as something more appropriate to democratic life. We have a lofty tradition of jurisprudence on the question of religion in American life, and the courts have described the contours of freedom artfully through a distinguished tradition of decisions on the First Amendment. But this dilemma invites us to remember also that judges are essentially referees and that a real accommodation is more likely to be arrived at through other processes of argumentation and conflict resolution open to a free society.

It would be helpful if some of the discussion could come through our normal political debate, but the evidence from the battlefield over the politics of virtue is that we should not hold our breath. By the way, it would be ironic if the Robespierres in the Republican revolution, brothers under the skin with the prayer amendment as spiritual cure-all advocates, resolved one aspect of this dilemma more equitably, the matter of funding, by creating a situation where all groups on a public university campus were denied, not just the religious ones, in the campaign to make government less of a provider of resources.

The volleys fired between strict separationists and religionists are roughly equivalent in the religious and moral sphere to attack-television advertisement politics. In fact, the two are in some way directly connected. Such commercials have been vehicles for missives about "family values," which has become a kind of code phrase for a larger set of moral and religious concerns. In assessing the havoc these ads can wreak in our political system, *New York Times* columnist Anthony Lewis conjured the conscience of Justice Louis Brandeis, who had stressed the importance of reasoned and full public discussion as essential to sustaining democracy.[4]

The same need to talk things through is evident in the quarreling over the place of religious values in American life. It is a complicated and at times legalistic subject that unfortunately is getting much of its airing in bits and pieces, when in fact it deserves and requires the fullest deliberation that our democratic processes allow. It is unsurprising, given this negative aspect to public discourse, that the real progress is being made down in the trenches of local communities, where one-to-one communication is easier to achieve.

The debate over the issue of prayer in the public schools that erupted late in 1994 was one illustration of the polarization. It arose because the Republican leadership in the House of Representatives was feeling its newfound clout in the wake of the overwhelming election victory in the midterm elections.

The floating of the proposal to revive a constitutional amendment itself was not a watershed event, and the idea had been around for some time. But the knee-jerk response to it from strict separationists and advocates of prayer in schools alike was a dramatic example of the need for context and argumentation in a democracy that is trying to work through difficult issues about which people feel passionately. In fact, some religious people have their own concerns that officially sanctioned prayer in the schools trivializes religious faith and undermines spiritual yearning.[3]

As mentioned earlier, the author James Davison Hunter has used the term "culture war" to characterize societal conflicts such as abortion, prayer in schools, the rights of homosexuals, freedom of expression, and community standards, and he says that we have no alternative but to address our differences head-on through civilized argument. Further, he holds that were it not for the presence of the churches, schools, synagogues, professional associations, and the press to serve a mediators, we might be in deep trouble.[6] African-American author Cornel West suggests similarly that the outcome of our national experience is on the line in this process of talking things through. He has written, "If we are to survive as a nation, the 1990s must be a decade in which candid and critical conversations take place about race and poverty, rights and responsibilities, violence and despair."[7]

THE RELIGIOUS RIGHT: FRIEND OR FOE?

Two extended installments of William F. Buckley, Jr.'s, public television program *Firing Line*—one of which, by the way, had West as a participant—were in the spirit of what the two authors say we need. If it is light we need and not heat, Buckley and producer Warren Steibel have shed illumination by advancing the understanding of complicated issues at the heart of religion in American public life. At the same time, the debates illustrated some of the divisions that are out there in our national discourse, and how acute the polarization can be among opinion leaders.

The two *Firing Line* installments, in 1993 and 1994, explored two essential questions. First, what are we to make of religious conservatives seeking to bring moral and spiritual values to bear on society's problems, and are they all to be categorized as zealots looking to supplant democracy? Second, where is the line between having shared values in a pluralistic democracy and going too far in mobilizing religion-based ideas? The debaters considered these questions through two resolutions argued on separate occasions, one dealing with real and imagined threats posed by the religious right and the other exploring the celebrated "wall of separation" between church and state.

The first debate, taped on September 9, 1993, at the University of South Carolina, considered the resolution: "We Need Not Fear the Religious Right." For Buckley, speaking first as captain of the affirmative team, the idea that religious people were trying to establish a state church was laughable; society's priorities were skewed, he said, when a rabbi could not pray at a high school but an artist could portray Jesus in a jar of urine. Moreover, he argued that secularism had already had its day and failed miserably as a dominant theme of American culture. The increase in crime, illegitimacy, and single-parent homes and the decline in educational standards were not addressed sufficiently by the scrupulous endeavor of keeping religion out of the public arena.

For Ira Glasser, executive director of the American Civil Liberties Union and lead speaker on the other side, citing Buckley teammate Pat Robertson's activities as a religious broadcaster was a way to show that the religious right was trying to subvert the constitution by restricting individual rights. Glasser argued that "the fusion of religion and politics has led to a situation where political differences are transformed into religious wars. We have avoided that in this country for 200 years largely because we have depoliticized religion."[8]

Barry Lynn, executive director of Americans United for Separation of Church and State, an ordained minister of the United Church of Christ, warned that religious fundamentalists were seeking to establish a theocracy in America and that their influence on public schools already was being felt in an effort to limit the curriculum and divert taxpayer dollars through voucher programs to their schools.

In his opening volley, Buckley had pushed one of the central buttons in the debate over the role of values in fixing what's wrong with America. It is, after all, just this concern over the unraveling of the social order that has motivated religious moderates to enter the fray in some of the communities we will examine later. He was framing a moral argument that plays to a large audience of Americans, not just those who think that whatever the religious right wants to do is OK. But Buckley went further by throwing a grenade at the left. The decline of American society, he said, was "in part the result of the new libertine values that have been introduced to America in the generation since Woodstock."[9]

Glasser conjured extremists of his own, envisioning the potential overthrow of science in the school curriculum and its replacement with the teaching of creationism. He said that claiming that "putting the teaching of creationism into the schools, the teenage pregnancy rates will go down and crime will go down and we will all be safer to walk the streets [was] a proposition that Mr. Buckley is too intelligent to believe."[10]

WHERE'S THE PUBLIC ON THIS?

Many Americans probably would fall somewhere in the middle of those early missives. Surely those who respect science, who accept evolution as fact and reject creationism, are concerned about the moral drift of the country. They may wonder if there are not fuller ways of expressing religious values and sentiments in our public life. Do they also hold Woodstock and all of the associations with the 1960s that event brings to mind responsible for the unraveling of the social fabric in American communities? Also, if they feel frustrated with politicians and judges they find hostile or at least inattentive to religious concerns, do they also want to reargue the Scopes trial? In both cases, the answer probably is no.

This debate demonstrated nothing if not an even-handedness in the rush to the poles. At one key turn, Lynn questioned Robertson about some of his previous writings and pointedly asked him about a statement once made that he would appoint only Christians and Jews to public office. Lynn raised two important concerns through those queries: first, whether such a standard would violate a constitutional prohibition on a religious test for office, and second, how "denying a job to a Hindu, a Buddhist or a humanist (would) be anything but an act of naked bigotry."[11]

Robertson had a golden opportunity at this moment to liberate himself and a cadre of religious conservatives who agree with him from the shadowy regions of American politics. It is worth remembering that this debate took place well before his publicized backpedaling from his book in 1995. All he had to do was affirm a commitment to the constitution and state that his primary concern was with establishing a better place for religious values in public life. Instead, he not only ducked the question but also appeared to lump an entire group of relatively newer Americans, Muslims, in the category of extremists. He did this by asking a rhetorical question in return: "Would you like to have the Ayatollah Khomeini in charge of health and human services?"[12]

While the answer elicited laughter from the audience for its absurdity, it confirmed any worries that people who saw the debate or read the transcript might have had that politically active Christian fundamentalists under Robertson's banner were intent on creating a government by and for those considered to be of acceptable religious persuasion.[13] The inability or unwillingness of somebody of Robertson's prominence to address diversity and tolerance of religious viewpoints in his stated objective of shoring up the moral fabric of America put him squarely outside the mainstream that he purported to represent.

HOW HIGH A "WALL OF SEPARATION"?

A year later, the second *Firing Line* debate argued the resolution: "Resolved: The Wall of Separation between Church and State Should Be Lowered." The show, taped at the New York University School of Law and aired on public television stations in September 1994, dealt with the nuances of the separation issue in a pluralistic society. Arguing for the resolution were Buckley; the Rev. Richard John Neuhaus, a priest who wrote a book on the secularization of modern American life called *The Naked Public Square* (and later was the lead interviewee in Peggy Noonan's "On Values" public television series); Lino Graglia, a University of Texas law professor; and Michael Paulsen, associate professor of law at the University of Minnesota. Arguing against were, again, Rev. Lynn; Alan Dershowitz, the well-known professor of law at Harvard University; Norman Dorsen, a New York University law professor and former head of the American Civil Liberties Union; and Ruti Teitel, a New York Law School professor.[14]

The concept of "the wall" had its origins in the colonial writings of Roger Williams. It became a focus of a constitutional debate with a series of Supreme Court decisions beginning in 1962 that played a significant role in ushering in religious conservatives as a force in modern American politics beginning around the time of the Carter administration. It had begun with the construction of "a wall" conceived as quite high—the banning of school prayer— and has been under discussion up to the present time with a series of other decisions focusing on "moments of silence," the issue of clergy- and student-led prayer, and the degree of "accommodation" permissible by a state legislature to meet the special educational needs of a religious sect. This constitutional debate has served as a taking-off point for a larger collision of perspectives between people who want to see more religious expression in public life and those who want less.

As was the case with the debate over the perceived influence of the religious right, there were sharp contrasts. Again, if viewers were not persuaded by the wisdom of either side from the merits of the arguments, they were left with at least the solid impression that some very intelligent people who are among the country's opinion leaders are very far apart on the proper role of religion in American life.

Buckley was first up again. He framed the discussion by attempting to reduce the arguments of the strict separationists to an absurdity; he envisioned a time when "the pearly gates" would have to be alluded to as "the allegedly pearly gates." He concluded, "We are here to protest the fanatical length to which the separationists have taken the First Amendment."

Speaking for those arguing to hold the line, Dershowitz observed that other countries had been awash in bloodshed because of fanaticism and that the United States ought to consider itself blessed that "the framers had the foresight to erect a wall." Near the conclusion of his team's opening statement, he asked, "What is wrong with freedom of religion being practiced privately?"

Neuhaus argued for a stronger involvement of religion in public life as essential to democracy and stated the case for the expression of religious sentiment in public life: "The American people believe morality and religion are conjoined in a way that, if they are going to participate in that democratic deliberation, they are going to have to bring their religiously based moral convictions to bear on our public argument."

Lynn, arguing on the other side, described the United States as a "worldwide oasis in the desert of religious intolerance and warfare." He fretted openly about what would happen if the government expanded its control over religion and that powerful religious forces would turn the country toward a theocracy. He saw the establishment clause of the First Amendment as a protector against such encroachment and expressed the preference that religion should exist in a free market environment, unaided by government.

Dorsen asked whether there was such a thing as a non-denominational prayer and stated that he wanted to see religion practiced entirely privately. Graglia supported a majoritarian view of the place for religious expression, but on the other hand worried that favoring the majority was not enough; the rights of minorities had to be protected because otherwise they would be trampled by zealots wearing religious badges.

THE BOUNDARIES OF OUR DIFFERENCES

These positions were deeply felt and expressed with passion, civility, and some wit. The debate gave viewers some of the parameters of the constitutional questions involved in religious expression. At the same time the participants were educating, however, there was not much common ground emerging from either of these debates. For example, the "lower the wall" forces in the second debate did not have a very convincing response for the assertions of Dershowitz and company that what they really had in mind was the Christianization of everyone. In fact, the revived idea of a constitutional prayer amendment that surfaced after the 1994 congressional elections did have as its antecedents some blatant attempts in American history to install Christianity as a national religion. There were attempts up until the 1950s to propose constitutional amendments that explicitly would recognize the sovereignty of Christ.[15]

Considering the history of attempts to "lower the wall," it is perhaps unsurprising that advocates of the premises that the religious right poses no threat and that the wall should be lowered also said nothing about ethnic and religious diversity. That would have lent some late-twentieth-century currency to their approaches to religion in the public square.

To make their argument stick, it seems they might well have argued that bringing all the faiths to the table was the desirable route. This could be done in a way that did not compel participation in any common devotional exercises or hold those with differing views captive in any way, say, by subjecting them to student-led prayer over a public school's intercom. Instead, the spiritual resources that Neuhaus wanted brought into "democratic deliberation" would be available as resources rather than relegated to people's private studies. It seems that doing this in a way that was truly broad would put a burden of proof on strict separationists to demonstrate that this somehow was harmful.

INCLUSIVENESS IS AN ANSWER

It is hard to uphold the argument for lowering the wall if those making that argument do not also relinquish some of their privileged status as members of dominant religions. On this question at least, the "keep the wall higher" group was right; the majorities are arguing for bringing religion into public life in part on the ground that they have the numbers to guarantee that their point of view will be the dominant one. This is hardly consolation for those who worry that there will be a compulsory environment, and it is disappointing in its inability or unwillingness to make the case for a broad-based inclusion of different religious resources.

Conversely, the sides arguing that the religious right poses a threat and that the wall of separation should not be lowered did not really have good answers for those who contended that efforts to drive religion from the public square give little evidence of any respect for religion itself. The "raise the wall" side, for example, had sparse acknowledgment for the capacity of religious values to enrich the quality of public debate or the nation's common life. If the challengers of Pat Robertson and friends did not regard religion with suspicion, or even as something potentially harmful, they did little to answer the Buckley argument that society has tried keeping religion entirely at arm's length from the public square and that what we have is a culture that seems depleted of spiritual sustenance.

In fact, a broad-based and inclusive approach such as we shall see in some local efforts would make a plausible case for some forms of public displays of religious expression. For example, as the holiday season approached while the nation debated the revived issue of prayer in the public schools in 1994, Rabbi Bernie King of Congregation Shir Ha-Ma'alot of Irvine, California, began the observation of Hanukkah by saying he was uncomfortable with seasonal religious observances in public schools "unless you include all the winter celebrations—then you have a very rich public school experience that's pluralistic and involves everybody."[16] There was a hint of accommodation in Rabbi King's observation, even though he made it clear that he was concerned with the problem areas inherent in public expressions of religiosity. There was no such suggestion that there might be areas of agreement in the extremes of the two *Firing Line* debates.

The debaters did seem to agree that something was terribly wrong in America's neighborhoods. And there was one brief hint of "accommodation" when the "young professors" of the second debate, Paulsen and Teitel, took the podium to examine each other's views and engage in a useful search for the meaning of that word in narrow legal terms. However, the larger exercise showed that rather than arriving at a moral consensus over a remedial course of action for the nation, we have become a society whose intellectual leadership is fractured on the very thing that presumably would help us out of the woods, namely, the prevailing spiritual values of American culture.

THE PUBLIC AND THE PARTISANS

The discouraging fact on the larger stage of society is that this kind of discussion is being carried out mainly in sound bites that aren't much help to anybody. A public argument conducted in that manner serves only the short-term interests of some politicians and demagogues who have recognized points to be made by jumping on the morality bandwagon at the same time that they avoid any complex argumentation over nuances.

We should not blame the public for being confused, for sensing that there is something missing in what both Pat Robertson and the American Civil Liberties Union are saying. These and others who joined them are the people who are out front on these issues, appearing to have the expertise in the nuances of church and state relations and in the larger role of religious values in society. It is disappointing to come away with a sense that they are so far from any resolution that might be instructive for the rest of us.

In fact, the public seems to be ahead of the partisans on the basic questions of the moral and spiritual direction of the country. There may also be a parallel between the general public's intuitive inclination for tolerance and accommodation on religious issues and what has happened on public policy issues. The public television program *A Public Voice '94*, aired before the watershed 1994 congressional midterm election, conveyed the sense through a panel discussion of political leaders and journalists that there was a dichotomy between how Washington views public policy problems and how they are seen down on the ground by ordinary Americans. There was a feeling, interspersed with snippets from focus group discussions of various issues by citizens, that opinion leaders in the media and government are talking about our problems in a very different way from ordinary working people—and in much more strident tones. For example, the author David Mathews, who wrote *Politics for People*, observed, "It's almost two parallel tracks going down that touch occasionally."[17]

Some of these themes showed their staying power as the 1996

presidential election year unfolded in such forums as the National Issues Convention held at the University of Texas and broadcast on PBS. We are left with a kind of paradox: A national conversation that ought to be very broad is somehow very limited and contentious. Not even a well-intentioned president could bridge the divide, especially one who was caught up in a host of his own political problems at a time when the public already was skeptical of moralizing politicians.

Chapter Four

The Bully Pulpit

Saints and Sinners in the White House

During the first half of the 1990s, the nation's pathways to spiritual renewal intersected in the Clinton White House. Partisans at any time in our history would have been unsurprised to find sinners in residence on Pennsylvania Avenue, even without the first couple's persistent veracity troubles. That there were aspirations of righteousness to be found only added to the current occupants' complexity.

In fact, the passions that Bill and Hillary Clinton stirred over questions of truthfulness and integrity existed alongside their distinct ambitions to improve the nation's moral climate. When all is said about conversations with Eleanor Roosevelt, consultations with Michael Lerner, and cloudy explanations about Whitewater and suggestions of scandal beyond, the Clinton administration quietly has broken new ground in a longstanding tradition of "civil religion" for presidencies. For all their controversies and self-inflicted wounds, the Clintons—on an ad hoc basis and through a measure of political intuition and eclectic piety—appear to have sketched a future framework for moderate alternatives to the activism of religious conservatives.

In the fall of 1994, the Republican congressional tide was followed by calls for renewed efforts to pass a constitutional amendment permitting voluntary school prayer. Democrat Clinton's earliest search for common ground under the new order was a hastily issued statement from Indonesia. He would consider working with the political opposition toward the implementation of such an amendment.

Soon, a retreat began. Aides tried to temper the president's position after its unfavorable reception from Democrats and civil liberties groups. The new "spin" was that what the president really favored was a law establishing a moment of silence during the school day.[1]

It would be easy to suggest that this episode was part of a larger presidential response to the results of the midterm elections, which included the sacking of the controversial surgeon general Jocelyn Elders and proposals aimed at moving the president toward the political center. The conventional wisdom on Clinton's move to the moral center—a perception encouraged by some religious conservatives like Ralph Reed of the Christian Coalition—was that it was a political makeover prompted by the 1994 election. But it would not be entirely correct to dismiss this reaction and adjustment as yet another example of the eternally compromising Bill Clinton. Rather than signaling some politically expedient jump by the president into the fray, it was a point on a continuum. Clinton weighing in on the moment of silence reflected a pattern of presidential forays into a fractious national discussion over moral and spiritual values in contemporary life.

In reality, if the president had gone left at the outset on policy matters and on such cultural questions as gays in the military during his first two years, his keen political compass on the question of "this whole values debate," as he termed it at the time of the amendment flap, actually had put him in the vanguard of politicians recognizing the significance of a restive moral center in the nation. The president, traveling his own spiritual journey, turned out to be attuned to some significant grassroots efforts, such as those conducted by The Pacific Institute of Community Organization (a misnomer by virtue of the organization's far-flung influence beyond a northern California base), which combines

Saul Alinsky-inspired community organizing with an interfaith flavor to improve the quality of life in dozens of communities.

In Anaheim, California, the local chapter actually engaged in successful collaboration with local government, and was doing so about the time Clinton was pondering aloud about how faith might be brought more openly into the public sphere. Clinton in effect was managing to wade successfully from the White House into the arena of religious values as the head of a secular government without prompting much more than modest protest from liberal constituencies concerned about church–state separation. While much of the national conversation about religious values in the public square was being conducted by extreme voices on the left and right, the president had identified almost intuitively with some of the actual concerns that were brewing in local communities.

Bill and Hillary Clinton both had interesting things to say during the early presidency about the spiritual resources and possibilities of the nation. Both seemed to have grasped the importance of this question at a particular moment in the nation's history when the issue was gaining importance in the confrontations over public religiosity and "family values." Both displayed a facility, from quite different perspectives as individuals, for addressing it from the White House platform. Kenneth L. Woodward of *Newsweek* was prompted to write in the fall of 1994, "… the Clintons are perhaps the most openly religious First Couple this century has seen."[2]

The president is a constitutional officer, embodying as much as any the traditional separation of church and state. But there is an undeniable moral quality to the presidency, and there is nobody better positioned strategically to attempt to bridge the divide between national perspectives and the interests of people in neighborhoods. The Clinton presidency is notable for its attempt to actually try this. It was on to something previously unexplored: the first draft of a new moral middle ground for a diverse nation. With all the president's other problems related to the character issue, there generally has been little recognition or credibility

placed in this effort. Clinton's reelection in 1996 was seen univer-
sally as a product of his deft move to the moral and political center
in response to the successes of Republicans in 1994. However, he
also clearly showed an interest in moral and religious questions
earlier in his first term. There seems to have been an element of
self-direction in his exploration that cannot be attributed solely to
the winds of politics or to the political advice of others.

"A RELIGIOUS DIMENSION" IN OUR POLITICS

The idea of a "civil religion" in America, which was advanced
some years ago by the sociologist and author Robert N. Bellah, is
crucial as a primer to White House involvement in the arena of
moral and spiritual values. The concept that there exists "an elabo-
rate and well-institutionalized civil religion in America" and that
this "religious dimension has its own seriousness and integrity"
appears in an essay published in 1967 in *Daedalus*, the journal of
the American Academy of Arts and Sciences, and later was reprinted in a collection of essays on religion in America.[3]

The concept of civil religion has its origins in the writings of
the French philosopher Rousseau, and its essential components
were described as including the positing of the existence of God,
the value of virtuous conduct, and the denial of religious intolerance, among other things. Most other religious opinion under
the banner of "civil religion" is considered none of the state's
business.

Bellah examined some previous presidential remarks for the
assumptions they suggested about the acceptable public sphere of
religion in a society that goes to some length to keep church and
state separate. An examination of the inaugural address of President Kennedy on January 20, 1961, for example, gives evidence of
homage to a secular religious faith, quite separate from Kennedy's
own private Catholicism or even his membership in a larger community of Christians. It is, says the author, a recognition in American life that there is a religious dimension to the political realm,

arising from "certain common elements of religious orientation that the great majority of Americans share."[4] This is so even with the guarantees of freedom of religious belief and association, and it is a separate religious sphere in American life apart from that of the state.

There also is an underlying assumption in the notion of "civil religion" that in America, despite the sovereignty of the people, there is a higher authority. That idea not only is found in the modern presidency, but also can be traced to the writings of the Founding Fathers, the early presidents, and the Civil War, when "a new theme of death, sacrifice, and rebirth enters the civil religion." Bellah observed that the concept needs continual restatement and reformation and to be "measured by universal standards."[5] In the more than a quarter century since that article appeared, we have had the religiosity of Jimmy Carter and the association, if somewhat at arm's length, between Ronald Reagan and Christian fundamentalists, among other things.

Clinton's Southern Baptist upbringing and his undergraduate education at Georgetown University, a Catholic school, shaped his view of community and personal responsibility, according to some observers.[6] Part of what is particular to the Clinton presidency is the attempt to speak over the "noise" of the fractious debate about the place of religious sentiment in public and national life and, in a sense, to begin redefining what the "civil religion" might mean in a vastly changed America and in the post-Cold War world.

Clinton had dealt firsthand with some of the public divisiveness over values because his views on abortion and gay rights set him at a odds with religious leaders in his own faith. He told ABC's *World News Tonight*, in a program aired on March 23, 1994, that he considered himself very religious anyway, as someone who recognized that he had sinned in his life, sought forgiveness, and regularly prayed for guidance so that he could do his job. Meeting with Baptist journalists during the fall of 1994, he said he found comfort in religious books and pared out any moral conclusions from such issues as abortion and homosexuality with the criminalization of conduct by the government, and talked about his familiarity with religious themes, churchgoing, and knowledge versed in Scripture.[7]

By the time the president gave these interviews, what might have been the most significant statement in this general area was already out there before the public. In August 1993, Clinton returned to Washington from vacation and, at an interfaith breakfast, told religious leaders,

> Sometimes I think the environment in which we operate is entirely too secular. The fact that we have freedom of religion doesn't mean we need to try to have freedom from religion. It doesn't mean that those of us who have faith shouldn't frankly admit that we are animated by that faith, that we try to live by it—and that it does affect what we feel, what we think, and what we do.[8]

Clinton acknowledged Stephen L. Carter's *The Culture of Disbelief* and underscored its subtitle for the assembled clergy: *How American Law and Politics Trivialize Religious Devotion*. The Carter book by itself drew considerable national attention for its themes related to religiosity in public life, but the president's active embrace of the concept of religious sentiment effectively updated the evolving "civil religion" tradition in the White House. In acknowledging religious diversity, he urged the clergy "to find areas where we can agree." He drew applause when he said, "If people of faith treat issues about which they disagree as nothing more than a cause for a screaming match, then we also trivialize religion in our country."

And then, foreshadowing future remarks about the moral health of the country, he seemed to embrace an approach similar to some of the interfaith community organizing efforts aimed at shoring up neighborhoods and cities. He said that "the national slaughter was not simply a secular issue," and deplored "what is happening to a country where we are losing millions of our young people and where they shoot each other with abandon." He ended with an appeal to "reach out to others who may disagree with us on particular issues."[8]

ON VALUES: A PRESIDENT SPEAKS OUT

These themes were restated, sometimes in secular settings, sometimes in an openly religious way. Some weeks after the White House prayer breakfast, Clinton deplored a "great crisis of spirit" in the country in a speech before a predominantly African-American audience in Memphis, speaking from the same pulpit where the Rev. Dr. Martin Luther King, Jr., had delivered his final speech before his assassination in 1968. His remarks well might have been delivered by somebody less prominent working in the local interfaith initiatives:

> Unless we deal with the ravages of crime and drugs and violence, and unless we recognize that it's due to the break-down of the family, the community, and the disappearance of jobs—and unless we say some of this cannot be done by government because we have to reach deep inside to the value, the spirit, the soul and the truth of human nature—none of the other things we seek to do will ever take us where we need to go.[9]

At a Hollywood fundraiser on December 4, 1993, Clinton urged entertainment industry leaders to consider what effect film and TV violence was having on the lives of impoverished young people.[10] The speech touched on a general theme that was to receive frequent attention in press coverage of the 1996 presidential campaign, and support for the V-chip to screen out offensive television programming that might be viewed by children was to become one of the modest "tools" in the Clinton campaign's pro-family agenda.[11] Several weeks later, on the same day that Clinton was pictured on the front page of *The New York Times* duck hunting with a board member of the National Rifle Association, the newspaper ran an article exploring the complexities of the issue of Hollywood's depictions of violence. It suggested that despite prodding from the president that got their attention, Hollywood executives were viewed by critics of violence as engaging in a "kind of double-speak," a willingness to reflect on a moral component of violence in films and then to return to business as usual.[12]

The Hollywood speech fell within the framework of the president's larger moral and spiritual themes. While its effect might be debatable, it signaled at least that he agreed with the general criticism of violent portrayals even if it meant sending a message to powerful campaign contributors to Democratic causes. Interestingly, perhaps in part because of the Republicans' studied identification with "family values" issues, and because of the Democrats' ability to become tongue-tied on a subject stirring concerns about censorship among powerful supporters, there was little if any public mention of Clinton's 1993 discussion of Hollywood when the consensus GOP front-runner, Senator Robert Dole of Kansas, addressed the same general topic in the late spring of 1995 and got so much media attention. But it was clear what thin ice "moral values" can be for any politician hoping to skate over it; Dole had only weeks before voiced an astonishing support for an assault weapons ban repeal, which put him awkwardly in the position of appearing indifferent to slaughter on the streets while he opposed it in films and recordings.

In early 1994, Clinton revisited themes of responsibility for shoring up society, delivering a pointed call for individual responsibility and local action in the values arena in his State of the Union address. In citing an epidemic of violence and in urging a moral renewal, he said: "Our problems go way beyond the reach of government. They're rooted in the loss of values and the disappearance of work and the breakdown of our families and our communities. The American people have got to want to change from within if we're going to bring back work and family and community." This attempt by a Democratic president to chart limits to what government can do was a statement that the values arena was not solely the province of politically active conservatives. It caught the attention of at least one liberal observer, the syndicated columnist Ellen Goodman, who wrote: "For a long time, the very word values was suspect as a code word used by the radical right. In the face of this, many others were tongue-tied.... Gradually we are now finding a way to the center. Not drifting right to some presumed political center. Reaching down to a psychological center. Finding a voice there."[13]

Days later, Clinton returned to a related theme. He told a group of junior high school students in a crime-ridden part of Washington that sex was not "sport" but a "solemn responsibility." He implored young women at Kramer Junior High School to defer having children until after marriage and warned the young men of their responsibilities in becoming fathers.[14]

In May of that year in Indianapolis, the president spoke at a groundbreaking ceremony for a memorial to Robert F. Kennedy and the Rev. Dr. Martin Luther King, Jr., in Indianapolis. The memorial would use metal from melted guns, and the speech was an appeal for improved political dialogue that called the memorial "a monument to peace where all of us can live together—not with walls coming up but with walls tearing down."[15] At UCLA later that month, he cautioned students against cynicism, urging them to take responsibility, and warned against a "citizenship of division and distraction and destruction" reflecting criticism of his own programs at a time when his own presidency was headed for a jolt by the strong Republican showing in the congressional election. It was a call for responsibility for community and family, pitched in a lament about negativism about the country.

In August of that year, mixing a political message with one on values, the president assumed the pulpit at a church in Maryland and said that the country was "coming apart at the seams" over violence and that small-mindedness over politics could be an obstacle to doing the right thing. The remarks were prompted by a stalled crime package, which the president said was needed, "Because there are too many streets where old folks are afraid to sit and talk, and children are afraid to play."[16]

During July 1995, as a presidential election year approached, Clinton decried extreme rhetoric in political debate and, several days later in Nashville at a town hall meeting, again took on the subject of violence in the media. Also that summer, the president instructed the government to distribute guidelines explaining what kinds of religious expression were permissible in schools under current law. In August, against the backdrop of a proposal from religious conservatives for a constitutional amendment on school prayer, the administration outlined alternatively how school boards might accommodate student religious activity.

ON VALUES: A FIRST LADY'S PERSPECTIVE

Hillary Rodham Clinton's activism in the moral and religious sphere predated her fateful meeting at Yale Law School with the man who would be her husband. But a vision that she brought to her role as First Lady found expression in a speech she gave at the University of Texas in Austin on April 6, 1993.

It began without any suggestion of anything more profound or unusual to come. She joked that following Governor Ann Richards as a speaker was akin to addressing St. Peter about the experience of living through a flood, and finding out that the speech would follow remarks by Noah. There was some Longhorn talk about sports and a tribute to Lady Bird Johnson. Then the speech made a transition to musing about how, despite the economic wealth of the United States, there was "this undercurrent of discontent," which led up to a statement that, "We are, I think, in a crisis of meaning." Mrs. Clinton rattled off a series of questions about the big picture: life in today's world, institutions, the meaning of education—nothing less that what it meant to be human.

She quoted a dying Lee Atwater, "architect of Republican victories of the '70s and '80s," as lamenting at the end of a losing battle with cancer about a "spiritual vacuum at the heart of American society." She went on to describe "a sleeping sickness of the soul" and wanted the "new politics of meaning" to provide "a new definition of civil society." In addressing the debate over family values, she insisted that it was important to recognize that children were shaped both by the values of their parents and by the values of the society at large. She suggested that it should be possible to have "the kind of approach that has to get beyond the dogma of right or left, conservative or liberal."[17]

These remarks provided an insight into the Hillary Rodham Clinton behind the more visible and politicized player in the public policy area of healthcare. She was bright, confident, willing to offer insight, but not entirely sure, either, that she had it all figured out. Despite this, she was willing to step up to the plate, mindful of history but reflecting a 1960s sensibility that some kind of new order was both necessary and possible.

In a remarkable pair of interviews for an article by Michael Kelly of *The New York Times*, Mrs. Clinton sketched her operative view of life from its religious base in Methodism, and as it had evolved from her days as a student at Wellesley College and later on. She was, suggested Kelly, a work in progress in the values arena, seeking "The Answer" or trying to come up with "a sort of unified field theory of life."[18]

Her Austin speech was described as the beginning of a crusade. The article traced her religious origins to Paul Tillich, Reinhold Niebuhr, Dietrich Bonhoeffer—who tied religion to crucial moments in public life, and the contemporary liberal Jewish thinker Michael Lerner. This mixture of ideas contributed to a basic outlook: "The very core of what I believe is this concept of individual worth, which I think flows from all of us being creatures of God and being imbued with a spirit."

Mrs. Clinton was mixing do-goodism and liberalism derived from religiosity, a progressive social agenda tinged with moralism and New Age and mainline thought. Her philosophy and approach throughout were eclectic; long before the election-year buzz about her relationship with the psychic Jean Huston, the Associated Press reported on Mrs. Clinton's consultations with a variety of friends, CEOs, academics, and gurus.[19] Through all this, she seemed anchored in the Golden Rule and the core values of her Methodism. She had focused on what *Newsweek* correspondent Howard Fineman called "the fraying of America's social fabric— once considered the crotchety preoccupation of the cultural right—[which] has become a national (even liberal) obsession."[20]

THE PERSISTENT CHARACTER QUESTIONS

To the unmasked delight of the Clintons' political detractors, lurking in the background of what is essentially a forward-looking and open-minded approach from the Clinton White House on values lies the persistent "character issue" and the need to compromise to survive in politics.

These are potentially troublesome areas for any political leader, but they are especially problematic for anyone who ventures into the tricky ground of moral and spiritual leadership. Perhaps a larger question needs to be asked: Given the harsh realities of political life, should any constitutional officer even try to provide moral and spiritual direction to a diverse nation?

Bill Clinton is not alone in seeming to believe that the answer should be yes. For example, in early 1995, Republican presidential hopeful Lamar Alexander, a former Tennessee governor, had as a cornerstone of his fledgling outsider campaign a belief that the presidency should have less to do with programs and politics and more to do with preaching grassroots connections. It was even rooted in his experience playing piano at revivals as a boy.[21]

The Republicans, by the way, have had their own set of problems with virtue in politics. At the time a beleaguered Clinton and the Democrats were wrestling with their own take on values, the Republican intellectual leadership had managed well enough in making connections between values and policy. In practice, however, their troops' courtship of the very rich, and their appeals to a narrow segment of the religiously motivated population, necessarily had consequences.

The need for big money, for example, was a factor given in the premature departure of former vice president Dan Quayle, the logical values standard-bearer of the party's right in the 1996 political campaign. There are questions about whether there was enough confidence to support a Quayle candidacy, but money was a factor that needed to be assessed in considering someone like Senator Phil Gramm of Texas. *The Wall Street Journal*, in describing his facility as a fundraiser, wrote, "The handiwork of wealthy backers ... is more significant than the common man of Mr. Gramm's populist rhetoric."[22] For all political aspirants, the cycle of promises and expectations that are intrinsic to having well-financed campaigns cannot help but affect the purity of intention of even the most idealistic public servants.

Then there is the elusive issue of "character," and it is certainly not the exclusive domain of Bill Clinton. On the Republican side, for example, as Gramm was courting social conservatives in the spring of 1995, he had his own little problem with the revelation that in 1974 he had invested in an R-rated film. In general, the disconnection between the espousal of values and the actual political behavior and conduct of public office by politicians likely is an element fueling public cynicism. In Bill Clinton's case, the writer Michael Kelly suggested that the president's problems came about "because the great goal of doing good gave him license" to indulge in compromises over the course of his political life from the earliest days.[23]

By 1994, Clinton seemed "dogged by amorphous but omnipresent public doubts about his steadfastness," wrote the late John Brennan, director of *The Los Angeles Times* poll.[24] A later poll taken by the newspaper after the president's State of the Union address in 1995 suggested that persistent questions about his personality and character, not his ideas, were a source of his problems with the American public.[25]

For all the president's talk about values and responsibility, he was scored poorly on "moral leadership" in a 1994 assessment of his presidency by the political columnist David Broder. He wrote, "Clinton has a clear sense of the nation's challenges, but he seems unwilling to trust the American people to take a similar long-term view."[26] Clinton's legendary vacillation may have eroded some of the strength of voice he might have had on moral and spiritual questions.

To some degree, he also was caught in the dilemma of his own administration's fumbles over ethics. He had promised to run an ethical shop, but ended up by early 1995 with a number of present and former Cabinet officers under investigation and waiting himself for developments on the Whitewater matter. Several lower-level officials left under a cloud; whether this was a result of failure in staff work to properly screen candidates, sloppiness, failure to consider a broad enough pool, or what, it was a problem serious enough to produce assessments that he had lost the handle on his presidency. In 1996, the controversy over FBI files surfaced, and later came the allegations of illegal campaign fund-raising.

Charles Lewis of the Center for Public Integrity, a Washington watchdog group, earlier said the Clinton Administration was very much like others, but was caught in the illusion that "this is Camelot revisited."[27] The conservative columnist Charles Krauthammer suggested, "This is a presidency that makes a public fetish of its virtuousness.... It is this contradiction between the claim to saintliness and the evidence of slickness that gives the Whitewater affair such drama and urgency."[28]

Both Clintons faced continuing questions about the bungled real estate venture, and before Bill Clinton became president the public already was acquainted with nagging questions about reports of dalliances. Nor was Hillary Rodham Clinton spared the scrutiny, especially in 1996, when the Senate Whitewater Committee turned up the heat. Her own explanations for her activities in Little Rock demonstrated the line she walked as partner in a leading law firm while being the wife of a small-state governor.

Even before a book tour found the White House playing defense for Mrs. Clinton, *Newsweek* quoted presidential campaign strategist James Carville as being horrified to learn during the 1992 campaign about a 1986 memo that indicated that Mrs. Clinton's statement about never profiting from state business was not entirely true. A *Washington Post* profile on January 22, 1995, found something enigmatic about her, and *Newsweek* concluded that she was neither "Saint Hillary" nor "Hillary Rodham Boesky."[29] Questions about the Clintons and Whitewater continued unabated during a partisan atmosphere of congressional hearings in 1995 and on into the election year.

At the same time, as 1995 unfolded, Mrs. Clinton seemed to find what would have made more sense from the beginning, a way of articulating "the politics of meaning" as First Lady. As her husband pointed out to the nation's newspaper editors in Dallas that spring, her focus on global issues of importance to women and children during a trip to Pakistan, India, and Nepal was entirely consistent with concerns she long had held. In the late summer of 1995, after China's release of Harry Wu, a human rights activist, the way was cleared for Mrs. Clinton to go to Huairou as honorary chairwoman of the U.S. Delegation to the United Nation's Fourth World Conference on Women. It was ironic that she was held most accountable for her modus operandi as First Lady as precisely the time that she seemed to be finding the handle on the job.

NEW DIRECTIONS IN THE "CIVIL RELIGION"

Bill Clinton's appeals to Americans to look within for the solutions to their problems covered ground already effectively staked out by conservative intellectuals in the Republican Party. But their agenda had a companion philosophical component that his generally did not: the idea that government itself was incapable of solving problems best left to individuals and communities.

Clinton was portrayed often as in a dilemma after the 1994 election, whether to pander to the conservatives or try to carve out some distinct alternative that either satisfied a political center in his party or protected a liberal base. Even before that, there was a legitimate question as to what degree the negativism he was deploring in the nation in those speeches in the spring of 1994 simply reflected concern about criticism of his policies and his presidency.

Whatever the accuracy of that picture, it would be unfair to suggest that the Clintons were anything other than mostly self-guided in their explorations on the religious values front. Clinton appeared early on to be appealing to the inner resources of Americans and preserving a role for government. For example, his Memphis speech in 1993 also carried a pitch for support of his legislative program for healthcare, job training, and education. The midterm election of 1994 was widely read by analysts as demonstrating that the voting public came down on the side of the conservative mantras about the problems with government, and it was only after being so chastened that Clinton began to shift away from the emphasis on government initiative as somehow interwoven with his calls for personal responsibility.

By the time he delivered his 1995 State of the Union address under the watchful gaze of a new Republican Speaker of the

House, Newt Gingrich, he was tying together a number of earlier themes related to problem solving that he regarded as starting with individuals—deploring the fraying of society, appealing to a common sense of purpose, and even directly citing and urging on the work of America's clergy. The speech generally seemed to play better around the country than it did in Washington, despite its length.

One big problem for making this kind of message effective is that presidential moral speech-making is at such a distance from the problems of devastated communities. That is, as Douglas S. Massey, a sociologist at the University of Chicago, said of Clinton's appeals: "At one level it is important to say these things are important to the society;" in cities, however, such appeals "will be seen as irrelevant unless you change the circumstances."[30] And by 1996, a State of the Union address that echoed previous themes of personal responsibility and family contained a full acknowledgment that, "The era of big government is over." But as he did in the budget battles with Republicans in Congress, Clinton sought to portray himself as a protector of programs for the needy and as someone trying to keep reform from excess.

As the first term drew to a close, the Clinton administration was still mired in controversy over "character." At the same time, its efforts to address the moral and spiritual health of the nation broke some ground within the tradition of "civil religion" because of the president's open appeal for finding ways of expressing faith in a diverse society. Indeed, Bill Clinton's lack of political debt to religious conservatives arguably liberated him to a degree to address broader spiritual themes in a changing society. Much has been said about the religious right's criticism of Clinton, but it is significant that he exercised restraint about criticizing them in return at a time when they were the favored target of liberals.

This most polarizing of modern presidencies, on the issues that are among the most polarizing in the society at large, ironically staked out a flexible moral middle ground. Some might consider it too flexible, in keeping with the Clinton habit of telling everybody a little something of what they wanted to hear. Perhaps it also was maddeningly unfocused in its lack of a cohesive vision, with the jumping from moral and spiritual theme to theme and audience to audience. Part of Clinton's inability to register also could arise from his inclination to talk too much.

Yet, despite the president's political troubles and for all the passion he and his wife stirred in a nation's fractious discourse, this may be the first American presidency to begin to reckon with the true diversity of national spiritual resources and how they might provide a pool of assets for approaching problems. This made for an unusual and interesting moral milieu for the White House, to say the least, when set against the backdrop of character questions. Indeed, once the public began in the late summer of 1996 to consider the choice between Clinton and somebody else, Bob Dole, the president registered some preference from religious voters along with his convincing lead among the general electorate.[31]

During that presidential election year, the doubts raised about the Clintons' veracity on the particulars of Whitewater and the firings of the staff of the White House travel office received widespread attention. A concern for historians well may be whether, given the Clintons' professed attention to spiritual questions at a time when Americans seemed to be looking to the White House for moral leadership, they squandered an opportunity to improve the climate of the country.

IS THE PRESIDENCY THE RIGHT PLATFORM?

It may also be that moral and spiritual themes are most effectively delivered not from the bully pulpit of the White House, but by leadership rooted in local communities.

If that is true, the message could be humbling for all politicians given to expounding from Washington on themes of virtue and could offer a suggestion of just how limited in scope people really want their government to be. Many Americans appear to be very much in favor of a moral and spiritual renewal, and while the polling suggests the White House has a role, the public may be of two minds. That is, ordinary citizens don't necessarily believe that politicians are the ones to lead the charge. An example is a response to an op-ed article in *The Wall Street Journal* on politicians and the will of God written by F. W. Meeker of Hampton Bays, New York. He wrote, "While we have a right to insist that our politicians act morally upright, we risk tyranny by insisting they don the mantle of moral authority. If we cannot be saved as a society but by politicians, we will not be saved."[32]

Clinton also may have been affected because of the inability of Democrats in general to make a convincing case that they are interested in advocating religious values in the public square. There seems to be a perceived disconnection in the public's eye between a liberal political agenda and the concerns brought before society largely by religious conservatives. Ironically, the Rev. Jesse Jackson and others in the African-American community who have provided Democrats with a traditional base of support generally have not strayed from the moral and spiritual premises of their political involvement. By the election of 1996, some Christians arguing traditionally "liberal" positions on such issues as poverty and homelessness began to be heard on the national stage as a countervailing voice to the religious right.

Liberal columnists and thinkers from time to time express some annoyance and even frustration at the degree to which Republicans were successful in seizing the values mantle, and they suggest correctly that Democrats too believe these things are important. At the same time, those who prefer to keep religion entirely out of the public sphere may have to live with the perception that they have understated its power to affect positive change, or that their ideal is not just a secular government but a secular society.

As for the Democratic president's own steadfastness, it would not be accurate to conclude, as many did, that he did not stand for anything in the values realm. Agree or disagree, his positions on abortion and gays cost him trouble with members of his own faith, and the issue of gays in the military was arguably one of a handful of issues that nearly cost him his presidency.

His voice was not lost on William Safire, a political columnist whose writing has not always given a boost to Democratic presidencies and who later became a lightning rod for criticism of

Hillary Clinton through a column in which he bluntly accused her of being "a congenital liar."[33] Bill Clinton was, he wrote, "a first-class political evangelist. He's a believer in people taking care of each other; it's a passion, not a pose, and [it] comes through in his rhetoric."[34]

By the time of the Republican ascendancy in Congress, Clinton presented himself as a president of paradoxes: sometimes weak and floundering, other times bold and restlessly curious in ways that seemed to peer into the twenty-first century. In his very public exploration of new ways of thinking about the country, one of the things he seems to have sensed was the spiritual restiveness at the core of the nation.

A lesson for the long term is that nowhere is it written in stone that the nation's moral and spiritual concerns are the province only of religious conservatives. In American politics, these preoccupations well could be a wild card depending on how they are handled by public leaders and political candidates across the spectrum.

Whatever history concludes about Clinton, he will deserve mention as a president who, though hobbled by questions about his personal character, employed a tradition of "civil religion" to argue for a new accommodation for the democracy. Even as he was seeking a new middle ground, he seemed to be in tune, especially during 1993 and 1994, with some things that were happening simultaneously down at the grassroots level. Americans were beginning to make their own pragmatic assessments, informed by their religious values, about how to deal with the country's moral dilemma.

Part II

Report from the Neighborhood

Seeking a Better Way

Chapter Five

A New Interfaith Spirit Holds the Key

On the night before voters went to the polls in the fall of 1994, the *MacNeil–Lehrer News Hour* queried leading political observers on the state of the electorate.[1] While there were different points of view expressed, the discussion cast a wide net that seemed to check the pulse of the nation's spirit.

Two of a number of panel members, former secretary of education William Bennett and journalist Haynes Johnson, appeared to agree on two important points, although they came from different places. The first was that there was a great deal of pessimism among people about the future of the country. The second was that Americans at the end of the Cold War, with no external demons to fight, were struggling to find a new sense of identity and, in particular, to find ways of being hopeful about what it means to be an American.

Johnson had pioneered a style of reportage during a long career with the *Washington Post* in which he wrote regularly about the nation's mood through the tides of upheaval in post-World War II America. Bennett, who has become a leading extoller of virtues for the Republican party, tapped a vein in the country's hankering for simpler basic values with his bestseller, *The Book of Virtues*. The conversation concluded without any substantive proposal of remedies, but there was a sense conveyed in the discussion that ordinary citizens, in their most basic attitudes and in their activities in local organizations and institutions, would hold the key to any new sense of American purpose.

The idea of restoring power to individuals and communities increasingly has gained currency in the nation's political discourse, and it is connected with the spiritual restiveness that is out there in the land. The election of 1994 was interpreted in various ways by analysts, but whatever messages it contained about the anger of voters and the desire for change, it seemed to confirm thinking found across the political spectrum that America was ready at the end of the twentieth century—after decades of governance by a professional class of politicians begun under the Progressive Era and after the experimentation with centralized government begun in earnest in the New Deal—to find ways of restoring decision-making to ordinary citizens.

Having lived a while with the outcome of that election, it is clear that while more limited government may be desired, it is not at all evident that dismantling it is what people have in mind. Many of the fundamental complaints about politics and politicians remain, and with them, a sense of uneasiness about the moral well-being of the nation.

We are now in our third century of the experiment with democracy, and we have learned painfully from experience that merely espousing or even exercising political freedom is not enough to make us well and whole. The modern lessons of the Los Angeles riots, the scourge of guns that have killed our children, the ravages of drugs, the corruption of government officials, the worship of materialism, the decline of taste in television and movies—all seem to affirm the idea that our ideal of "freedom," merely standing alone, doesn't guarantee much.

Coming on the heels of the business scandals and the unraveling of some of the television evangelists in the 1980s, many mainstream Americans now find themselves sharing some of the concerns about the spiritual health of the nation that politically active Christian fundamentalists have been expressing for some time. No treatment of our collective sense of well-being could be complete without either acknowledging or fully addressing the changing role of moral and spiritual values as a force in society.

NEW DIRECTIONS IN COMMUNITIES

Many Americans are tolerant of other religious and moral viewpoints, and some, as we shall find, are working quietly with the country's diversity. A decline of civic participation and a preoccupation with the narrow concerns of individuals have been linked to voter apathy and other ills. But there also are signs that embryonic new relationships already have been forming at the grassroots level.

The mobilization of small groups of citizens, in churches and schools and clubs or activist groups, is an idea in vogue among contemporary conservative intellectuals like Bennett as alternative to the philosophy of the welfare state. However, it is an idea that cannot be claimed exclusively by any particular ideological group on the political spectrum.

The rejection of exclusively governmental solutions to our national problems and the growing concern with individual responsibility across the political spectrum have come at a time when the stage was set for the transformation of moral and religious sentiment as an active force in American life, irrespective of political philosophy. In a society cracking at the seams with concerns about values, community activists and local religious leaders are in a historic position to influence the nation's agenda and to affect the country's future in profound ways. We know from several decades of political activism by fundamentalists that the seeds for this grassroots involvement are already in place and that this kind of activism certainly has managed to work in ways that advance a narrow rather than broad-based social and cultural agenda.

In recent years, politically active religious conservatives, the worker bees of the religious right, have stepped up their involvement by organizing to conduct voter education campaigns, to seek and win election to boards of education, and to take positions on policy matters. Much has been said about them. The activism of more mainstream faith communities in shoring up neighborhoods and in conducting interfaith discussion has received far less attention, but it is no less important. It suggests that a broader group of Americans has the capacity and inclination to apply their spiritual energies to societal problems.

Traditionally, our secular creed's answer to the bloody conflicts, suspicions, pogroms, and misunderstandings that religion has fostered over the centuries has been a practical one: to keep religion at arm's length from our public agenda. But those who argue for a fuller place for religious values in our common life say that we have paid too high a price. The *Firing Line* debates discussed in an earlier chapter showed the depths of the division over this question. The religious right, as we have seen, has gone ahead and taken up its agenda anyway, citing the amorality and the bankruptcy of traditional liberal approaches. This has hardened the resolve of well-meaning moderates and liberals in the process and has made them suspicious of religious ideas in the marketplace and justifiably worried about what fanatics will do with a hard-won right of privacy. It also has created some apprehension among the moral and religious leaders of the new immigrant groups, whose spiritual perspectives are new to the arena and must be included.

Despite these challenges, some fledgling work has taken place against the backdrop of a tense and continuing constitutional debate on the national stage over the proper place of religious concerns in a diverse society. While the debate over the proper place of moral and spiritual values in our collective life is easily polarized, that is not necessarily the case in communities trying to grapple with very real societal problems. The evidence of success in addressing common problems at the local level not only suggests the power of community organization, but also hints at the potential for a new and broader-based spiritual dialogue that eventually might alleviate some of the tension that has existed between separationists and religionists and bridge some of the gaps between ethnic and denominational groups.

Having looked at the conflict on the national stage, it is worth looking at some of these examples in local communities. In southern California, the search for a new community-based sovereignty has begun in earnest, even as the discourse on the larger national stage has remained polarized over just whose moral and spiritual values ought to prevail.

RELIGION AND THE NEW PRAGMATISM

In Anaheim, California, local faith communities, desperate to bolster the family and to get beyond rhetoric, have found a way to address problems without putting people in opposing camps and without straining the separation of church and state. In Los Angeles, the seat of an already established interfaith conversation, a stark reassessment of race relations and civic consciousness came after the rioting in 1992. It awakened a profound realization that religion provides the very building blocks of a multiethnic community.

California is associated with new national trends, but it is fair to ask up front whether what is going on there is unique to a place often regarded as removed from the mind-sets of the nation's heartland or its older centers in the East and Midwest. It is not. There are in fact many other instances around the country of productive interfaith initiatives that are either beginning or already under way, but that may be getting far less attention than the political activities of religious conservatives on the national stage.

Here are some examples. Missouri is a state described by the *Almanac of American Politics* as being "at the center of America in so many ways."[2] In St. Louis, former Senator John Danforth is heading a group called Interfaith Action for Children Today (Inter-ACT), which is bringing congregations from across denominational and racial lines to help inner-city youngsters. The idea is modeled on a partnership between the African-American and Jewish communities from Cote Brilliante Presbyterian Church and Central Reform Congregation that is already successfully up and running. Members of each congregation serve as mentors for elementary school children. InterACT will expand on such efforts to include such things as after-school programs.

In New York City, some 150 representatives of different faiths gathered at a service at the Cathedral of St. John the Divine on October 16, 1994, dedicated to focusing attention on violence against children. The event was part of a regular national observance held by the Children's Defense Fund and was organized locally by an Episcopal priest, the Rev. Peregrine Murphy, now an assistant minister at the Church of the Incarnation and a clinical researcher who works with victims of Lou Gehrig's disease at Columbia University.

The idea of getting so many different individuals together from Christian, Jewish, and Muslim faiths around a common liturgy has proved to be a help to participants who work with children's programs in New York by reinforcing their work and has inspired new initiatives. The minister described the impact of the event as "phenomenal" and as an achievement in bridging barriers. Meaningful interfaith initiatives, she notes, pose a formidable challenge because of the potential for misunderstanding when "what one person holds to be absolutely true" may turn out to be offensive to others.

The Pacific Institute of Community Organization (PICO), a misnomer by virtue of the group's present far-flung influence beyond its northern California base, is a network of 25 autonomous groups around the country that emphasizes interfaith approaches to improving the quality of life in communities. With origins in Saul Alinsky's neighborhood organizing strategies in Chicago, PICO has evolved since the 1980s into what is termed a "church model" of community organizing, with activist congregations in places as different as Mobile, Alabama, and Denver, Colorado. In Kansas City, Missouri, for example, some 10,000 families are involved in addressing the city's problems with drugs, neighborhood blight, prostitution, and traffic safety.

The executive director of PICO, John Baumann, a Jesuit trained in the early 1970s by one of Alinsky's lieutenants, has worked to teach and support local staffs in the mobilization of large groups of church-based congregations intent on improving their communities. Baumann reports that the demand and interest from community activists around the country for such groups outstrips the capacity of the organization to keep up and still meet its own standards.

About the time the Christian Coalition was getting the attention of politicians for its "Contract with the American Family" in the spring of 1995, National Public Radio reported from Boston on an alternative group called The Ten-Point Coalition. This grassroots coalition of about two dozen religious leaders—many of whom are minorities from the inner city who have stepped forward as an alternative to the religious right—was introduced to House Speaker Newt Gingrich by Governor William Weld of Massachusetts, a Republican with a libertarian streak, who is well to the left of many in his party on social issues. Weld said what would be especially attractive about this ecumenical group for conservative politicians like Gingrich was that it was community based.[3] In Boston, The Ten-Point Coalition received considerable media attention and at times brushed up against established leaders in the black church because of its response to the perceived needs of alienated young people.[4]

DIVERSITY AND TOLERANCE AS ASSETS

Christian fundamentalists understood early on in the current cycle of concern over "family values" that many Americans wanted to apply their moral and religious beliefs to improve society. However, many have advanced a narrow spiritual vision, and some have exceeded the boundaries observed by more mainstream faith communities by running stealth political campaigns, producing "voters' guides," and spending lavishly to influence the political system. Their involvement in electoral politics raises questions of church–state separation, has put others on the defensive, and ultimately undermined the clout of faith communities by putting them on a track to become one more special interest group among others.

To date, the groups we will look at in Part II of this book

wisely have tempered their moral fervor with restraint in the political arena, and their tolerance is a great resource in the effort to apply religious values to America's problems. If they can stay the course, their diversity and openness must be considered the way of the future in a country that cannot and should not return to some imagined Christian nation or relinquish its fundamental optimism about the future to biblical fatalism. By contrast, the successful involvement of religious groups in constructive interfaith efforts ought to provide reason to think that differences over social and cultural positions do not have to result in divisiveness.

In Anaheim, a sense of urgency has produced a practical outlook that is encouraging for what it suggests about the potential role for religious values in modern democracy. Members of faith communities that may be opposed on abortion and gay rights have put aside differences in favor of occupying common ground on survival of the community. The size of the city and the manageable scale of the effort not only are an asset for the undertaking, but also provide a suitable case study for others to consider.

In the post-riot world of Los Angeles to the north, there is a far more complex political and religious environment. Some of the lessons learned in Anaheim seem to apply on a larger scale. It is a religious environment in which the interfaith dialogue, one of the nation's longest-running and most extensive efforts, shifted gears when it became clear that old concerns about racism were unresolved as the city changed. The religious community has begun to identify its many traditions as assets that can facilitate communication and, in the process, to strengthen the influence of messages heard within a range of congregations.

These local experiments suggest that instead of getting bogged down in rancor, the country at large has the capacity to identify and foster what is good and enduring in all our religions and value systems. It can do so in a way that is helpful and does not divide people, water down the strengths of individual religious traditions, or trample minority rights.

Also, while the mobilization of church and civic groups is generally an idea promoted in our national discourse by conservatives, the evidence suggests that there is a limited but meaningful role for government in partnership with faith communities. The cooperation and shared objectives that are making progress possible at the community level belie the ideas that government is a liability or that solutions are best left entirely in the hands of local charitable and religious groups.

This may sound like walking the razor's edge in a world that has seen too much religious intolerance. However, people of good will and democratic temperament are concluding at the end of the twentieth century that the radical separation of religious values and civic community is a bankrupt approach to our common affairs in a modern multiethnic society. We shall meet some of those activists next.

Chapter Six

A Town Meeting Near Disneyland

The road north from Disneyland, with its audacious sign proclaiming it "The Happiest Place on Earth" and its motels and
restaurants, passes swiftly into a world of more modest possibilities. Here summer skies in the evening burst forth in Disney-
colored fireworks, as if the Fourth of July were a nightly occasion.
Harbor Boulevard rises over the bustling Santa Ana Freeway,
which crosses below, shuttling an unending stream of traffic north
to Los Angeles and south to San Diego. On the horizon, beyond a
sign marking access to the freeway, it is possible to imagine this
world as its settlers must have seen it.

On a clear day, the San Gabriel Mountains are visible in the
distance, and below stretches a plain that since has grown into the
central area of Anaheim, worn for wear suddenly after all the
post-World War II growth, but a target in recent years of some
ambitious redevelopment. It is to this patch of southern California
that a band of German immigrants in the nineteenth century set
foot after coming through San Francisco, first to work in vineyards
and later in the citrus groves that gave Orange County its name.

In the extended light of a balmy evening on June 20, 1994,
people gathered in the parking lot of St. Boniface Church. They
represented congregations from around the city and elsewhere in
Orange County, and had arrived for a meeting sponsored by First

Presbyterian Church and St. Boniface Community Organization, under the umbrella of Orange County Congregation Community Organization (OCCCO).

A church sign badly in need of a new piece of glass announced services going on during the week in three languages, English, Spanish, and Vietnamese. The ethnic composition of the parish was an indication that old images of Orange County as a mostly white enclave that had incorporated in response to the perceived ills of Los Angeles had been overtaken by new realities. The agenda was a reflection of just that: what the churches and the city government together could do about deteriorating neighborhoods and turning around the lives of troubled young people.

Inside the old church, which was built by the early German Catholic settlers, a mass in Spanish was winding to its conclusion, capped with a rousing song of praise to the Almighty. It echoed through the cavernous candlelit sanctuary and lingered like a fine mist as communicants drifted out into the early evening to mingle with the arriving people from OCCCO who would meet that night with Mayor Tom Daly and representatives from city government.

A COMMUNITY ORGANIZATION OF CONGREGATIONS

OCCCO was founded in 1985 after members of the Oakland-based PICO were invited in by local religious leaders and the Orange County Human Relations Commission. The goal was to work in Anaheim and Santa Ana and bring the grassroots organizing power of churchgoers to bear on community problems. By the time of the 1994 town meeting at this old church near Disneyland, OCCCO claimed 50,000 families in 15 congregations and said it was dedicated to the principle of "Iluminando el Camino, Lighting the Way." A mission statement committed the group to improving the quality of life in communities by empowering people and mobilizing them for neighborhood action. According to local staff director John Gaudette, the ethnic makeup of the group in Anaheim is about 55 percent Latino, 35 percent white, and 10 percent Asian American.

James T. Walker, at the time Anaheim's gang and drug program coordinator and the city's liaison with an associated group of activist clergy, likened the local efforts of the group and the city's religious leadership to a much older idea, the activism of community organizers in Chicago; OCCCO's parent PICO has adapted Saul Alinsky's strategies for faith communities. In fact, Gaudette, the son of one of Alinsky's lieutenants, grew up learning firsthand about community organizing. He believes that these strategies are particularly well suited to churches, because those institutions have invested in the fate of their communities.

Walker, whose perspective was based in city government, described the milieu as one where, "We're back in the 1990s to discovering the innate potential of what the faith community can provide." OCCCO is inspired by just such an idea: "Nuestra fe nos llama a la accion. Y es por medio de nuestros esfuerzos unidos que las vidas de nuestras familias y las condiciones de nuestras comunidades se transformaran." ("Our faith calls us to action. It is through our united efforts that the lives of our families and conditions in our communities will be transformed.")[1] Its work in Anaheim is associated with the Anaheim Religious Community Council (ARCC), a group of clergy and lay leaders from a cross-section of churches. The latter group includes some of the Christian groups on hand that night and also the Baha'is of Orange County, representatives of a local Jewish synagogue Temple Beth Emet of Orange County, the Council on Islamic Education, and Buddhists.

The larger OCCCO group is committed to "come together in the best traditions of our country to create opportunities which reflect that which is most precious to us: human dignity for our people, justice for our families, and a future filled with hope for our children."[2] Beyond that, the group was motivated by a resolve to shore up the city's flagging quality of life. On the evening when the mayor made a guest appearance, its enthusiasm created an atmosphere of electricity in St. Boniface's old octagonal parish hall, festooned with bingo scoreboards.

This group was committed to using religion as a taking-off point, but to do so without fixed ideology. At a time of polarization in the fuzzy "family values" debate in Washington and regional capitals like Sacramento, they had reduced their agenda to the rescuing of young lives and the restoration of families and communities. They were assembled not to advance social and cultural agendas, such as the crusade for or against abortion rights, for prayer in public schools, or against homosexuals. Many agreed with some of the positions of the religious right, while others had been targets of protest mounted by the anti-abortion group Operation Rescue at a church down the street.

Here, however, in their concern for shoring up the fabric of society against youth violence, drugs, and gangs, they had settled on an inclusive agenda. A poll by *The Los Angeles Times* conducted that summer identified a segment of the population similar in outlook to these. They were Americans worried about trends in morality, who said too many people in the country had "lifestyles which are harmful to themselves and society" and who concluded that urban problems arose more from a lack of personal responsibility than from other causes. At the same time, many respondents seemed unalarmed by the perceived threat to society from conservative religious groups.[3]

One resident there that evening, Dianne Horn, an administrator by day and a congregant at the First Presbyterian Church, said in a later interview that the families of six of her seven grandchildren had moved away from Orange County because of the seriousness of the area's gang and drug problem. She had made a commitment to an ecumenical approach to bolstering families: "The children in our country need help. We have some serious problems, and do not have a stable home life. We as a community need to offer alternatives," she said.[4]

By the end of 1994, OCCCO had convinced the city council to pay for more than $250,000 worth of afterschool programs. While they did not get everything from the city they asked for, they did receive funding to expand an anti-gang program called Kids in Action, see the hiring of a person to work with female gang members, get summer recreation programs expanded to year-round, and more.[5] In this manner, they effectively were reshaping the relationship between church and state at the grassroots level.

TESTIFYING BEFORE THE MAYOR

On the night of the OCCCO meeting, the mayor, a trim man in his early 40s, mingled with the congregants who were registering. He was accompanied by Steve Swaim, the city's community services superintendent, and his associate, Walker, who both worked out of the city manager's office. They represented a city that in the years after World War II had a good deal more experience thinking big than thinking about neighborhoods and church folk.

Grand designs in Anaheim previously had meant Walt Disney planting his dream for a new kind of amusement park in one orange grove and Gene Autry putting home plate in another for a major league baseball franchise. A significant factor contributing to the modern expansiveness was the construction of the Santa Ana Freeway, which literally paved a path to new communities of grid-style housing tracts, schools, and shopping malls a manageable distance from Los Angeles.

The topic of this evening was the resuscitation of neighborhoods and the redirection of lives, a different kind of challenge in the 1990s. It was a far more introspective undertaking for a community that had marketed itself as a magic kingdom, and it was inspired by a frank assessment that all was not so sunny. The meeting took place at a time when the fate of Anaheim as an entertainment and sports capital had drawn much of local government's attention on some ambitious plans to expand Disneyland and to find a solution for the future of the Los Angeles Rams football team, which at that point had all but booked its flight to move out of town and later did, and for the restiveness of the California Angels baseball team, who were wondering what the city would do for them.

The mayor was given a hot seat of honor on the stage, and as he looked out, there were hundreds of people sitting and standing in the hall, a few bearing signs from their congregations. An interpreter shared the stage with him, to recast each statement into Spanish or English. Daly, like mayors in other cities who deal not only with movers and shakers, but also with people in neighborhoods, was aware intuitively of the power of foot soldiers in political terms, even, or perhaps especially, if they are led by people of the cloth. His presence was a recognition of the political importance of paying attention to neighborhood concerns.

Daly also brought a secular counterpoint to the vision of the faithful. As a public official dealing with a host of interest groups, he reminded the OCCCO representatives that even the best intentions must be tempered by political reality. It was essentially a message for the politically uninitiated or naive in the hurly-burly of politics: Decisions about what government can and cannot do for people, however meritorious or important or well-intentioned their causes, turn on the limitations of the budget. He told the group what those among them schooled in the political world knew already, that a budget is a statement of what a community considers important. Learn how the budget process works and attend budget workshops where important decisions are made, he said. One could understand a lot by getting in on the ground floor of the competition for dollars.

Daly's presence constituted a recognition that no politician delivering a lesson in priorities could afford to ignore the chorus of 350 people gathered on a weeknight in his city. Beyond its values and resolve, the group brought numbers of people who vote.[6] Moreover, whatever the group might be lacking in sophistication about the budget process, it was not simply a neighborhood group convening around a single issue and then dissolving back to the world of schools, malls, and minivans. It consisted of citizens who had transformed themselves into grassroots activists. They had prepared for this meeting and pointed it in the direction of getting the city to commit to a bill of particulars for young people. By the time the meeting was over, the group had extracted from Daly a solemn pledge to work toward achieving their laundry list of objectives.

FIELD RESEARCH FOR ORDINARY CITIZENS

OCCCO foot soldiers in Anaheim previously had held sessions in people's houses and claimed to have surveyed more than 3000 residents. The group had done its homework, and its speakers were authoritative when they took the microphone to assert that the city was cutting programs when gang membership and youth violence in central Anaheim had increased. It was not quite the same as one or two persistent activists or gadflies rising at a city council meeting to provoke elected officials to action.

The group that night provided charts showing that gang membership in Anaheim had exploded since 1990, increasing more than six times in four years. In the meantime, it described city staffing for parks and recreation and community services going the opposite direction, from 171 in 1990 to fewer than 134 in 1994. As for the number of felonies and murders committed by young people, they had nearly doubled between 1991 and 1993. Swaim later said that while the group's figures on youth violence and city resources might not be precise in every instance, they presented a generally accurate picture.

The group's facility at bridging the gap between public officials and their constituents has been evident elsewhere in Orange County. Two months earlier, the mayor of Santa Ana and the superintendent of that city's school district had met with an even larger OCCCO group of about 1500 people. In Santa Ana, with a large Latino population, Monsignor Jaime Soto, the vicar for the Hispanic Community for the Diocese of Orange, has observed that even in the face of propaganda and political conflict over immigration, this kind of activism has the potential to unite communities in their approaches to urban problems.[7]

The Anaheim group, following the momentum in Santa Ana, said it had held 54 meetings with experts on education, law enforcement, and crime prevention. On the night it met with the mayor, the most compelling moments were a bit of theater.

On the agenda it was listed as "testimonio de representantes comunitarias," the testimony from community representatives, delivered and then translated according to the language used by speakers who approached a microphone to address the mayor as if they were hand-picked delegates to one of Bill Clinton's town meetings. In deploring the cuts and asking for new programs, they described their own experiences in the troubled neighborhoods of the city.

One person lamented that a friend's youngster was shot and killed in their neighborhood and pleaded for a community center because people were afraid to go out on the streets. Another talked humorously about being a "couch potato" without community programs to divert his attention. A parent described two drive-by shootings on his street; he had lived in the city for 25 years and for the first time his wife was in panic and his children were terrified. A mother said she feared for the future of her children, that they lacked activities, that a homework center was needed to help youngsters with their education, and that without such proactive measures youngsters inevitably would continue turning to antisocial behavior and to a life without hope.

Sister Vickie Brady, a nun at the host church who works with the community, asked the audience to affirm its commitment to the programs with applause, a request that was complied with in two languages and two rounds. The mayor then made his pitch about the demand of the budget, but he agreed to make a commitment to meet more regularly with the group and to provide a detailed action plan and said he was looking for the churches and the families to provide help. He concluded, "The churches are a central part of solving problems; one of our best assets is an active and large church community. The key word is 'partnership.' "[8]

Father John Lenihan, the host parish priest, rose to say that he had buried ten young parishioners who died from drug overdoses or shootings in the past year, and he was intent on holding the mayor's feet to the fire. He said to Daly, conjuring the TV ad about the investment house that claims to get people's attention, "You are more powerful than E. F. Hutton." Of the churchgoers, he said "We're in this for the long haul."[9]

ACTIVISM AND ITS RESULTS

While Daly suggested the group had some things to learn about the political process, Lenihan's comment about the churchgoers' commitment was telling. As early as 1986, a delegation from OCCCO had worked with the city to develop traffic alternatives to unsafe conditions along a street traveled by trucks after the group's research indicated that senior citizens and school children were endangered. Working with the city that year, St. Boniface had managed to get $60,000 for renovations of a park and to address crime, drug dealing, and youth gangs. The city's United Methodists had obtained pledges of "community responsibility" from ten liquor store owners not to sell to minors. The next year, the First Presbyterian Church met with the director of redevelopment and won agreement for free parking in city structures at night and on weekends.

In 1989, 200 leaders of the group met with the county and had a hand in the adoption of an agreement to coordinate drug strategy. And then in 1990, the local OCCCO effort came of age. It alerted the city to deplorable living conditions in Anaheim's troubled Jeffrey Lynn neighborhood behind Disneyland, an area inhabited by service workers at the park. By working with the police department and parks and recreation code enforcement, a new community center and playground were built.

In 1991, the group labored for the adoption of a local drug and gang strategy by reenacting Las Posadas, the journey of Joseph and Mary searching for sanctuary. The next year, there were four forums for the newly created Anaheim Gang and Drug Task Force, which grew directly out of the lobbying, and the city council adopted a $5.8-million strategy. That year, a coordinator was hired and the money was earmarked for implementation. Three hundred representatives heard a report on the use of community redevelopment funds. Long before it received counsel from the mayor on a June night in 1994, the group already had begun to mobilize the power of its faith effectively to transform the nature of local government in Anaheim and to restore a sense of well-being to the city.

ORANGE COUNTY RECKONS WITH CHANGE

Putting religion in the context of the pursuit of happiness is a very Orange County-like way of looking at things. The area has grown since the nineteenth century as a frontier at the edge of the continent where the pursuit of personal happiness and satisfaction was taken at times to libertarian extremes. St. Boniface lies in the heart of a congressional district that is described in *The Almanac of American Politics* as an area where "a distinctive civilization was implanted ... mostly white and middle-class, confident of its traditional values and its market capitalism, proud of American principles and American military might."[10]

Many of the more conservative members of the old parish are descendants of those first German immigrants who arrived in the middle of the nineteenth century. They fashioned a city that jockeyed a century ago with Santa Ana to be the seat of a new county. As voters in what is now Orange County, they elected to have their rural society secede from Los Angeles in an effort to have more local control.[11]

The area has gone through various periods of upheaval at the same time it has developed as a formidable and increasingly cosmopolitan global economic center. In Anaheim, reactionary sentiment set the fun-loving German Catholics against the prohibitionist movement sentiment stirred by the local Ku Klux Klan, which seized on that issue as a focus for their conspiracy theories. There was a brief period in the 1920s when the Klan actually won municipal elections in Anaheim. Throughout the years, reactionary voices were heard from time to time—the John Birch Society, opponents of sex education in the schools, and recently, the religious right.

Orange County's colorful politics drew national attention in the 1950s and 1960s because of the activities of the John Birch Society, and some recently retired editors at *The Los Angeles Times* who remember the period tell of interviewing candidates for political office and routinely asking questions about Birch Society involvement. But the county, despite its waves of reaction and nativism, has been propelled in progressive directions by an expansive economic engine and by new freeways and housing developments as Californians spread southward. The sense of optimism found expression in military aerospace and high-tech expansion—and its bedrock conservative values tinged at times with a libertarian streak that surfaced in some of its politicians and in the editorials of the *Orange County Register*.

The seal of the city of Anaheim contains to this day a romantic vision of Orange County as an American frontier of promise and plenty. It portrays the distant mountain range, some agricultural fields spreading in the benevolent sun, and in the foreground, a harvest of citrus fruit to conjure a Shangri-la. It is the view that one can imagine on Harbor Boulevard before descending into central Anaheim on a day when the smog in the Los Angeles basin has lifted.

Such an optimistic view of Orange County, almost as a state of mind, took root as the place developed. One Times Orange County Poll, conducted on the centennial of the county's founding, produced some astounding findings as recently as 1989.[12] The polling appeared just before the unanticipated onset of recession and, with it, a new period of economic uncertainty and social problems in southern California. It found that 96 percent of respondents in Orange County were happy living there. It also found that, true to the tradition of its legal separation and psychological distancing from its more urban cosmopolitan neighbor to the north, it was considered by residents to be self-consciously an alternative to Los Angeles.

The prevailing values of the culture were clear enough in the polling, although they were not entirely consistent with the archconservative political stereotypes of Orange County. The area did take shape as a place that put a high premium on free enterprise and personal liberty, and residents held a deep suspicion of government but a friendly attitude toward the military. However, the survey found Orange County residents more inclined than its national image would suggest to oppose banning abortion and more accepting of homosexual rights.

While the poll identified broad-based conservatism, there was a decidedly mainstream cast to some of the county's thinking on the national political spectrum. Indeed, presidential candidate Bill Clinton, running as a centrist, ventured into Orange County two years later in search of votes in an area that had been Ronald Reagan's starting and ending place for political campaigns in the

1980s. In the 1992 election, a group of prominent Orange County Republicans caused a stir by abandoning George Bush in favor of the Democratic candidate.

URBAN TROUBLES FOR A PLACE IN THE SUN

Moreover, the poll also detected a streak of pragmatism about the limits of growth that did not indulge personal liberty all the way to the point where the environment would be harmed. As the 1990s unfolded, Orange County began to reckon with new perceptions of itself; it was no longer only a place blissfully pursuing individual freedoms and set apart from the problems of the rest of the country. It was beginning to look more like the more complicated world that Lenihan surveyed from his post at St. Boniface Church in Anaheim. It was beginning to look more like the rest of America.

In earlier times, the news that the city of Los Angeles was positioning itself in the autumn of 1993 for the anticipated verdict in the trial of two men accused of beating Reginald O. Denny, a truck driver assaulted during the riots the previous year, might have served to reinforce the perception of Orange County as a trouble-free place apart. If the reaction to the Denny case was not the most important concern on the weekend of October 16 and 17, when the verdict was anticipated, it was because other pressing concerns close to home had crowded it out.

That weekend, from Anaheim to the country's southern community of San Clemente, six people were killed and eight others wounded in gang-related attacks, with the city of Santa Ana, a community with a large immigrant population, bearing the brunt. In Anaheim, Eusebro Elizalde Arteaga, a 16-year-old, was one of those killed. He was shot in the back during a drive-by shooting, for no apparent reason, as he and his brother walked home after visiting with an uncle. In another incident that came to epitomize trouble in paradise, a 17-year-old high school student named Steve Woods in San Clemente to the south, which had been known primarily as the escape for President Nixon during his presidency to a "Western White House," lay in a coma near death after being speared by a paint roller in a hostile encounter between groups of youths in a beach parking lot.[13]

The Woods case ended up bringing to the surface racial tensions between whites and Latinos that had gone unattended in San Clemente, a very different and much newer community than Anaheim. Nevertheless, such incidents as the drive-by shooting in Anaheim and the beach parking lot attack in San Clemente were suggestive of some of the cracks in the foundation of the belief that all remained well in Orange County as a limitless frontier of suburban freedoms. A group that cosponsored the controversial California anti-illegal immigration ballot measure, Proposition 187, asserted at one point that the Woods case actually had been a catalyst for the initiative.[14] Woods, who eventually died, had been white, and his assailants had been described by police as gang members. Parents complained that Latino youngsters were being stereotyped after six teens were arrested in the death and two were convicted of second-degree murder and sentenced to the California Youth Authority by a judge who concluded that the youngsters still had hope of turning their lives around. A third youngster was later sentenced to 26 years to life in prison. The case produced a great deal of resentment, and the community found itself in the throes of pain and soul-searching, a sign of change in suburban Orange County.

A similar concern about the social fabric had enlisted the interfaith group and the city government in the older community to the north of Anaheim, but it was just beginning. Collective angst found expression soon after the Woods attack at the University of California, Irvine, where results from the annual survey conducted out of the campus' School of Social Ecology were released. For the first time ever, an urban-style angst about crime had topped the list of public concerns.[15]

Actually, by 1994, it became clear that crime was on the decrease in Orange County as a whole, but some urban areas like Anaheim and Santa Ana were caught in the grips of recurring bouts with gang violence, and there were unmistakable signs of a deteriorating social structure. By this time the recession had sunk in, and suddenly the sense of optimism and boundless possibility for the future that had characterized much of the growth of Orange County were being questioned. Mark Baldassare, chairman of the urban and regional planning department at UC Irvine and the pollster who had found such remarkable satisfaction in earlier years in his survey for *The Los Angeles Times*, observed in late 1993 that the combination of crime and economic concerns had resulted in new perceptions about the quality of life. Perhaps more important, he reported the crucial finding that people were "more pessimistic about what the future holds."[16]

Separate polling done in the fall of 1993 by *The Los Angeles Times* addressed some of the same concerns about relationships between ethnic groups that Lenihan had suggested were present within the confines of his parish, even though his was by definition a community bonded by faith and committed to such values as "love of neighbor." Overall, residents of Orange County believed that race relations were better in their own bailiwick than in post-riot Los Angeles, but there was strong evidence of dissatisfaction. A full 52 percent of the county's residents thought that race relations were either "poor" or "not so good" and that rapid ethnic change that had to be reckoned with in a previously homogeneous county had set in.[17]

In touching down on the area of personal satisfaction and in exploring whether the political, social, and economic environment was producing "quality-of-life" returns for people, such survey research explored much of the same terrain upon which the Anaheim interfaith group and that city's gang and youth violence people were focusing their attention. It was an intersection of the findings of social scientists and the conclusions of members of a faith community, and also of city officials who saw the benefit of using the churches as a resource.

THE MODERATE ACTIVISTS ARE DIFFERENT

All the talk about "family values" in recent years makes it clear that many agree society needs to be shored up, but the

Anaheim group's foray into political waters has been refreshingly short on ideology. There is no shortage nowadays of professed piety in politics and over the public airwaves, but here was an alternative to the so-called "culture wars" playing out in the heart of Orange County, an area where the religious right has had a great deal of influence.

Several blocks away from the meeting place, for example, are the offices of the Rev. Louis P. Sheldon, whose Traditional Values Coalition has warred publicly against homosexuals and has participated in political campaigns across California, including several Orange County legislative races. In 1995, Sheldon took a leading role in developing a "religious equality" amendment. Also in recent years, Orange County has been a major seat of sophisticated church-based lobbying in conservative politics, according to a Times Orange County Poll on religious beliefs and practices conducted in 1991.[18]

Activities of these politically active religious conservatives differ in key areas from those of OCCCO. The former have become the foot soldiers of the "new" Republican party and at times have operated invisibly in local races, for example, by quietly interviewing political and school board candidates to determine their fitness to carry forward a political and social agenda that is tied to a narrow interpretation of a uniquely "Christian" culture. The OCCCO effort includes other groups and moves openly into the public stage at forums and through direct dialogue with city government.

OCCCO does contain some evangelical members, and there is evidence to the north in Los Angeles of the participation of some of these groups in broader community empowerment activities. However, most Christian conservative activists in Orange County appear to have steered clear of broader partnerships such as OCCCO, which share a basis in spiritual values but are strikingly different in their multiethnic and interdenominational makeup. Although they espouse a return to "family values" from the kind of broad-based coalition building that OCCCO represents, the religious conservatives do not in fact seek to negotiate with the city of Anaheim, even though it is wrestling with similar concerns about the fabric of society.

One difference between the two camps of faith activists is money. OCCCO and its companion ARCC are rich in the existing infrastructure of church facilities, but lack financial resources. While its participants tend to be conservative, the group has not been directly active to date in political campaigns. The religious right's modus operandi has been to spend generously in political races all over California, but to obscure the true sources of funding through political action committees with names that do not suggest their ties. In contrast to the very public "testifying" at St. Boniface Church, politically active Christian fundamentalists have tended to conduct "stealth" campaigns for local school boards, where candidates are financed but do not specifically identify themselves by religious affiliation.

Chapter Seven

Is There Common Ground for Church and State?

After the interfaith meeting at St. Boniface Church, Steve Swaim, Anaheim's community services superintendent, said that his city was witnessing a new fundamental relationship between city government and constituents. "No longer is city government up there on a hill," he said. "We are much more in the role of a facilitator now."[1]

The idea of a "city set upon a hill," John Winthrop's vision for a community in the New World, is older than the nation. It has quite a different connotation from the relationship conjured by Swaim, a city official working in the sprawling urbanized culture of southern California at the close of the twentieth century. The latter was intended as a far less flattering image of modern city government that stands apart from the citizens it serves, functioning as a remote central bureaucracy, like the big-city school systems around the country that consolidated power after the turn of the century and made decisions in top-down fashion, thus becoming targets for reform movements. The older colonial model is more the goal for what has been happening in Anaheim in the 1990s.

Because of the prevailing culture of the colonial period, the more optimistic vision of a "city set upon a hill" was exclusively Christian in focus. However, implicit in the notion is also the idea of forming sound working relationships between government and people of religious faith, and by today's standards, that includes a much broader group.

If the effort to bring religious sensibility to the public arena in Anaheim represented a new direction in a centuries-old American concept, "the city set upon a hill," then the prayer offered at the beginning of OCCCO's meeting with the mayor was offered by someone who provided the direct link with the past. Before the parade of speakers approached the microphone, the Rev. Stephen Mather of the First Presbyterian Church rose from his seat about midway back in the audience and strode to the microphone. He offered an invocation from St. Augustine, an author appropriate for such a moment because of his well-known considerations within the Christian tradition of the alternative cities of man and God.

The prayer noted that there were obstacles and dark moments on the road of life and that the inspiration to get beyond them arose from some wellspring of light and hope beyond people's immediate grasp. These words contained not just a statement of religious belief. They also suggested an acknowledgment of a deteriorated condition in the city that would require the best thinking of those who had come to meet from both sides, the late-twentieth-century versions of Augustine's secular city and his city rooted in higher purposes.

Mather's commitment to this coming together of representatives from the city and its communities of faith had personal and historical significance. A descendant of the Puritan leaders of colonial Massachusetts, he thus had a direct line to the earliest experience with local self-governance in the New World. His ancestors later moved from the New England of the early Congregationalists to the Midwest with a young nation's westward expansion; eventually Mather, in his mid-40s at the time of Anaheim's peak period of faith activism, had come to California.

Increase and Cotton Mather, leaders in some of the colonies' earliest religious activism, were no strangers to controversy. That inclination seems to have survived westward expansion in the person of their descendant. On the abortion rights question,

Mather had jumped feet first into the fray of the clash over societal values by assuming the role of president of the board of directors for Planned Parenthood in conservative Orange County.

ADVERSARIES TABLE THEIR DIFFERENCES

Less than a week after the interfaith meeting with city officials, Mather's church was picketed yet again by about 50 anti-abortion demonstrators from Operation Rescue—at a time of increasing concern about the safety of and right of access to abortion. As it turned out, the police outnumbered the protesters on that particular day. In a short statement, Mather appealed to freedom of conscience, echoing his ancestors in a principle rooted in American history. He asserted that Planned Parenthood was a voluntary organization, that it was promoting responsibility through education in sexuality, and that it provided other important health services to women.[2]

Mather joked that his work on behalf of abortion rights was in part a way of making restitution for the ways that the Puritans treated women. His personal card lightened the atmosphere of heat in the kitchen of his ministry; it said his line of work involved having: "Saints created, elephants tamed, dragons slain, lost sheep found, sins forgiven, pagans converted, missionaries sent, pilgrimages arranged, marriages validated, wars ended, cathedrals built, lions fed."

The presence of Mather with other clerical voices in OCCCO made for a complicated alliance. As "Father John" Lenihan observed, some of his own parishioners at St. Boniface Church who held strong anti-abortion views were among those demonstrating from time to time at Mather's nearby church. Lenihan, in assessing his association with Mather, said, "I don't want to come across as soft on our 'pro-life' stand, but there is a deeper level that unites us."[3]

Indeed, even as the faithful and the clergy have stood shoulder to shoulder in OCCCO and ARCC, they have affirmed the right to worship and congregate freely. Lenihan said that differences over social and cultural issues never came up because the participants were so focused on community survival that they effectively learned to table areas of sharp disagreement. The united clergy subscribe to the idea that when the well-being and safety of society is at stake, there are more important things than even abortion to be attended to, and other differences on social matters or theology are tabled.

THE ANAHEIM EXPERIMENT

Steve Swaim knew about higher common purposes, since the very existence of his office came into being in the early 1990s as part of the recommendations made by a task force of citizens influenced strongly by the local clergy. The group, working in 1992, was conscious of the rioting in south central Los Angeles to the north that had erupted after the verdict in the Rodney King beating case, and it sought to head off urban unrest in one of Orange County's oldest cities.[4]

Although Anaheim by that time had achieved the status of a national entertainment capital, the task force findings painted a stark portrait of a city at risk. It found that existing city programs were woefully inadequate and that there had been a proliferation of gang activity since the late 1980s. An estimated 700 members were found to be operating in 35 gangs, and in the first quarter of 1992, the number of narcotics-related arrests had doubled over the entire previous year.

The work of this group was aired at a series of large public forums. The city then set for itself ten priorities for action. The first was, predictably, more and better use of police, courts, and corrections resources. But close behind was a more basic perceived need to improve dealings with interpersonal, family, and community problems. These were the very "quality-of-life" considerations that traditionally are some of the concerns of religion. Trying to improve the way people in Anaheim related to one another was listed ahead of obtaining money for dealing with guns and drugs, ahead of the laments over poor coordination between city institutions and government, and ahead of a lack of housing and community facilities.[5]

In this plan of action, bearing the imprimatur of the city of Anaheim, a significant statement about reordering priorities and connecting religious institutional aims to improve family life became the officially stated public policy of a major southern California city. This declaration, focusing intensely on the survival of a community, came rather quietly into being, and without much agonizing over whether there might be potential constitutional hazards inherent in church involvement with civil matters.

This happened at a time when the "family values" debate raged on the larger national stage, with its distracting ideological conflicts over abortion rights, gay rights, officially sanctioned prayer in the schools, and the teaching of creationism. A city in Orange County, an area of much ferment on the politically active conservative front, was committing itself to a full and nonideological partnership between St. Augustine's city of God and city of man. It did so without ever mentioning religion specifically, except to list the churches conspicuously along with other groups as participants and to borrow directly from the language of religion and psychology about personal and community well-being.

The Anaheim experiment suggested the possibility for a more dynamic role for religions in American public life. We are a secular society that professes to allow the free exercise of religion or even the practice of no religion. But this does not necessarily mean that there can be no meaningful dialogue between church and state.

A CITY THAT LEARNS FROM ITS CITIZENS

The seventh-floor window in Steve Swaim's office adjacent to the Anaheim city manager offered a panoramic sweep of some of the symbols of Orange County. Spreading from west to east were the sprawling Disneyland complex and the nearby Convention Center; the Crystal Cathedral in nearby Garden Grove, whose pastor, the Rev. Robert Schuller, started preaching at a drive-in theater and developed a global TV ministry; and the Anaheim Stadium complex where the Angels and Rams professional sports franchises were once lured from Los Angeles, before they began to get restless in a changing sports environment.

Swaim had his desk pointed away from that window, and above it the wall was populated by the art of children. There is symbolism to be found in that positioning. Others in city government were focusing on reaching out for new development and sports teams or for the retention or redevelopment of old tourism areas. Swaim had a more interior view, focusing on neighborhoods.

Looking back out over the city, he outlined his philosophy:

> The skills of city employees are changing, now they are facilitators and problem solvers, and interest in bringing the best out of people so they can solve their own problems … City managers used to be experts in finance and paperwork, now we are finding city managers are those who have the people skills, and are good at consensus-building. That's my job, to facilitate throughout the community.[6]

Swaim, whose career began in the parks and recreation department with the city, came to his assignment in 1992 when the city was gearing up for its war on gangs and drugs. He readily acknowledges the influence of the local clergy in establishing his work as a priority within the city's executive branch. He was quick to recognize what activists had brought to the city's efforts in a time of dwindling fiscal resources for municipalities. The initial progress made in improving the impoverished Jeffrey Lynn neighborhood outside Disneyland, where Swaim was instrumental in implementing a new city policy, alerted the city to the extent of its community problems. Those problems came to the attention of officials because of the pressure of citizens, and that experience educated the city in the importance of listening to what ordinary people, without any expertise in city policy and planning, might have to say.

Mather believed that for city officials like Swaim, the activism of the faith community came as a revelation. Here, suddenly, were ordinary people coming forward who had made themselves knowledgeable about public policy. "They were not used to hearing the churches talk this way, but that they spoke from power, in effect were a resource for government, and that the ideas from the grass roots would percolate up to affect policy ... The sense of participation is new. Most churches have either a jaundiced view of the civic arena or ignore it," he said.[7]

This realization, coupled with a recognition that the city had money available to make a difference, transformed the dynamics between city and the churches. When church members moved into the public arena, they would begin their involvement in a manner deferential to city officials, but as they did their homework and developed expertise they became more confident. The city began to treat them differently.

Swaim said that the city and the churches discovered they had identical agendas both in recognizing a slippage in the community quality of life and in reversing it. It was, he said, the city's intention to make planning for children and families a priority in the budget. Part of this new awareness resulted from interaction with the churches. They had a track record and the authority to influence the behavior of citizens. Also, the resources of people are supplemented by the existence of church facilities in places that could be used to meet critical city needs. Swaim was candid about wishing it were easier to have more of them made available by the churches.

With tight city budgets, the churches already had in place the physical plant, or infrastructure, needed for implementing programs. Swaim noted with satisfaction, as if he were a recreation official counting swingsets and ball fields, that Anaheim has some 108 churches, many with community space and outdoor play areas. He said, "If you can energize six to eight clusters of churches in parts of the city influencing young people, and if the city provides a coordinated effort, you would be amazed at how effective this can be."[8]

Swaim would not comment on the absence from the community meeting of some of the nearby politically active Christian fundamentalist groups, except to say that anybody with an interest in improving the city's quality of life would be welcome at the table. However, he observed that it was essential for church groups to "have a broad involvement in the community," and that only those with long-established traditions were likely to be in a position to participate. Those churches happen to be the ones with the facilities, and they happen to be those considered "mainstream."[9]

AFTER COMMUNITY SURVIVAL, WHAT NEXT?

If the politics of having the churches work more effectively with the city could be worked out, Anaheim was poised to take a unique partnership between the public sector and private religious groups in interesting new directions. Money almost certainly would be a factor in what the city can do for groups of citizens coming forward with demands grounded in even the best of intentions. Were OCCCO not already well established, it would be much harder to get such a partnership going in the current fiscal climate. The declaration of bankruptcy by the county government after the collapse of its investment pool in late 1994 sent shock waves of alarm rippling through the cities about what the future might hold. Anaheim seemed to shake, but it also appeared rather quickly to be in a financial position to right itself over the long term. John Gaudette, OCCCO staff director, later said he believed that it would continue to be possible to work with the city toward the creation of a teen center and meeting other goals envisioned by the community activists.

By 1996, there clearly was a change in strategy, which Gaudette said was a hopeful "indication that we were not concerned with just the basics anymore." By that he meant that the early activities of OCCCO had to do with community survival and had found expression in lobbying for community policing and after-school programs to keep youngsters out of trouble. With these things coming on line, the group began to focus at a new rung on the hierarchy of needs: the promotion of job training and opportunity. He said, "What a kid needs to get on track is not there, and we're starting to get into that."[10] Special attention was being given to summer programs and how resources were being allocated among students during the school year.

There also were plans to begin working in the newer sprawling suburbs to the south. Orange County is well suited for church communities to figure in the spread of the suburbs. The area lacks traditional ethnic neighborhoods grouped around church communities, which bound people to their early American experience in older parts of the country, the places that sent migrants west to southern California. Its sprawling nature linked only by freeways and retail and job centers fueled the development of "full-service" churches, which provide people with a sense of connection that they might not otherwise be able to get in the vast, grid-pattern development that dominates the landscape.

As early as 1991, a Times Orange County Poll found that more than 91 percent of church or synagogue members thought that their congregations were doing a good or excellent job of providing for their needs.[10] Some of the churches, like St. Boniface in Anaheim, have provided substantial services to the community, such as food for the homeless, schools, and religious services that reach out to an increasingly diverse group of residents who speak many languages.

This acceptance of churches' ability to be providers of services that benefit the community provides a crucial element for the city's involvement. A mutuality of interests has been spawned at a time when church and community are drawn to stake out common ground because of concerns with violence and drugs a shared perception that community life is eroding.

THE NEW "CITY SET ON A HILL"

Swaim was mindful of the city's need to maintain arm's length from the religious content that inspires a diverse group of churchgoing participants. However, he said there was no denying the depth of the city's commitment to the effort either, considering that "a percentage of our community is turning to behaviors with drastic consequences, and somebody has to figure out what's wrong with kids today."[11]

The problem, from Swaim's perspective, is that too many young people inevitably are exposed to "risk factors"—gangs, single-parent families, dangerous neighborhoods, lack of direction, and little hope of future economic opportunity—that put them in trouble's reach no matter what. He said that law enforcement officials and other city officials agreed that the problem begins with weak family units. The family is an area of traditional concern for the churches, and this gives the churches and the city a common starting point in trying to address what is wrong.

For Swaim, the problems generally were reducible to a lack of supervision, a lack of discipline, a failure to set goals in healthy family settings, and instances of child abuse. He observed that there were about 15 neighborhoods in the city that he described as "disenfranchised," and he hoped eventually to mobilize them toward the goal of making youth and families a priority, perhaps with the aid of the city's seven school boards.

Anaheim is hardly unique, but the perspectives of its city officials and clergy, and their methods for approaching their problems, provide a window on some national trends. Not long after the Anaheim meeting at St. Boniface, the Census Bureau reported that the traditional "nuclear family," with both parents in the home, was close to becoming the minority in the United States, a sign of powerful societal forces placing children into single-parent or alternative situations.[12]

Swaim, who undertook his efforts drawing from 15 years' previous experience with the city, said it was unusual for a city with a population of less than 300,000 to have someone acting as a community facilitator, but saw it potentially as the beginning of a national trend. Through his city hall perspective, he recognized the potential of churches as partners.

Religious leaders nationally clearly have come to their own conclusions about the need for church involvement in a hostile or deteriorating social environment. Martin J. Marty, who teaches the history of religion at the University of Chicago, has observed that churches across the country have been seeking to provide alternatives to a secular mall culture by providing community services to meet spiritual and social needs.[13]

As a priest, Lenihan saw himself walking a fine line, to be socially active without being openly political, and mindful that some of the more conservative members of his own parish react unfavorably to efforts to involve the church in such activities. At one point his parish's luncheon giveaways to the homeless had to be moved to another site because of concerns about the appearance of "undesirables" mingling so close to children at a parish school. Neither did Lenihan have illusions about the crumbling of some of the neighborhoods. He believed it was an emergency situation calling for emergency measures. He regarded religion as bringing resources of compassion, discipline, and hope as bromides for the aimlessness, disappointment, and cheapening of life.

The question remains whether there will be a lasting success in turning lives around in this collaboration—or whether it will make a difference soon enough. Swaim acknowledged a certain frustration with the slowness of building an effective partnership and a politically effective component to OCCCO. He believed there were times when a phone call might be preferable to a grand presentation before the mayor or the city council.

If success did not come swiftly enough for idealistic city workers, the evidence of progress was undeniable. It could be found in the small victories achieved in targeted neighborhoods and in the existence of an arm of the city government pledged to work with these groups. For whatever politicization may result from involving mainstream religious groups in city problems, there also was evidence that slow and steady wins the race.

A LIGHT IN THE SANCTUARY

The assumption of a new and updated view of the much-discussed concept of "personal responsibility" was a thread running through the relationship of the city with the churches, and it was at the core of the churches' ability to reach their own accommodation.

Lenihan's early participation in OCCCO was premised on the idea that it is possible to bridge the gap between Sunday rituals and what happens the rest of the week in the city's neighborhoods and families. He talked about the need to set parameters for young people by encouraging them to defer gratification. He acknowledged that the ideas of sin and guilt in the Christian tradition might be seen as adding yet another burden to lives that already were bogged down in the concerns of basic survival.

But his was a more nuanced view than simply demanding the postponement of sensual enjoyment because to do otherwise would be morally unacceptable behavior. It posited a constructive outcome. It was the idea that happiness is to be pursued not through immediate satisfaction but through longer-term striving for worthwhile objectives. It was premised on the notion that entire communities could be strengthened by lifting their sights. Lenihan said he never had discussed theological differences or nuances of positions on social issues with other participating clergy. He said, "We rarely spend time on the things that divide us."[14]

If affirmation is central to Lenihan's ministry, justice turned out to be crucial for Mather. The pursuit of just ends bridged the perspective of Mather's faith community and linked it with the larger aspirations of a modern democracy. This sentiment was shared by one of his parishioners active in OCCCO, Dianne Horn, who said that a sense of social justice informs the idea that "We have to live our faith."[15]

Just blocks from city hall, Mather worked in an office tucked behind giant wood doors leading to the church's courtyard, and its cramped quarters gave the feeling of entering a stateroom on an old ship. Crossing to the sanctuary one day at the height of the interfaith effort, he was reminded that literally and figuratively a light shined in his church and on his city.

In the 1950s, a time when Orange County was going through the convulsions of its John Birch Society phase, the sanctuary of the First Presbyterian Church was built. At that time, a period when interfaith dialogue in the city was unheard of, the parishioners of St. Boniface Catholic Church before Lenihan's time had donated to Mather's predecessors a sanctuary light as a gesture of goodwill that today still hangs from the rafters of the Presbyterian Church.

It is a beacon from the early days of local efforts to cross denominational lines and carve out the earliest new expanded boundaries of interfaith acceptance. It is in a sense a street lamp for the "city set upon a hill," a signal of a broader view of community. The light hangs high in the rafters, spreading dim illumination in a quiet sanctuary of subdued colors. Showing it proudly to a visitor, Mather looked up and said, "I don't know how we will ever get up there if we have to change the light."[16]

His statement was testimony to the sustaining power of good intentions and to the wonders of a well-made bulb. The light has continued to glow without interruption since the time it was given decades ago.

Chapter Eight

Identifying America's Emerging Moral Middle

In the discussion of the interfaith effort in Anaheim, it was noted that a poll by *The Los Angeles Times* in the summer of 1994 found that while many Americans did not always agree with the solutions advanced by religious conservatives, few believed that they posed much danger to society. At the same time, by a five-to-three margin, respondents worried more about trends in morality than economic concerns.[1] As *Newsweek* political writer Howard Fineman observed shortly thereafter when the Christian Coalition was convening in Washington, much of the polling leading up to the November 1994 elections and laying groundwork for the 1996 presidential election gave evidence of a concern about moral issues among mainstream Americans. That included some surveying done by People for the American Way, a liberal group that monitors religious conservatives, which found that most Americans embrace traditional moral and religious values.[2]

In 1995, Republican Ed Goeas and Democrat Celinda Lake found 40 percent of Americans concerned about the links of Democrats to radical liberal groups and 39 percent worried about Republicans links "to conservative special interests like the religious right and the Moral Majority."[3] A poll by *The Los Angeles Times* taken in the spring of 1996 found that 78 percent of respondents said they were dissatisfied with current moral values, and these concerns spread across lines of race, age, gender, income, region, and political boundaries.[4]

Efforts to achieve interfaith understanding in Anaheim had their roots in the 1950s in the simple granting of a sanctuary light from one congregation to another. It developed into a full partnership between the city's faith community and its city government and offered a case study of insight into areas of overlapping concern between politically active religious conservatives and mainstream Americans. By the early 1990s, the religious right successfully had identified that because of such problems as out-of-wedlock births, high crime rates, and youth gangs and violence, many Americans were feeling anxious about the moral climate of their society. They advanced a coherent but simplistic and constitutionally troubling response, a direct challenge to those who at the same time were insisting that religion and the state ought to be completely separate.

THE MORAL CENTER: TOLERANT AND FLUID

The struggling partnership of the churches and the city in Anaheim and similar efforts being made elsewhere suggest that there is some mainstream territory providing more room to maneuver on America's moral and spiritual landscape than might be apparent. In that zone, people from various cultures and backgrounds can wear their religious sentiments on their sleeves, and do so even with some government involvement in ways that do not threaten to bring democracy to its knees and replace it with something else. This middle ground has the potential in modern times to be what the nineteenth-century observer Alexis de Tocqueville saw in the America of his day, a place where religion operated as a positive force, practiced freely and keeping the government on its toes.

There is evidence of this possibility for religion-based activism in the other new interfaith experiments around the country. For example, former Missouri Senator John Danforth's group that has been mobilizing congregations in St. Louis to help inner-city youngsters reports no church–state friction arising from its early efforts to work with school officials. Liz McCloskey, who directs the group called InterACT, said in an interview, "I was sort of expecting that, but everybody I am talking to seems very supportive of the power and capacity of religious congregations to positively impact people's lives."[5]

If groups like Anaheim's could identify a tolerant middle ground, it suggests that injecting religious values into the public arena need not aggravate differences between liberals and conservatives on social issues or public policy. It may be that this group of Americans is fluid, with people moving in and out to occupy areas of agreement where concern about the well-being of society's fabric is so strong as to compel grassroots activism and override differences on particular divisive issues. For example, people in Anaheim opposed to abortion on moral grounds stood shoulder-to-shoulder with abortion rights advocates on after-school programs and, having achieved some of those goals, today seek further improvement in education and job training.

The presence of shared religious values in this effort is clear. It was not apparent for the long term whether the Anaheim effort would succeed in its stated policy goals, stemming youth violence and turning around deteriorated neighborhoods. New participants would have to continue the efforts of those in on the early efforts, people like "Father John" Lenihan, who was assigned to a different parish in south Orange County in the fall of 1995. Sustained efforts with results to show along the way would count for a lot in answering the concerns of strict separationists who say that the full flowering of religious sentiment is best left to private homes and churches. John Gaudette, staff director of OCCCO, reported in 1996 that he believed that with a systematic approach to community problem solving in place, it indeed was possible for new players to enter the arena and pick up the work of those who had established it. "We are pulling in new leaders," he said.[6]

However, even for those who recognize a place for religious values in the public arena, there may be limited areas in the larger society where agreement on objectives is possible. Former New York Governor Mario M. Cuomo raised this question in his much-publicized 1984 Notre Dame speech: "The values derived from religious belief will not, and should not, be accepted as part of the public morality unless they are shared by the pluralistic community at large, by consensus."[7]

One of the things that turns people off to the religious right is the idea of church activism in politics, with all that it might portend about the erosion of the principle of church–state separation. But if the right has been a force in seeking to impose church-based solutions on everyone else, the left also has tended to be unwilling to acknowledge the potential for a comfortable accommodation of faith activism in modern democracy. The people in the middle are the ones who appear most open to real change through the application of moral and spiritual perspectives to modern society's problems. The others, for vastly different reasons, are holding fast to outdated views of religion in society that create and sustain some of the polarization that we examined in Part I of this book.

CONFLICT OR RESOLUTION?

The search for common ground has been going on rather quietly, even as the debate of the so-called "culture war" raged over abortion, gay rights, abstinence, interpretations of scripture, and the role of government in the lives of Americans and as politicians homed in nationally on public concern about morality and values. Much of the debate over values seems to be going on today in a highly charged environment.

By contrast, what is significant about Anaheim's interfaith initiative is that it gave evidence of meaningful conversation between religiously inspired Americans being conducted at the local level. The same can be said of the dialogue on interfaith religious content in Los Angeles that will be discussed in subsequent chapters. This is happening at a time when the country seemingly is confused about its moral direction and appears ripe for a broad-based and nondogmatic spiritual dialogue.

As the debate over values has become highly politicized at

the national level, we have people acting in ways that cross cultural and denominational lines, even if their belief systems arise from different concepts of the Ultimate Ground of Being, or God. Moreover, while the moral middle seems to share some of the concerns of fundamentalists, election results in nearby Vista, California, in late 1994 suggested that mainstream Americans do not necessarily want to embrace a narrow religious-based agenda in the quest for a better moral foundation for society. After a divisive time in the school system, fundamentalist members of the school board were recalled, and all five Christian conservatives who ran for three vacant seats on the board were defeated.[8]

The tolerant moral center provides flexible ground for citizens, religious leaders, and institutions to move in and out at any given time and to have an easier time achieving consensus as the action moves into specific communities and neighborhoods faced with immediate problems. For example, Lenihan and the Rev. Stephen Mather were light years apart on abortion, and yet they and the multilingual congregations participating in OCCCO and ARCC have explored ways of working together in the moral sphere that presumably would be unthinkable for, say, a preacher who told young people at the Anaheim Convention Center in the summer of 1994 that tolerance and diversity were social liabilities.

MORAL PERSPECTIVES AND INTERFAITH ACTIVISM

At the same time, there are common threads evident in the interviews done with the two clergymen for this book. For example, Lenihan's interest in encouraging the postponement of enjoyment for getting one's life in order and Mather's "alternative to the ethic of consumption," were somewhere on the same page and yet quite different in tone and character from the pledges of abstinence taken by those thousands of evangelical teenagers at the Christian youth movement gathering.

Mather, like Lenihan, believed that churches were positioned strategically as concern mounts about the social fabric to talk in modern terms about topics such as what it means grow as a human being and resisting temptation. He agreed that the time was ripe for the kind of attention to the human personality that is the province of religion traditionally and for the healthy involvement in civic affairs that the interfaith group seeks.

Although he and Lenihan disagreed strongly on abortion rights, both found a receptiveness in the soil for the traditional concerns of churches as custodians of a way of living disciplined and moral lives. Mather did not favor simply telling young people not to do things. Rather, he said, "Our appetites will always exceed what we can do, so some other discipline has to be part of life. We're in a key place to back an alternative to an ethic of consumption."[9]

The mainstream effort's pragmatism arises in response to a self-destructive tendency in modern life identified dramatically by Father Greg Boyle of the Dolores Mission Church in Los Angeles, who has dedicated his life to working with gang members in one of the toughest pieces of real estate in southern California. It is the idea that certain behavior is counterproductive for the individual *and* society. That idea provided the bridge with the city officials in Anaheim who were trying to get the government involved in turning lives around. Boyle, who met with officials and clergy in Anaheim, went so far as to describe what he saw in gang communities as collective suicidal behavior. It develops, he said, from economic conditions and from an irrational and debilitating mind-set that leaves young people and entire communities with a feeling that there is nothing to live for tomorrow.

In that sense, the moral compass of the new multiethnic middle ground points toward the transformation of hopeless situations into more positive and fertile ground for the long term. The undertaking is significant for its attempt to marry broad-based religious impulses and democracy at some deep level. It seeks to replace an existential view that nothing matters beyond the immediate moment, because there is nothing more purposeful to live for, with the idea that a democratic society is worth investing in for the good of its individuals and for the collective welfare of all its members.

The experience in Anaheim likewise arose from a perception

that all was not well with the family or with society's collective life. But it was premised on the idea that people of good will need to stake out areas of agreement that can be found more easily than arguing over social and cultural issues. If religious sentiment in the public arena can be misguided and cause harm, it also makes a strong case for being a constructive force.

Because it was centered in concepts of love and positive images of self, it had the capacity to do more than even well-intentioned discussions of bringing our "common democratic values" to bear on our problems. This did not mean that it would prevail in the short term, or even that the process itself would be without a political component. As Mather observed, the drama of giving testimony and the ritual of lobbying were necessary and effective as pressure tactics, even if frustrating for bureaucrats. However, religious motivation makes practitioners bold enough to try this even against the odds and in the face of daunting experiences in life on the mean streets. Religion posits a view of human nature that can be quite realistic about man's capacity for evil or to do harm to himself. At the same time, it looks beyond limitation to affirm something exalted within.

DEALING WITH OUR DIFFERENCES

In a sense, there is nothing new under the sun. Church activism was central to abolitionism and the civil rights movement, to the nation's protests against nuclear madness and the Vietnam War, and, going back to colonial times, to fanning the flames of revolutionary ferment. The difference in the current climate is that the politically active religious conservatives were first into the fight in addressing the country's current moral malaise, boldly bringing the discussion of "values" to bear on a society perceived as being in decay.

The enlistment of mainstream people from different faith communities, and from different cultures, is a much trickier business. It raises new considerations about how the country deals with its new diversity, since any broad-based discussion of values necessarily raises the question of whose values we are talking about. For these efforts in a democracy, Anaheim has been instructive.

While many in the Anaheim group would be described as politically conservative, their efforts were not quite like what many conservative intellectuals have been saying in recent years. In the rhetoric of the right, government is the bad guy and ought to be entirely out of the business of social programs, leaving the churches and concerned individuals to do what they can privately. Alternatively, secularists argue for keeping the religions at bay. While the conservatives don't trust the government, the liberals don't trust the churches.

In fact, the Anaheim experiment was much more accommodating of government, more open about applying pressure to achieve policy objectives, and ultimately more centrist in political terms. The faith community sought government assistance and generosity for an anticipatory agenda of afterschool programs, community centers, computer labs, and homework centers. These are all the kinds of preventive programs that were so controversial nationally as measures in the 1994 crime bill that some Republicans objected to as "pork."

ARCC listed among its membership Baptists, Catholics, Baha'is, Lutherans, Muslims, Methodists, Presbyterians, Christian Scientists, and others. Not only has it been a mainstream effort, but it has also differed markedly from the political activities of fundamentalists because of its inclusiveness. When ARCC formed in response to the city's gang and drug citizens task force strategy, it sought either to be a leader or a resource in making the city a better place to live.

In this effort, the group seemed to be charting fresh meaning for the concept of freedom of religion. The wall of separation between church and state and the free exercise clauses of the First Amendment inform the role of religion in American society. Clearly, the wall of separation envisioned in the constitution was being tested in Orange County, as the religious right pushed its agenda. In the Capistrano Valley School District in the growing southern part of the county, for example, an effort was made to import creationism into a public school classroom. The fundamentalist biology teacher involved in that case, John Peloza, went beyond even what pressure groups in state legislatures elsewhere had tried to do in seeking equal treatment for creationism in the classroom—he sued his own school district.

If California provides harbingers of things to come nationally, the Anaheim experiment evidences the country's willingness, maybe even desperation, to get beyond the rhetoric of "family values" and cultural clashes. While the initiative has its moments of grandstanding and speech-making, it seems relatively free of the polarization that characterizes most of the discussion about values in the country today. The group had been active long enough by the time it met with the mayor of Anaheim that it was not an entirely "new" movement, either. One telling question for the long term is whether it can survive and flourish in the polarized atmosphere that exists in Orange County and whether similar efforts can flourish nationally in the country's charged political landscape. It will be especially difficult to do these things at a time when money to do even proven social programs is even harder to find.

In Orange County, during the 1990s, the competition from worthy causes for public dollars intensified as the recession sank into a region where once it appeared that the sky was the limit. The county's declaration of bankruptcy after its investment fund collapsed cast a pall over many dreams. Moreover, the particular nature of the problem the group has been trying to address in Anaheim, gang and youth violence, may be so intractable as to defy remedies. The people involved in this effort on both sides, in the religious communities and at city hall, knew what a daunting undertaking it was to aim for the transformation of the culture of the city from the inside out. One answer, at least for the near term, is that there may be no alternative left but to try.

The ability of the Anaheim group to evolve from a concern with basic community viability to quality-of-life questions associated with education and job training programs surely was an encouraging sign. However, if efforts like it falter, one place to look will be in the shifting political and moral center. It is a place between ideological extremes where people with views as different on abortion as Catholics and Presbyterians are trying to share space. Such fragile alliances are susceptible to collapse or manipulation when there is as much political hot air about as there has been in this country in recent years. A key question is whether the light shining in Anaheim amid the heat will be overcome in the shouting.

The Anaheim group's efforts show that tendencies to accommodation and compromise are at the heart of making our system work in practice. This is, after all, a plan of self-governance that for all its flaws turns on the premise, much tested and strained, that things can be worked out. Democracy does not have much of a chance over the long haul if it gives way to mistrust or proves unwilling to put faith in some fundamental quality of goodness at the core of its individual members.

On the eve of the twenty-first century, multiethnicity is a fact of life in the social activism of all people of faith, and it is going to challenge government to adapt with fresh understanding and to contemplate new working relationships within the American system's framework of church and state. As we shall see in Los Angeles, this effort in the social and political sphere can be supported by the search for areas of agreement on an even deeper level, in the identification of what a community is all about and in core spiritual values themselves.

Part III

L.A. Story

How the Riots Got People Thinking

===============================

Chapter Nine

The Search for a City's Soul

When the light dawned on Los Angeles on July 1, 1993, a city battered a little over a year earlier by rioting awoke to a different political era with the inauguration of a new mayor. The suggestion that the city was looking for its spiritual coordinates was richly evident.

Richard Riordan preceded his arrival at city hall with a private Mass presided over by Cardinal Roger M. Mahony, followed by a prayer breakfast sponsored by the Interreligious Council of Southern California. The new mayor's support for abortion, his status as a Catholic estranged from his second wife, and his participation days earlier in the Los Angeles Gay Pride Parade might on the surface appear to be issues in his own relationship with the conservative cardinal. The latter had kept his distance from gay and lesbian groups and had declared several years earlier that all Catholic government officials had a moral obligation to work for laws on the repeal of abortion. Yet, on that day of new beginnings, Mahony told the archdiocesan newspaper, "We need a [mayor] who can keep his spiritual values and principles strong. And I believe Mayor Riordan is that type of person."[1]

The relationship between the two leaders, as *The Los Angeles Times* pointed out, was well established by the time Riordan became mayor through his efforts as a businessman, as chairman of an archdiocesan education foundation, and as a member of the cardinal's finance council formed to modernize the finances of the archdiocese.[2] There is always a certain amount of pragmatism evident in relationships between Catholic politicians and their church's spiritual leaders, but the day also gave hint of a potential for a changing dynamic for religious institutions within Los Angeles.

The Rev. Vivian Ben Lima, at the time president of the interfaith group and director of the archdiocese's Commission on Ecumenical and Interreligious Affairs, later concluded in an interview for this book that the mayor's relationship with the cardinal had facilitated the important task of introducing an interfaith component in addition to the celebration of the Mass, which was a Catholic affair. Mahony by that time had demonstrated considerable political skill by leading religious leaders in an effort after the riots to extract promises in the midst of the recession for an antigang program, over the opposition of former Mayor Tom Bradley.[3]

On one level, the interfaith component on inauguration day reflected the evolution of the discussion between the Roman Catholic community and others in the city's religious and governmental power structure. Under Mahony, for example, the Catholics had forged ties with the city's Islamic community that were so solid that the two faiths generally had identified areas of agreement on moral positions related to abortion, crime, gang wars, immigration, and the like. By the summer of 1994, Lima could say without hesitation, "The cardinal speaks for them in matters of ethics" (but not politics).[4] Dr. Maher Hathout, the president of the Islamic Community of Southern California, later confirmed in an interview that this comfort level had been achieved. That this faith-to-faith dialogue within a diverse city seething with racial tensions could move so far beyond the mere formalities of acceptance represented a substantial achievement.

The mayor early on forged political relationships not only with the cardinal but also with conservative religious communities elsewhere, such as in south central Los Angeles where the rioting had occurred, as a study by the University of Southern California later noted. Both the mayor and the cardinal by 1994 also were trying to invigorate mainline religious involvement in the renewal of the city through programs like the church's anti-gang program, Hope in Youth. Although different in its top-down structure from the more broadly based OCCCO, it espoused similar populist tactics of inspiring faith communities to community organizing.[5] In the competition for scarce resources, the cardinal's Hope in Youth program came under heavy criticism from the city's Community Development Department for overstaffing and alleged poor management in early 1995, but received a funding reprieve from the city council.

On a broader level, the interfaith community's involvement on inauguration day was a significant moment for the city's long-running interfaith dialogue, born in the late 1960s in response to a perceived need for better contacts between the major religious institutions of the city. In the aftermath of the riots, everything suddenly appeared in a different context to participants, as if the city's spiritual need somehow was crying out urgently despite years of dialogue. There was a sense that new approaches to old and festering problems of racial suspicion and tension needed to be tried.

In 1992, there was a recognition that the city itself had changed, and there was an assessment that the role of interfaith efforts should not be merely to conduct dialogue and attend to social needs. Those things were important, but perhaps more important was the realization that the city's own soul, its very sense of self and identity, needed a massive injection of spiritual renewal.

WHAT THE RIOTING REVEALED

Rabbi Harvey J. Fields recalled about a year after the riots that when the unrest broke out, he had been standing before 350 teenagers of different ethnic and religious backgrounds gathered in the sanctuary of his Wilshire Boulevard Temple for a Seder, a feast marking the exodus of the Jews from bondage in Egypt. It was, he told *The Los Angeles Times*, a moment of realization. "I know the city is coming apart.... It dawned on me in that moment that ... somehow the religious community had to get more deeply involved in turning this city around."[6]

At the time of the riots, the energetic Fields was president of the Interreligious Council, an 18-year-old organization that was generally considered to be among the nation's most advanced interfaith dialogues and a model for other cities in major institutional contacts between faiths. But Field's sense of immediacy arose in part from the relatively closed nature of this exchange. He later said in an interview for this book, "It represented the major religious elements within the community, the old-line religious groups, and representation was by appointment."[7]

He suggested that an organization that initially had been innovative had come to represent the establishment for many. A program of dialogue in a city bursting with different ethnic groups and local congregations was still to be explored at the grassroots level. The Interreligious Council, for all its considerable achievements as a pioneer in interfaith dialogue in the United States, was suddenly behind the times and poorly positioned to respond to site-specific neighborhood needs. Recognizing the need for change from within might be the difference between the revitalization of an organization and the establishment of alternative groups to do the job. The alternative would be the gradual irrelevance of an existing institution.

About a week after the unrest, an event sponsored by the council and attended by about 300 people produced a sense, as Fields later described it, that "We've got a major revolution here and we have to throw open the doors." The idea for the Interfaith Coalition to Heal Los Angeles was born. A project of the larger umbrella council, it would operate on the premise that the effort to make religious organizations more responsive to the needs evident in the rioting would have to be something more inclusive and accessible.

All would be welcome. The coalition would attempt to combine efforts to get people thinking differently about the city. There would be mentor relationships established between individual congregations and programs in the schools to improve understanding between ethnic groups. Direct congregation-to-congregation dialogues would be tools designed to facilitate communication in a crisis.

Hathout, later a president of the interreligious council, said, "The riots showed how incapable we are as a body to deal with an emergency volatile situation." He characterized the establishment of the more flexible Interfaith Coalition to Heal Los Angeles as "a rapid deployment force."[8]

Efforts for low-income housing and youth shelters were launched. Donated food was given away, prayer vigils were held, credit unions backed churches, and entrepreneurial assistance programs were started. A program in the public schools to foster understanding of different ethnic groups was instituted. Pulpits were shared, bringing rabbis to inner-city platforms and ministers to synagogues. The liberal group the American Jewish Congress met with African-American and Latino clergy to discuss the videotaped beating of Rodney G. King and, after hearing allegations of abuse incidents at the hands of the Los Angeles Police Department, called for Police Chief Daryl F. Gates to resign.

On short notice, a symbolic event called "Hands Across L.A." was assembled. An estimated 15,000 people held hands across Western Avenue in a demonstration of religious unity. The event was significant for what it suggested about the conclusion reached by some clergy, especially Fields, about the task at hand. The selective use of the media event was considered for its capacity to perform the larger function of fostering a sense of unity in the community. The idea, literally, was to encourage people to love their city.

Fields had concluded that communicating the need for an improved sense of community "is not done magically, and it's not the religious establishment versus the media." He believed that what religious communities in Los Angeles needed to do was get people thinking about what they had in common, and the media was something they already shared. In his assessment, one of the central post-riot needs was getting people thinking beyond their individual neighborhoods and congregations and beginning to see the city in its entirety.

RESEARCHERS IDENTIFY A NEW CIVIC SPIRITUALITY

The search for ways of healing a city's soul was ultimately an effort that involved human emotion and passion about a place undergoing profound upheaval. In 1994, a study by the Religion and Civic Order Project at the University of Southern California and the University of California Santa Barbara identified some of the bubbling enthusiasm and evaluated its effects over the short term.

On the one hand, it found that "Los Angeles' emergent politics of the spirit is drawing mixed reviews among religious leaders and parishioners, both on the right and left."[9] That is to say, among other things, that some liberal members of the clergy thought that the conscious attempt to get people thinking positively as a premise for improving life in the city constituted a kind of diversion, or even narcissism, that might district from the hard work of focusing on political or economic issues and programs. There was also concern among evangelical Protestants that religion and politics should not be interchanged.

On the other hand, however, the study suggested convincingly that these criticisms might be "undervaluing" the effort because of the despair that many people were feeling. Fields, a man of infectious enthusiasm, later said he thought that modern-day marketing strategies were required to get messages out, even those calling for people to think of themselves as part of a body of citizens united in spirit and purpose. "We live in a media world," he said.[10]

L.A.'S LONGTIME INTERFAITH WORK

The larger interfaith effort in Los Angeles, the Interreligious Council of Southern California, celebrated its 25th anniversary in 1994. It has aimed to promote understanding and respect among all faiths, to share concerns about problems, and to provide moral leadership on various issues. While the smaller interfaith coalition arose in 1992 as a direct response to the civil unrest, the parent organization had developed not so much from any specific event as from conversations that were already taking place. Rabbi Alfred Wolf, director of the Skirball Institute on American Values of the American Jewish Committee, present at the creation, recalled in an interview a feeling that "the community was ready for an across-the-board, lasting organization."[11] Originally, it consisted of the Roman Catholic Archdiocese of Los Angeles, the Board of Rabbis of Southern California, and two Protestant church councils.

Essentially, it was an interfaith organization of Protestants, Catholics, and Jews. The Islamic community later asked to join, and efforts were made to enlist the participation of Buddhist and Hindu organizations. Later came the Baha'is, the Mormons, and the Sikhs. The organization has been supported with staff help from associate members, the American Jewish Committee, and the National Conference of Christians and Jews. Over the years, there have been retreats, workshops, and educational events.

In retrospect, Wolf said that while many religious leaders who had little interest in the past became involved routinely in the dialogue, the effort "still has not trickled down into the pews." While those leaders who had been involved actively in interfaith work had achieved a great deal of understanding and communication, there still was not any substantial participation in this work by congregations. By the mid 1990s, the larger goal of increasing the involvement of ordinary citizens in interreligious activities largely remained unfulfilled. "We're nowhere near that yet," Wolf said.[12]

The relatively informal nature of the interfaith dialogue in Los Angeles in practical terms has meant that the focus and effectiveness of the organization at any particular time has depended on the personality and interests of whoever is president of the Interreligious Council. Fields' tenure coincided with the riots, and the fact that he had the gavel facilitated the implementation of the effort under a different name to establish more immediate contacts between congregations and to mobilize the religious community toward the goal of creating in people across a vast basin, teeming with different ethnic groups, a better sense of identification with the city of Los Angeles. Lima, during his tenure, was able to work from the platform of the archdiocese's own interfaith efforts and build on the cardinal's relationship with the mayor.

MUCH WORK TO BE DONE

Lima later returned to his parish-based ministry, but reflecting on the experience in an interview, he noted that cultural differences in a city as diverse as Los Angeles present daunting obstacles to understanding between religious groups, and even within religious groups. He observed that the United States is nowhere near as literate in intercultural dialogue as his own native India. He regarded the riots as the product of intercultural encroachments in the city of Los Angeles that, left unaddressed, amounted to "a ticking bomb."[13] For him, the verdicts in the Rodney King case were merely the excuse for something that would have happened anyway over something else.

Lima said that while the Interreligious Council for years had dealt on the larger plane of theological and spiritual matters, the riots brought an awareness that religion could play a role in bridging cultural divisions within the United States, an acute void in Los Angeles in contact between Koreans, Latinos, African Americans, and others. This was essentially a confirmation of what Fields had perceived in the early formation of the Interfaith Coalition to Heal Los Angeles.

The priest also suggested that the partisan political debate over "family values," to the extent that it focuses on a "1950s, *Father Knows Best*" model, has little relevance in the complicated and multiethnic society of modern-day Los Angeles. He said, "Today you have families where two sisters or a grandmother are taking care of children." However, he noted that at the root of these different arrangements could be found traditional democratic aspirations and values of decency, respect for others, and a sense of justice.

Indeed, Lima said that although some of the newly arrived ethnic groups might be organized by different family structures, there was as much alarm in those immigrant communities about the breakdown of social fabric as was being expressed by white religious conservatives. His successor as president of the council, Hathout, echoed this sentiment in an interview by challenging any assumption that the religious right was sole custodian of any franchise on moral and spiritual concerns. Both Lima and Hathout, who is from Egypt, are immigrants, and each represents a faith outside the orbit of Christian fundamentalism that has deep and abiding concerns about "family values." Referring generically to the Moral Majority, the largest and most influential of the early groups of politically active Christian fundamentalists that entered the fray in the 1980s, Hathout gave this blunt assessment: "We don't know if it's a majority, and we don't know if it's moral or not."[14]

The common denominator in the Los Angeles dialogue, according to Hathout, has been a "feeling of a crisis situation as far as the moral health and family well-being are concerned." For Hathout, pragmatism and a recognition of the value of others occupying similar moral ground informed the discussion, just as in the city of Anaheim concern with the social fabric inspired the cooperation between denominations that might have differences on social issues. He said, "A person who allows his or her religion to form the personality is a good person. In America, life does not allow you ivory tower conversations. In America, things are changing every moment, and people are interested in peace of mind and safety."[15]

The Coalition to Heal Los Angeles would attempt to take this idea to the level of direct contact between specific congregations. Rabbi Fields recognized that, for example, there are substantial differences in perspective between the city's liberal and conservative congregations, but that each side has moved toward some of the outlooks of the others by necessity. Citing the conservative evangelical groups' increasing involvement in the social sphere, he believed that there had been a recognition that "We don't have to convert every person we touch, but we do have to make the city a better place." And conversely, "Liberals have been saying you can't change the society without changing individuals, and you have to care for the individuals and be concerned with their spiritual well-being."[16]

STUDY FINDS GRASSROOTS INITIATIVES

For the religious leaders, the riots brought renewed attention to the feelings of racial injustice, cultural division, and institutional unresponsiveness that were out there in a diverse city. If the cooperation and conversations that resulted were only a beginning point, the riots did produce a profound recognition, across a spectrum of congregations and denominations differing in size and social theology, that there was a greater need for the community to take matters in hand.

The study by the Religion and Civic Order Project reached some important conclusions about the fundamental capacity of religion to shape community identity and responses to crises. It noted that the response to the riots began on April 29, 1992, at a house of worship, the First African Methodist Episcopal Church in South Central Los Angeles, under the leadership of the Rev. Cecil Murray, who was a powerful local and national presence in the days after the rioting. The study said that "in the spirit of the religiously inspired American civil rights movement, with which he had long been associated, Murray invited the citizens of Los Angeles to join together in acts of reconciliation and healing."[17]

The study, by Professor John Orr of the USC Department of Religion and colleagues, found that the city's religious community already was well aware of the tensions beneath the surface in the period after the Watts riots in the 1960s, and as Lima had suggested, was cognizant of the explosiveness of the situation before the match was lit. But the study took note that efforts of the Interfaith Coalition to Heal Los Angeles mirrored something that had been going on for some time, namely, a large shift in the city's religious and political leadership to a style less top-down in character, less institutionally cumbersome, and "more decentralized, more neighborhood specific, more coalitional, more populist, and more organizationally experimental."[18]

The study discovered this grassroots initiative across a range of congregations, but found an increase in programs in evangelical Protestant churches and nondenominational Christian fellowships. There was a sense that while it might be accurate to say that what churches were doing was not enough to address the scope of the problems in Los Angeles, it also was true that not any one institutional group could do enough and that the architecture of a better city had to be built from the ground up in a mosaic of various neighborhood- and congregation-based efforts.

These responses were strengthened in resolve by the bitter experience of frustration about promises unkept under traditional political arrangements and by a sense that community organization was a tool for getting things done, that it was not only the province of organizers on the left. In this new environment, the study suggested, autonomy of local churches to act with others in an entrepreneurial fashion had become crucial to the evolving nature of religion as a social force in Los Angeles.

Old mainline churches were ceding more power to local congregations to develop strategies, and the framework of leadership in the civic area was not comprised only of these groups. It was being shaped by the participation of evangelical Protestant leaders like Michael Mata, director of urban Ministries at Southern California School of Theology, who were found to be "performing a civic miracle" by building coalitions encouraging "blurring of boundaries between Right and Left" and arguing against a leaning too far in the direction of liberal issues.[19]

The study also found that many storefront churches with less clout than the city's more visible church activists were doing important community work, although badly handicapped by their lack of visibility and funds. Moreover, the ethnic transformation of communities with a new influx of immigrants from Central America and elsewhere challenged older churches with space to make specific sites available to multiple congregations and, in some cases, to find common ground in their approaches to the diversity of the city.

Key players like Fields and Mata were described as "civic spiritualists," leaders attuned to mass communication and holding the view that the concept of unity was itself a way to combat balkanization in a sprawling, ethnically and religiously diverse community. While the researchers pointed out the concern about whether such efforts would be merely cosmetic, they concluded

that this aspect of interfaith work had identified something important "because the city so desperately needs a moral/spiritual
ideology that encourages comfort with multiethnicity."[20]

AFTER THE RIOTS, "THE DAILY REALITIES"

Today, the energy that arose from the urgency and emotion of
the post-riot period has given way to more permanent strategies
to meet what Alvin Rudisill, retired chaplain at the University of
Southern California, has called "the daily realities" of meeting all
the needs that were so glaringly apparent after the rioting in 1992.
In 1996, he headed up a new organization called the Interfaith
Coalition of South Central Los Angeles, which, while not a direct
offshoot of the original coalition, was endeavoring to work in its
spirit for the long haul. Also, the University of Southern California
received a grant from the Irvine Foundation for a new Center for
Religion and Civic Culture. It would work on public policy development to ensure that the spirit of the post-riot activism would be
built into the approaches to long-term urban problems in the
future. In 1996, Professor John Orr, an author of the earlier USC
study and a codirector of the center, was urging Los Angeles
County's public health system to make better use of existing
community-based health centers that were associated with faith
communities.[21]

"A MYSTERY GREATER THAN OURSELVES"

The religious response to the riots was well under way by the
spring of 1993, when Lima took the reins as president of the
Interreligious Council. But for all that had been said and written
about the riots by that time, religion's unique perspective in times
of community crisis had been stated with remarkable brevity and
clarity by this immigrant clergyman.

In a brief article noting his appointment in *The Los Angeles*

Times, Lima was asked about his philosophy of interfaith relations. His answer was:

> I think, ultimately, that whatever the dogmas and doctrines we so possessively cling onto, our icons are like windows through which we see a mystery greater than ourselves. The interreligious council seeks to discover the commonality in all religions. Los Angeles is like a microcosm of the world. If we can do it here, we can do it in the world.[22]

Lima, as a Christian, has some strong ideas about the strength of individual traditions and the need to avoid watering down messages. However, his words suggested a place lying beyond even the efforts to build coalitions and a sense of civic unity within a city. It was the mystery beyond the individual faiths, the divine ground itself, and the need for dialogue on the actual messages of the faiths.

In that statement was an implicit suggestion that moving toward common ground on the content of religion also might have profound consequences in the social and political life of a multi-ethnic society.

Chapter Ten

Can Religious Diversity Be an Asset?

The concept of the free exercise of religion in the United States has allowed spiritual ideas to flourish, but because of its implicit neutrality, we have been left to decide for ourselves whether to undertake any attempt to reckon with diverse perspectives.

Now the nation finds it has all these religious and ethnic groups clamoring in full view for a full share of American life. Many, viewing the catastrophes around them through the prisms of their own value systems, find themselves every bit as appalled at the deterioration of the social fabric as the religious conservatives who have been active in politics.

The Rev. Vivian Ben Lima's vision of Los Angeles as a microcosm of the world and of interfaith relations as approaching some common mystery beyond the doctrines and dogmas of particular denominations quietly set a tone upon his election as president of the Interreligious Council of Southern California for the city's interfaith efforts after the riots of 1992. The council's response to the civil unrest was well underway by that time, and Lima, a product of a diverse religious environment in his native India, was particularly conscious of a need to bridge the city's cultural divides, sometimes even within the same faith. Within the Roman Catholic archdiocese alone, Masses were held in 52 languages.

The priest was interested in moving the dialogue toward a

place where the power of individual faiths was not watered down in the eagerness to find common denominators. The difficulty of achieving this objective was apparent in a city the size of Los Angeles, but the council over a long period of time had made slow progress.

One of the things that the civil unrest after the Rodney King verdict in the spring of 1992 may have made more clear was that there was a distinction to be made, at least on the surface, between programs and strategies aimed at improving the quality of life in the city and the actual dialogue over the content of the faiths themselves. Most of the response related to the post-riot period, from Rabbi Harvey J. Fields's Interfaith Coalition to Heal Los Angeles on, was geared toward the former.

The experience in Los Angeles demonstrates that when different faiths search for common ground, the focus actually can be on different levels. The first is how people all get along. The second, which is the original and older province of local interfaith conversation, is the substance of those religious ideas themselves, and how they apply to a sense of commonality. The latter, a long-running conversation dating back to the origins of the Inter-religious Council of Southern California's beginnings in 1969, was not rooted so much in crisis and the immediacy of a particular set of profound urban concerns.

The approaches to this second discussion, however, proceed inevitably from the excesses of history, that is, centuries of religious intolerance, hatred, and warfare. Indeed, in the current climate, progress in such conversations is likely to be slow at best, and at times hampered or affected by the self-absorption and dogmatism of particular groups or by the agnosticism or outright cynicism and pessimism of some who are concerned with the role of religion in communal life.

But the conversation itself began in Los Angeles and was sustained over the years with the affirmation that it may be possible to have a productive interaction while still having areas of disagreement. And there is at least consideration given on occasion to an ancient idea, one certainly not widely incorporated, that all religions are fundamentally true at the core, even though their various doctrines, dogmas, and rituals may have the effect of obscuring the common points. This latter idea, at least as old as Krishna's counsel to Arjuna in the *Bhagavadgita*, remains a provocative concept for modern religion. There is suspicion that this idea dilutes cherished principle and is therefore a threat to the integrity of the various perspectives.

However, in the main, the dialogue on religious content in Los Angeles for over 25 years has been predicated successfully on the notion that a productive conversation is possible even with differences. Dr. Maher Hathout, president of the Islamic Center of Southern California and for a time in the mid-1990s president of the Interreligious Council of Southern California, assessed this work in an interview for this book. He said he believed that, in this manner, the Los Angeles interfaith effort set a national standard through its adherence to a guideline that participants "are not there to convert or preach, but to understand."[1]

In the realm of social relations, Hathout was encouraged by the ability of small groups of Christians and Muslims to produce guidelines on interfaith marriages even though there was strong sentiment within both camps that such unions were not a good idea. He characterized relations between Muslims and Jews in Los Angeles as demonstrating "sanity" through even the worst times of international conflict, and claimed that participants had discovered that "nobody needs to sell out to dialogue."[2] While the riots provided evidence of disturbing balkanization within the new multiethnic environment of Los Angeles, the city long had a base for institutional discussion between religious groups with different and even conflicting perspectives.

As for the content of messages about spiritual values, Hathout said, "When it comes to moral codes, I almost find it identical across the board." He said it was possible to reach a point on overall religious perspectives where people could say, "I am true; I know that others will reach a different conclusion, which I respect."[3] Dennis Prager, a Los Angeles radio talk show host who regularly engages listeners in conversation about moral and religious issues, succinctly expressed a similar viewpoint one afternoon when a caller asked him, "Which religion is true?" Prager, who is Jewish, answered, "Mine is true, but I am not prepared to say that others are false."[4]

A CENTENNIAL CELEBRATION IN HOLLYWOOD

The Parliament of the World's Religions in Chicago 1893 was an unprecedented event in interfaith dialogue in the United States that foreshadowed the society of multiethnic religious groups we have become on the eve of the twenty-first century. The gathering was part of the Columbian Exposition, which focused on achievements in science and the arts, but the gathering of religions provided a benchmark near the end of the nineteenth century in a largely Protestant country for the substantial advent of Catholicism and Judaism and also brought Eastern religions to the attention of Americans.

On the occasion of a centennial observance in 1993, when 6000 participants would gather in Chicago, Peter Steinfels, a *New York Times* religion writer, took note of the event by citing the legacy of remarks made a century earlier by one participant. An Indian monk named Swami Vivekananda preached,

> "Do not care for dogmas, or sects, or churches, or temples. They count for little compared with the essence of existence in each man which is spirituality." It was a message that struck chords in an America where schoolchildren encountered similar thoughts in the writings of Ralph Waldo Emerson and Thomas Jefferson.[5]

Preparations for the centennial observance, which would address themes of economic and social injustices along with its broad themes of "a global ethic," were underway about the time of the anniversary of the riots in Los Angeles. The need to further religious understanding against the backdrop of a recent experience with civil unrest was explored in Hollywood on May 2, 1993, when representatives from various local religious organizations participated at an interfaith service designed to mark the centennial of the parliament.

The host of the gathering, Swami Swahananda of the Hinduism-based Vedanta Society of southern California, set the stage by saying that Vivekananda a century earlier had urged an understanding of all religions. His fellow monk in the Ramakrishna Order of India, Swami Shraddhananda of Sacramento, California, opened by observing that religion had not been planned as part of the Columbian Exposition, but that its addition later constituted a recognition that it "gives impetus to human progress." He suggested that unity was an old idea, but one difficult to implement, and observed that Vivekananda "did not see religious diversity either within or outside as negatives. A world with uniformity of thought is a dead world. The more religions there are, the more opportunity there will be for man to think of religion." He also said that "each religion must assimilate the spirit of the others and yet preserve his individuality and grow according to his own law of growth." He asserted that "the life of religion is deep inside the heart of man, and that fact is universal."[6]

Rabbi Daniel Swartz, at the time assistant rabbi at Temple Israel in Hollywood, picked up on the theme of diversity of religion as an asset for America in the next 100 years by telling an anecdote. He said that when somebody who had studied the South American rain forests was asked to sum up what he had learned, the response was: "God has an inordinate fondness for beetles." The rabbi observed that dealing with a similar diversity of religious perspectives posed a unique challenge. He said that at the original Parliament of the World's Religions, the idea of universalism was a search for bragging rights about how universal each denomination was, that it alone was the most "tolerant." Tolerance could be misconstrued if it implied that somebody tolerated somebody else, and the challenge was to identify "the value of particularism," that is, to understand that there was great value in each individual tradition.

Lima, who was there that day, observed that the Second Vatican Council had signaled the Roman Catholic Church's evolution by producing a recognition of "the authentic presence of the Holy Spirit in these religions," which had changed Catholicism's fundamental relationship with other faiths.[7]

The Buddhist representative, the Venerable Havanpola Ratanasara, president of the Buddhist Sangha Council of Southern California, engaged in some good-natured bantering about his host's linkage of Hinduism and Buddhism on Indian soil, but asserted that when members of the Interreligious Council of Southern California got together, "I am now happy to tell you, when we meet, we meet as one family." He emphasized his religion's view of man as the product of his own actions and issued a challenge in the face of modern society's problems—and locally in the presence of gangs and violence—to teach and live by the core message of religions. He said, "It is not enough that the Bible says to love one another. We have to put it into practice. With love and kindness we can have a safe society. In the future, these ideas are needed and need to be disseminated."[8]

Hathout, who also was present, opened with a tribute from Islam's bible, the *Koran*, to the ideals of the day. First, he alluded to the spirit of religious diversity embodied therein: "And if God had pleased, he would have made you all [all mankind] one people [people of one religion]."[9] Hathout said that the reference to diversity in the *Koran* "means that part of the belief in God is to believe in the diversity and pluralism of his creation." Second, he said, "Every human being, regardless of race, creed, or color is entitled to dignity." He said that religion provided an antidote to "absolute human relativism," the idea that everything is relative. He said that relativism was leading to confusion in a world that needed points of reference to guide it, and that religion would provide "a very important reality of the future."[10]

NEW AGE PERSPECTIVES AT LAX

The bouillabaisse of religious perspectives to be found in Los Angeles was very much in evidence at another interfaith gathering, which was widely advertised in area newspapers. It was a Science of Spirituality session held at the Los Angeles Airport Hilton on August 1, 1994. About 300 people gathered for what was advertised widely as an "interfaith spiritual dialogue." The ascending airplanes bound for global destinations, the tables outside the banquet room that turned the halls of the hotel into a sprawling bookshop, and the adoring followers of a Science of Spirituality teacher, Sant Rajinder Singh, gave this event a decidedly New Age cast.

The host group said it had over 800 centers open to the public and retreat centers with main headquarters in Delhi, India, and a western headquarters in Naperville, Illinois. It affirmed a "deep respect for all religious traditions and draw[s] upon the teachings of the great saints, mystics, and teachers of all faiths," and Singh, who held meditation seminars and gives lectures around the world aimed at promoting "inner and outer peace through spirituality," addressed these themes in his talk.[11] A Baha'i representative likewise spoke in universal terms and said that people were yearning for peace. She urged a recognition that humanity was "organically connected."

Along with this expressed hope for a new era in world spirituality, there were some traditional messages heard at the session. The Rev. Vernon Robinson, an associate minister of the First African Methodist Episcopal Church in Los Angeles, stood in for the Rev. Cecil Murray, the church's pastor who had been so central in his city's response to the rioting in 1992. Robinson, an African American, set the stage for the future by reminding listeners of the history of racism within religious traditions in the past, and he emphasized the benefits of the multiethnic outlook of his church. He talked about prayer and said it was necessary to pray not for narrow interests but for everybody. He said, "Regardless of skin color, regardless of what we believe in, we must know God abides within us, and we must teach that to our children."[12]

Swami Sarvadevananda, of the Vedanta Society of Southern California, included a story from Ramakrishna, a nineteenth-century Indian saint who was the spiritual teacher of Vivekananda and who had tested individual religions in performing his own spiritual disciplines to conclude finally that they were all valid. The parable was about blind people being asked to touch and describe an elephant, a pointed reference to humanity's quest to know the totality of a godhead that is not immediately visible through the senses. Each gives a different answer depending on the part of the animal he came in contact with, even though obviously, it was one and the same elephant.

In its somewhat novel and unusual exploratory nature, the talk on this evening was suggestive of new ideas and directions for humanity in a world reduced in size by modern technology and communication. Was this just heady optimism? Many Americans certainly would not have been entirely comfortable with all that was said on this night of futuristic thinking about religion. However, the search for a better way was not exactly adrift from the reality of history, either. The presence of the African-American minister, whose faith had been forged in the history of injustices in America, and the swami, who was linked directly to ancient ideas about universality, was a reminder that even with the arrival of New Age ideas and experimentation, universality and diversity in religious matters are deeply embedded in human experience.

This session, while highlighting some of the newer religious movements, was striking for its juxtaposition of self-help ideas with the more established messages that are now rooted or transplanted into the spiritual culture of the United States. This dialogue was possible, if only for a few hours, because it arose from a conscious renunciation on the part of participants of any claim on the exclusive possession of ultimate truths.

Much of this kind of conversation around the nation may remain outside the mainstream, but the essence already is informing the spiritual ideas being absorbed by ordinary Americans, and it is likely to do so even more in the future as many from different backgrounds live and work side by side.

Are the cynicism mentioned earlier and negatives such as an unwillingness to do the work to learn about others drawbacks to progress in this area? Yes. The task for religionists in the future, if they are to do anything more than preach to the choir, will be to demonstrate that it is the diversity and force of the many spiritual resources now available that can shake loose the cobwebs and get Americans thinking in new ways.

Chapter Eleven

Comparing Beliefs

Why "Our Best versus Their Worst" Is Wrong

While there are many miles still to travel in the interfaith dialogue in Los Angeles, the events since 1969 suggest new directions for the interplay of religious values in the new multiethnic American society.

In 1948, the national World Council of Churches was focusing on struggles over the merits of capitalism and communism, and in 1950, the domestic ecumenical movement centered on the founding of the National Council of Churches. We have seen the reforms of Vatican II, the civil rights movement, and other developments. The interfaith dialogue in Los Angeles has come a long way since those times.

Even if the Los Angeles discussion that began at the close of the tumultuous 1960s has made modest achievements to date, the implications of this effort as society tries to make room for its new diversity are significant for the long term. The Los Angeles interfaith effort long has been recognized as a model for other cities.

In recent years, part of the dialogue evolved after the riots into a more grassroots movement, the Interfaith Coalition to Heal Los Angeles, and the long-term work it inspired several years later in south central Los Angeles. This has been conducted against the backdrop on the national stage of the increasing political activity of the religious right, beginning with the Moral Majority in 1979 and 1980, the activities of the television evangelists, and the like.[1] Interestingly, the Ten-Point Coalition in Boston, a response by younger clergy and church leaders to youth violence, was another, although somewhat different, example of grassroots, religion-based activism arising in urban centers to shake things up. The widespread dissatisfaction in the early 1990s with the spiritual condition of society has inspired a new faith activism that is not exclusively the province of conservative white Christians.

The conversation in Los Angeles, both in its attention to the social fabric and in its longer-running focus on what the faiths have to say, makes it apparent that the debate over the role of religion in the public arena is also an exploration of how we deal with the ways in which we are different. Los Angeles provides evidence of the potential for the full play of religious ideas in the United States in ways that enable local communities to envision and work toward a new civic cohesiveness.

It is in this kind of cultural and ethnic interaction that the nation may find a response for the inference of some civil libertarians that the national preoccupation with "family values" is somehow an exercise in trying to return the country to some narrow, imagined past. Equally important, the faiths' common messages about what it is to live a moral life ought to address the concerns of religious conservatives who lament that religion has abandoned its claim on influencing behavior by focusing less on personal conduct and more on vague liberal notions of social justice.

This religious ferment in Los Angeles was rooted in tradition, and yet the search for a healthier city and common truths showed in crisis that it has a capacity to generate a sense of renewed possibilities for the future.

Religion is acknowledged as a custodian of the building blocks of civility in a democracy. When the social order was in jeopardy, the response in Los Angeles across a broad range of denominations—both conservative and liberal, mainline and evangelical—centered around establishing a vision of a city as a city, and not as a mere aggregate of neighborhoods and ethnic groups.

FOCUSING ON THE CONTENT OF IDEAS

The steady evolution of the discussion of the content of the faiths separately challenges groups either to recognize some validity in what others have to say or to persist in asserting that theirs is the only true custodian of truth.

There are many no doubt who will reject such efforts to find unity in different religious perspectives as an attempt to gloss over irreconcilable differences. They may do so either because they think that only their ideas are correct or because they are pessimistic that the search for common ground will produce results. Even those who participate have questions that are never far below the surface of the discussion. Some of the believers in a personal God have been candid about trying to reconcile their beliefs with the Buddhists, who begin with man's condition and posit no deity as an answer and whose view of ultimate reality seems to them totally different. There are questions for others about, for example, what "liberation" really means in the Hindu tradition, a concept that requires careful study and understanding, and there are concerns about the implications of a "Christian" vision of a better world.

However, it also is clear that all such discussion begins with the reality that there are many faiths and that they talk about many of the same things. The Rev. Vivian Ben Lima, the Catholic who spoke at the interfaith service in Hollywood, made the crucial observation that in the competing claims of religions and cultures, "We always compare our best with somebody else's worst." He said this was a mistake. As an example, he argued that when Christians assess destructive fundamentalism within the Muslim world they should remember that their own traditions have histories of excesses and intolerance. "When we look at our neighbor before us, we have to look in terms of their ideals, their best,"[2] he said.

Lima also noted that love was a universal message in the various religions. The Venerable Havanpola Ratanasara, a Buddhist, without specifically mentioning Jesus, made reference to the biblical call to love one another as he urged his listeners to work toward putting the message into practice as a means to "a safer society in the future." Ratanasara and Dr. Maher Hathout, a Muslim, while having very different perspectives on ultimate reality, were practically finishing each other's sentences on the threat of materialism in modern society. Rabbi Daniel Swartz gave the wonderful image of "God's inordinate fondness for beetles."

WHY VALUES MATTER FOR COMMUNITY

Because of the complexity of the city's culture and because of the level of distress of the community, some religious leaders in Los Angeles were approaching common ground—in effect, beginning to talk in new ways about how religious values play out in society. Religious ideas were seen not merely as values that stand out among others in a restless world; they are in fact the defining values that make a community viable.

A crucial question in this area for the long term is whether the impetus provided by a particular crisis can be sustained.

Los Angeles certainly has had problems enough to unsettle its spirits since the post-riot interfaith effort was launched. It has been mired in budgetary woes, among other things, and despite reform efforts, the old questions about racism in the Los Angeles Police Department emerged in the O. J. Simpson murder trial.

By 1996, Mayor Richard Riordan's administration, which began in the bright dawn with an interfaith breakfast, had become entangled in a testy relationship with the city's African-American community.

Nevertheless, the experience of Los Angeles's interfaith efforts is instructive for a nation struggling in anxious times with the basic ideas around which it organizes its democratic efforts. What happened in Los Angeles and in Anaheim received very little attention from Washington, but as noted earlier, these efforts were very much in tune with some of the thinking aloud that President Clinton was doing in 1993 and 1994, and they certainly provided some basis in experience for the focus on families and children that came into full bloom during the political season of 1996. This local example makes a very powerful case for the crucial idea that a civic sense in American life arises from religious principles.

The content discussion suggests that interfaith dialogue is not only about trying to get religions to talk to each other. It is also a profound effort at understanding individual traditions more fully by learning from others.

While not all agree, it is not too great a leap to conclude that it is actually possible for more than one religion to be true; indeed all of them can be valid in all their richness of ideas, tradition, and ethnicity. The slow and steady advent of comparative religions, as not only an academic exercise but also a grassroots way of relating to one another, is a significant development. In it lies the possibility of learning some new things about life's ultimate mysteries in addition to the obvious immediate benefit of increased understanding.

The idea that unity may not be merely a nice idea around which to build an occasional prayer gathering addresses common concerns of the human spiritual condition. The new proximity in which diverse traditions must coexist in the United States seems to compel the exploration of this approach to religious understanding. As one of the speakers observed at the local centennial observation of the Parliament of the World's Religions in the spring of 1993, variety and diversity are to be considered assets in the world of religion, not points of contention.

In Los Angeles, we saw a microcosm of a nation doing some of the stretching exercises that must be done as it reckons inevitably with the true scope of its pluralism. Moreover, the energizing of congregations and neighborhoods—and their spirit of experimentation—seemed to have a way of tempering the extreme rhetoric evident on the national stage. John Gaudette, executive director of the OCCCO, said this approach was what differentiated community-based faith activists everywhere from the ideologues.

What seems obvious is that there is no turning back to an earlier time. Those who are preaching a return to exclusively Christian traditions are swimming against the tide and arguing a very limited version of what the moral mainstream really is.

In many ways, Los Angeles by the time of the riots was

already a national pioneer in interfaith cooperation, but its longevity also had served to point out some of the difficulties. These included the different perspectives of the faiths, the institutional dialogue that had broken considerable ground but did not filter down to the grassroots levels, the sense that some congregations were more adept at gathering media attention than others and hence got the money, the top-down mainline church approach versus new grassroots efforts, and the basic ethnic divisions.

For all these complicating factors, this local dialogue appears by contrast far more progressive and effective overall than what the national quarrel over religious values has produced. If the quality of commitment and results are mixed down on the ground, they at least represent an attempt to bridge some of the dangerous divisions that exist and to that degree are successful simply for their existence.

THE KEY TO RELIGION AND CIVIC RESPONSIBILITY

The pervasive notion of "empowerment" on a scale beyond individuals and even individual congregations has interesting ramifications. This is "empowerment" beyond the seductive idea that life in America should be a grab bag, where enhanced "self-esteem" has become a euphemism for self-indulgence. It has to do with taking the responsibility along with the opportunity to better one's self, an idea now strengthened by the range and diversity of moral instruction available within various religious communities that are working toward the building of a sense of one city.

If the accommodation of the faiths somehow were to be summarized for export to other cities and communities, a few significant conclusions might be drawn:

First, in the new multiracial and ethnic world into which we have been catapulted, it will not be necessary for people to abandon core religious ground. The pleasant irony of taking a broader view of world faiths is that it can strengthen understanding of one's own tradition.

Second, in the diaspora that the United States has become, we may need to filter these religious messages through American culture. That is not to say that the full power of moral and spiritual ideas should be diluted. Rather, core ideas and themes must be identified for those who are unfamiliar with the trappings of customs and rituals in which they are encased when brought to these shores by various immigrant groups. These new religious resources may seem at first inaccessible to many Americans. It may be tempting in some cases to lump the new arrivals all together as "Eastern religions" or New Age movements. They need not be so exotic. The nation ought to be able to develop ways of helping sift through these resources so that core principles are decoded from complicated cultural settings and are made accessible to ordinary Americans.

Third, the nation will need to reconcile some of the differences. There are important obstacles that lie at the heart of perspectives of major faiths, to be sure. These positions are deeply felt and will have to be approached carefully and with sensitivity. However, there may be more room for accommodation than some partisans think. The absence of a personal God in Buddhism is a case in point. The difference with other faiths over a deity seems profound, and to some it is both that and seemingly insurmountable. But as cosmologists and theologians explore more common areas in their considerations of reality, and as Westerners understand more of what it was that the religious reformer Buddha actually said and why, this apparent obstacle may be less problematic for the long term.

Much confusion arises from ignorance about the common points and messages inherent in other traditions. At the interfaith gathering on the centennial of the Parliament of the World's Religions in Hollywood, for example, Dr. Fred Register of the United Church of Christ observed that the fact that many Americans had grown up in insulated communities is changing and that there are "a variety of religious expressions now, and it is difficult to stay in a religious cocoon." He also made the point that historically, "politics and power often get tangled up with religion ...

politics tends to shape our religion, when it ought to be the other way around."[3]

The efforts in southern California stood in contrast to this polarization on the national stage. Rabbi Harvey Fields of Wilshire Boulevard Temple said in an interview, "On the national level, there is a lot of puff and staking out of name and territory for all the wrong reasons. On the local level, we are able to get some work done."[4] The discussion may wax and wane, but once certain milestones are reached, it is no longer possible to retreat permanently and say that finding common ground is beyond people's capacity. It may exceed what they are willing to do at any particular moment, but it is not ever possible again to say that a sense of harmony and unity is beyond reach.

When the sledding gets rough, as it has for this nation early in its third century, we are likely to find also that an exclusively secular discussion of morality and values is fine as a starting point, but, without the active accommodation of the faiths, it can be dry stuff. As we have seen, the moral high ground can be politicized easily as those advancing narrow agendas square off with others who are wary of the varieties of expression of religious values in the public square.

The religious impulses offer the sustenance to keep the fires of resolve burning to do the work to improve communal relationships in modern democracy. The nation should thank its lucky stars that it has these people who are working from the bottom up instead of from the top down. The country at large is awash in rhetoric that arises from the misunderstanding or outright manipulation of moral and spiritual perspectives, as we saw in the first part of this book.

An emphasis on virtues based in religion can give us structure as civility is fragmented, but we also need from religion the hope, inspiration, and sense of purpose to carry forward. We as a society have come up short on answers to the plaintive question of Forrest Gump: Do we have a destiny, are we just floating, or is our condition some combination of both?

The cautious haven of the secularists, "moral renewal," will give us some direction, but religion in full bloom assures us that the effort is worth it. In all its diverse forms, it reminds us of our place in the grand scheme of things. It teaches us that we are at home in the universe and that we have the capacity not only to choose between right and wrong, but also to improve the quality of our collective lives through such nourishing concepts as love and compassion and by connecting with something beyond ourselves.

Part IV

Cultivating the "Moral Middle" for Our Future

Chapter Twelve

Closer to Answers
Than We May Think

The proper place for religion has become one of the crucial debating points in contemporary society, and some of the most interesting things are happening at the local level, as we have seen. On the national stage, much of the argument has been conducted in the courts, where the constitutional tension over church–state separation has found expression in the legal search for appropriate "accommodation" of religious practices in public life.

All in all, isolating religion from the larger democratic culture lest somebody be offended hasn't done much to bring on "the good society." Indeed, the general feeling of moral urgency that pervades the nation has made it ripe to consider fresh ways of looking at the role of religion.

If there is ever to be a new accommodation of moral and spiritual values in the modern American democracy, what will it look like? How do we come up with something better than Pat Robertson versus the American Civil Liberties Union as the defining image of religion on the stage of a nation's common life?

The United States needs to think about an "accommodation" that is not entirely the construction of judicial review. If mainstream Americans do not engage in this exercise, politically active religious conservatives will do it for them. At the same time, some on the left are inclined to view "accommodation" as a sign of weakness or political pandering or to overgeneralize and overstate perceived threats to separation of church and state.

We might begin in the most obvious place, the broadest area of agreement. The idea that religious values are important in modern society is largely uncontested nowadays in view of the pervasive concern about America's well-being. Even the strictest separationists recognize the value of religion, but talk about having it flourish in private. Agnostics and atheists have their own perspectives and active concern with humanistic values and seem mostly interested in being left alone, and they should be. But there are far-reaching implications to the question of just whose religious values should be mobilized, if it is appropriate to do so at all, and what place they should have in a modern democracy.

To this point, we have seen both the capacity for misunderstanding and division over ideas based in religion and the potential they have to bridge differences and address a common perception that society is coming undone. It is easier said than done, but if we understand that religion is at the heart of many people's organizing principles and that it provides democracy with important ideas, then finding meaningful ways of making it work better for democracy is not simply optional. The journalist Bill Moyers, who grew up in a small Texas town where his church's "priesthood of believers" served as "an apprenticeship in politics," has said wisely, "A society cannot survive without a story that provides it with common moral ground."[1]

Striking the proper balance will require a fuller degree of participation by a much broader group of Americans in the future. There are at least four general areas where this might happen:

The first is one we already have examined in detail, namely, grassroots groups determined to work through their social and denominational differences and even to enlist the support of government on occasion to achieve practical goals within the political system.

The second is argumentation and dialogue, the traditional democratic methods of conflict resolution outside the court system. This is the arena where discourse has been polarized at the national level, but where we should not give up, at least not yet.

The third is a commitment to use traditional institutional resources—a nation's universities, think tanks, and the like—to help develop new ways of looking at old problems. This approach takes time, and the big breakthroughs may not make a splash commensurate with their importance. The press has a role to play in making sure that important stories here are not underplayed.

The fourth, touched on in the Los Angeles discussion and to be developed more fully in subsequent chapters, is the adaptation of ideas from the "new religions" in our midst. They in fact are quite ancient in their own right, but have been imported to modern American culture fairly recently, and now are available as spiritual resources.

As we have seen, the first of these methods is the most proven response religion-inspired Americans have fashioned to date. It also happens to be taking place along a track parallel to that of the political involvement of religious and cultural conservatives. It is what mainstream people of faith do to express their moral concerns in the "public square."

Whatever the noise level, the mainstream well may have time and tide on their side. The religious right for too long allowed too many questions to gather steam about its commitment to pluralism and separation of church and state. Even when the latter's leaders employ language that appeals broadly to common concerns about the state of our society, they are hard pressed to capture the imagination of the larger American public. This is likely to be so as long as the religious right focuses on litmus test issues and fails to be truly inclusive in its expressions of religious sentiment.

There has been a lot said and written about the narrowness of the appeal of Christian conservatives. A broader spiritual outlook holds a key to the place of religious values in democracy's future. The glaring absence of inclusiveness is an underlying reason many Americans are turned off by the religious right but agree on what's fundamentally wrong with the country.

Local success with accommodation between faiths and between religious and governmental interests provides evidence that people can work together to shore up the social fabric. We know also from experience that the political process tends to reward those who can build broad coalitions, and it tends to drive single-issue politics off center stage sooner or later. It is just such pragmatism that seems to be working at the local level. The experience of Anaheim, California, for example, suggests that there is also a kind of priority-setting that goes on with this approach.

The idea is that as deeply as people feel about some issues, such as abortion, there are others such as the future of neighborhoods and safety on the streets that are so important that they have the power to create a constituency on moral ground among people who have fundamental disagreements on other issues. It is possible for a society to put aside some of its most basic differences if only to address a particular transcendent task.

If these things are so, then it should follow that a new national understanding of the broad place of moral and spiritual values is not entirely beyond our grasp. Since the American political system has a way of marginalizing those who cannot be inclusive, it ought to be possible to have more of a religious accommodation for the larger democracy.

The First Amendment is broad enough to mean, "Do what you want because we'll never agree," at the same time Americans are invited to broaden their view to, "The more the merrier, and the better for all of us to have this diversity." The conversations of the interfaith clergy in multiethnic Los Angeles showed that the full richness of that diversity itself can be a source of insight into the nature of what the faiths hold in common. This ought to encourage Americans to believe that, rather than neutering religion in an effort not to offend, these ideas can contribute to the health of the democracy through the celebration of distinct traditions.

We will get some but not all the answers from our constitutional arguments about church and state. It may be, for example, that government funding for certain religious activities would violate a court-constructed test of suitable government involvement. But it is also possible at the same time that the unintended effect of such a test is to relegate the role of religion to an inferior standing alongside secular activities, and thereby to deprive it of its nourishing role in democracy.

In fact, the free exercise of religion in modern America probably is not going to rise or fall on such narrow questions as the Supreme Court decided in the spring of 1995, when it ruled that the University of Virginia was bound to subsidize a student religious publication on the same grounds as other student publications. Many such constitutional debates are important indicators of the political wrangling going on between Pat Robertson and strict separationist groups, or people like them on the poles. But they are instructive as much as anything for their lesson that "accommodation" is something that must be worked out by a much broader group of Americans than lawyers and judges.

Some of these battles may go unresolved, be decided differently by different courts, or be revisited with cases presenting a different set of facts. The society, rather than achieving some golden court-constructed definition of "accommodation" is more likely to achieve satisfactory results through the kind of pragmatic tabling of differences we have seen in some of the southern California and national examples. The middle now has become the progressive heartland on values because much of the left and right remain locked up in ideology. The country has a great resource if it can tap into the flexibility and reasonableness of those in the center.

We know already from the earlier examination of interfaith dialogue and efforts to improve communities that the society at ground level is moving toward this new consideration of religious sentiment in public life. The Clinton presidency, for all its shortcomings and distracting questions about "character," suggests that the discussion has been joined on the national stage—and not just in the writings of academics, clerics, and lawyers about the proper place of religious sentiment in American life. Indeed, the administration had begun by early 1995 to explore ways of putting the Justice Department on the side of allowing a larger play for religion in public schools within the parameters of First Amendment considerations.[2]

Some of these shifts in attitude may be seeping into the larger society, and even into the arena of the litigation itself. For example, in the closely watched oral arguments before the Supreme Court in the University of Virginia case, the lawyer for the university appeared to anticipate the concerns of swing justices about accommodation when he steered away from an unconstitutional "establishment" of religion argument that had prevailed in a lower court and argued that universities must pick and choose in the allocation of scarce financial resources.[3] By the way, one of the ironies of our time may be that scarce public funding for anything has the potential not only to privatize jails and landfills, but also to accomplish the privatization of religion, which is what the separationists have said they want all along.

PROGRESS IN THE NATIONAL CONVERSATION

A larger task remains the resolution of the polarized national debate over the role of religious values. In the activities of the Clinton administration, and in the concerns of two Supreme Court justices, Sandra Day O'Connor and Anthony M. Kennedy, it was possible in the mid-1990s to see crucial public figures in the executive and judicial branches of government beginning to struggle with the new possibilities of accommodation. This was a sign within the federal government of activity similar to what has been happening at the grassroots level. This requires pragmatism and a willingness to reconsider fixed orthodoxies of the left and right. Accordingly, this approach will take time and likely will not be free of conflict.

One of the most contentious aspects of the debate over the role of religion in public life emerged in the spring of 1994 with the release of the Anti-Defamation League report discussed earlier. *The Religious Right: The Assault on Tolerance & Pluralism in America* was an indictment of religious extremism and all that it might portend about hostility to religious freedom and to specific groups. It threw down the gauntlet early on with its very definition of the religious right as

> an array of politically conservative religious groups and indi-
> viduals who are attempting to influence public policy based
> on a shared cultural philosophy that is antagonistic to plural-
> ism and church/state separation. The movement consists
> mainly of Protestants, most of them evangelical or fundamen-
> talist, a far smaller number of Catholics, and a smattering of
> Jews.[4]

The latter reference suggested that Jewish and Christian perspectives on public policies are more complicated than a clear
division over church and state roles and the question of anti-
Semitism. While many Jews understandably are alarmed about
these matters and about the targeting of Jews by evangelical cru-
sades, there also is support for some fundamentalist Christian
objectives among Jewish conservatives.[5] The presence of Jacob
Neusner, a prolific Jewish scholar, alongside Pat Robertson on the
Firing Line debate team arguing that the religious right did not
pose a threat was a case in point.

The Anti-Defamation League study goes beyond being a
mere reaction to the threat on church and state posed by extremists, an argument heard in the *Firing Line* debates. It is not
surprising that the book has been criticized on the right, but there
is a measure of irony in this response because in fact it derives
considerable moral weight as a document from its underlying
acknowledgment of the power of religious and moral sentiment in
American life.

The book early on concedes that there is a vast array of
fundamentalists and evangelicals who are not members of this
group, and it takes pains to point out that popular assumptions
that devout Christians are only diehard Republicans is incorrect.
But perhaps more important, in a foreword, Abraham H. Foxman,
the national director, sets the tone for the examination of the aims
and organizations of the religious right by acknowledging that
"… many Americans find in their religious faith and vision the
resources they need to address contemporary moral crises" and
that the First Amendment enhances "the sanctity of personal faith
and the determination to achieve a better world—a determination
that often arises from faith."[6]

The book makes the classical argument that the vitality of religion is enhanced by the separation of church and state and details its case that the religious right has attempted to reconstruct the basis for civil law and deny church–state separation. It also discusses anti-Jewish perspectives and notions of a "Church age," with the implication that God has turned from the Jews for their rejection of Jesus.[7] It observed that tension over the proper role of religion in society arises in part from one of the nation's earliest diversity challenges, the need to protect a religious minority, Jews, from encroachment in a young democratic society from the over-zealousness or persecution by members of a majority, Christians.

In Part I of this book we saw that much of the national dialogue over religious perspectives was being conducted in polemics. The Anti-Defamation League report's portrayal of the religious right as a threat to democracy and as at times hostile to Jews was answered by the Christian Coalition with accusations that it was filled with fabrications and half-truths. The rhetoric escalated during the fall election of 1994, but afterward Jewish and conservative Christian leaders met in Washington over a kosher lunch for five hours of discussion. The session was organized by Rabbi Yechiel Eckstein, president of the Chicago-based International Fellowship of Christians and Jews, to address a "crisis situation that has been dividing the two communities."[8]

The parties agreed to disagree and to respect each other's right to participate in the political process. Perhaps most interesting, both said the angry rhetoric itself posed a threat to the nation's declining moral health, which was after all, an issue everybody was concerned with. Both Foxman and Christian Coalition Executive Director Ralph Reed acknowledged that the dispute had been painful. Foxman said the report stood up, but that it might not have been issued if there had been more open communication; Reed wanted the dialogue to continue. Later came the flap over Pat Robertson's book.

Whatever meeting of the minds occurred over this period was a hopeful step forward in addressing antagonism, and it brought clarity to the deeper question of the country's moral well-being. What they learned in the end was how far from a meaningful dialogue on the national stage they really were. The good news was that a lunch that stretched on a bit, five hours, was time well spent in addressing common concerns. And those common concerns turn out to be very much those that already are shared by many mainstream Americans.

About the time these two parties from the religious sphere were taking stock, the country moved into the period of Republican ascendancy in Congress. If anybody thought after the watershed election of 1994 that the country therefore was moving to an ideological extreme, a dose of reality awaited in the results of a poll by *The Los Angeles Times* conducted before President Clinton's 1995 State of the Union address. Along with the uncertainty it found about key elements in the Republicans' "Contract with America," it identified a substantial concern in the land about the direction of the country and found people still worried about its moral well-being.[9]

The conversation the Christian Coalition had with moral and spiritual leaders outside its orbit offered a political lesson as well as a religious one for anyone engaged in polemics on the national stage. To survive politically under the dome of American politics, religious conservatives have been drawing fire and finding out the hard way about the need to temper their language and their perspective.

For example, when the Republicans first were jockeying for position in the 1996 presidential race, Reed warned Republicans against putting an abortion-rights supporter on the ticket. But by that time, some lessons may already have been learned. *The Wall Street Journal*'s columnist Paul A. Gigot noted that social conservatives already had demonstrated they would support "nuanced pro-choice Republicans" and that Reed himself had been "privately encouraging" of Republican William Kristol's effort to offer compromise language on abortion for the 1996 GOP platform.[10] The hard-liners eventually won the day on the platform language at the 1996 convention in San Diego, but broadening their appeal remained a central challenge for religious conservatives.

Reed has been a pivotal figure on the "faith politics" landscape not only because his Christian Coalition has stuffed the envelopes and walked the precincts for Republican candidates to become a force to be reckoned with. It is also because he professed much more interest in ethnic diversity than many others on the religious right. As some political observers have noted, Reed's organization ran a risk of marginalizing itself by focusing on single-issue politics. His perspective also is limited by an apparent lack of accommodation with religious viewpoints beyond the mainstream orbit of mainline conservative Christians and Jews. But Reed himself appeared to have understood the larger point that "the emerging faith factor" can be a potent force in American life.

Bill Clinton, ironically, seemed also to understand intuitively this potential, despite his political troubles. Clinton's travails may, among other things, provide the evidence that it is not possible to be all things to all people united only by a chord of faith. Reed's group already has had to reckon with the political problems arising from single issues, and that is only within the Republican Party. The mobilization of religious faith in the political realm seems to be with us, and while we have seen it before in American politics, this time it is supported by broad concerns about the moral health of the country.

HOW UNIVERSITIES CAN HELP

A third method of accommodation is to remove the debate over the role of religious values in society from the political arena and to consider it in the calmer setting of a university or think tank. A case in point is some work that has been done quietly over the role of religion in the schools.

A *U.S. News & World Report* poll found in 1994 that nearly 65 percent of Americans would approve if the Supreme Court found a moment of silent prayer in schools to be legally acceptable.[11] But while there are arguments in favor of common prayer, there are questions about what it might accomplish even if nobody were made to feel uncomfortable by it. And the talk about a school prayer amendment, whatever its constitutional questions, is an attempt to take a short cut around the hard work of striking the right balance for religion in public education. Nobody has put the larger question of prayer in American life in better perspective than the Rev. Jesse Jackson, who at the end of the National Rainbow Coalition's meeting on January 7, 1995, said at a news conference, "Let's not have a prayer amendment. Let's have a prayer life."[12]

But incorporating the values themselves into the public education curriculum is a different matter. A pragmatic assessment of this difference comes from Nina Fue, the 1990 New Jersey teacher of the year, who teaches responsibility, perseverance, and compassion to her fourth graders without much fuss about a formal values curriculum. Although she was a religious woman, she took the view that a moment of prayer was insignificant compared to what happens in the values arena during the rest of the school day.[13]

While the political debate over a school prayer amendment was raging immediately after the mid-term election in 1994, a report was released with little notice that belongs on the agenda of every of school board, on the desk of every district superintendent and principal, and in every classroom in America. It is as important a statement as the nation has ever had on the role of religion in the public schools. It is a guidebook for public schools put together by Charles Haynes, a visiting First Amendment scholar at the Freedom Forum First Amendment Center at Vanderbilt University called *Finding Common Ground: A First Amendment Guide to Religion and Public Education*. It suggested some ways out of the dilemma over the role of religion in the schools.[14]

Perhaps most important, the document made some fundamental assertions about the sorry state of religious education, despite all the conflicting rhetoric about the need for prayer in times of moral decay versus the perceived threat to church–state separation. Haynes noted that religion usually was left out of curriculums because of fear by teachers and administrators of the constitutional conflict. The study suggested that "Failure to understand even the basic symbols, practices and concepts of the various religions make much of history, literature, art and contemporary life unintelligible" and asserted that interest in a prayer amendment would disappear if schools found the right way to deal with religion in learning.

The following useful points also were made: that we have to think about the public schools in their role of nation-building, that we have to own up to the fact that public education throughout our history has failed to "find a constitutionally permissible and educationally sound role for religion in the schools," that "the exclusion of religious perspectives from the curriculum and the adoption of 'values clarification' and some self-esteem programs fuel charges that a particular world view is being consciously promoted in the schools—be it 'secular humanism' or more recently, 'New Age religion,'" and that "avoidance of religion and exclusion of religious perspectives is anything but neutral or fair. Students need to learn that religious and philosophical beliefs and practices are central to lives of many people." Finally, there was this powerful assertion: "A secular view of human life and history pervades the curriculum, and ... some widely used approaches to values education are rooted in psychological theories antithetical to many traditional religions."[15]

Haynes drew a sharp distinction between the study of religion as an academic subject and the involvement of the schools in the advancing of particular beliefs. The report acknowledged the useful influence of the Williamsburg Charter, "a return to first principles" issued in 1988 on the bicentennial of Virginia's call for a Bill of Rights, which was intended to reaffirm the role of religion in American life. Because the charter was put together in consultation with a wide range of political leaders, scholars, and members of various faith communities, it represented precisely the kind of broad-based democratic approach to the role of religion in American life that is needed. As for the report itself, Rabbi David Saperstein, director of the Religious Action Center of Reform Judaism, seemed to summarize the need for a fresh look at accommodation when the report was released in 1994. He said, "Right now, there is nothing in the middle, so the extremists on all sides come in and pull people from the middle. When you get people thoughtfully speaking to the concerns of people in the middle, you take that middle ground away from the extremists."[16]

WHOSE FIRST AMENDMENT IS IT?

Haynes suggested in a chapter of his book entitled "Strategies for Finding Common Ground" that "We need to remind ourselves that First Amendment Religious Liberty clauses do not belong only to lawyers and judges; they belong to all of us. The principles of rights, responsibility and respect that flow from the First Amendment are obligations of citizenship for 'every' American."[17]

The discussion of these responsibilities broadened to say that no religious consensus was possible in the United States. It acknowledged the ground rules for negotiating differences over the place of religion in American life in part resided in Supreme Court decisions. But wisely, Haynes concluded that legal rulings were not the best starting point for establishing guidelines; rather, the starting point lies in an affirmation of the rights, responsibilities, and respect for others that are inherent in the nation's commitment to religious liberty. He suggested that schools needed proactively to build comprehensive policies to chart a course for religion in the schools.

The distance the society yet has to travel to get to that point is evident enough. For example, CBS's *60 Minutes* reported on a Mississippi public school district where Bible classes were part of the curriculum and prayer conducted over a loudspeaker had prompted a legal challenge from a woman who had moved her family to the area. The report focused on the constitutional problem of this open violation of the Supreme Court's 1962 ruling and elicited the acknowledgment from some Southern Baptist parents, who agreed with the school policy, that they too would be uncomfortable if they moved to a school district where, for example, Jewish prayers were recited by speaker phone.[18]

Somewhat less obvious in the controversy was the affirmation of community leaders, which came through in the language of their own faith, about the importance of values education in a troubled world. If such a community, largely isolated from the currents of religious diversity, could recognize and accept that it is moral and religious values, not a particular set of beliefs and rituals, that inoculate it against a host of social ills, it might be possible to incorporate education about religion in the life of the school in a way that does not infringe upon minority views or cross the line of church and state.

COMMON SENSE ABOUT RELIGION IN POLITICS

Another example of the academic community as a resource for accommodation comes from the chairman of the department of religious studies at California State University at Fullerton. In arguing that religious groups have a legitimate place in politics, Professor Benjamin J. Hubbard cautions that guidelines are needed to ensure fairness, to temper passions, and to allow religious groups to be more credible in bringing their moral concerns to the public arena. High on the list: Positions should be based on reason, not religious doctrine, so as to be persuasive to a broader public beyond the closed circle of true believers.

Also, says Hubbard, it is important to stick to relevant issues that have bearing on a particular political office. Faith activists should avoid religious tests such as Pat Robertson's appeal for the election of "Christians" to public office, and they should offer candidates the opportunity to explain complex positions rather then forcing them to give "yes" or "no" responses on surveys intended as voter guides.[19]

Mark J. Hanson, associate for religious ethics at the Hastings Center in Briarcliff Manor, New York, makes a similar point: "A basic tenet for the liberal society of both Democrats and Republicans is that laws and policies should not be publicly justified by the moral and religious truths of any particular segment of that society. This is especially important in the pluralistic society of today's America, even though the moral and religious perspectives of various communities in fact might inform particular policies."[20]

ONE'S PERSPECTIVE IS EVERYTHING

Uniform standards can be helpful as the nation wrestles awkwardly with perspectives in religion-based political activity. In the *Firing Line* debate on the real or imagined threat of the religious right, Representative Henry Hyde (R-Illinois) and the Rev. Richard John Neuhaus, one of the country's best known scholars of religion, focused in their questioning of the other side on the circumstances under which it might be considered constitutionally permissible to make political appeals to church members. What was clear from this discussion was that one's point of view tends to be everything; for example, for some on the left, the involvement of the Rev. Jesse Jackson with church groups is viewed in an entirely different way from the activities of Pat Robertson. What is also needed in the overall search for accommodation is to decide on which issues there is a legitimate constitutional concern and on which there can be give and take. Keeping the big picture in mind is important to this task when, for example, affirming the constructive place of values in American culture. The historian Gertrude Himmelfarb, among others, suggests that to begin dealing with social problems, we first need to "relegitimize morality."[21]

A more symbolic issue is the question of a moment of silence. Few separated out the issue more clearly from the question of a prayer amendment than the columnist John Leo of *U.S. News & World Report*. He suggested that school prayer raised concerns even for those who might like it but found merit in a moment of silence when "students are invited to take stock of their lives and think about where they are going, even if this results in some ethical or (gasp!) religious thoughts not shared by all."[22]

The needs and views of the agnostics and professed atheists must be respected, and there is no doubt that democracy can survive without a collective moment of reflection in the public schools. This is not an issue to go to the mat over in assessing the role of religious sentiment in our public life. If the objections to the moment of silence are overstated, so are the arguments for it. However, it is also the case that opposition to the idea stands on shaky ground.

SILENCE WON'T HURT ANYBODY

It is difficult to see why an accommodation can't be made to satisfy those who believe that a moment of calm and quiet in a world traveling at top speed would be a useful statement about getting control over our collective lives. To say that the moment of silence is somehow intrusive diminishes the more compelling argument against compulsory prayer. For what it's worth, none of 20 "teachers of the year" *The New York Times* interviewed, ranging from conservatives to liberals, opposed the former, although the vast majority opposed the latter.[23]

One of the best points made by Haynes in his report is that the legal side of complicated questions regarding religion in public education takes us only so far. The larger community must decide how we will manage questions of public religiosity. Again, this may be one of those instances where the "tolerant mainstream" identified earlier can lead the way toward agreeable common ground. For example, a majority of people surveyed by a *New York Times*/CBS News poll in late 1994 were in favor of prayer from many religions in the public schools led by students or parents, not school officials, and yet they seemed reluctant to amend the Constitution.[24]

Somewhere in these areas lie the seeds of a new accommodation. The questions that go before the courts tend to be much more narrowly drawn than those that present themselves for resolution by the society at large. As we have seen, the evidence is coming in from James Davison Hunter's "culture war," and from the polarization of America's intellectual elites, that we are not yet succeeding at identifying the common ground. How America views the role of religion in the larger society, or in the schools, to name just one focal point of contention, is too important a question to be decided by lawyers for either Pat Robertson or anyone else.

In the case of the role of religion in the public schools, it ought to be possible to design programs that are not hostile to religion. As Haynes points out, the guideline for determining what constitutes excessive government involvement in religious activity—the Lemon Test—already is under reconsideration by the court, with some revisionist thinking being explored by Justices O'Connor and Kennedy.

What the larger society must do is figure out how it wants religious values to fit into the framework of our common life. Hubbard, by the way, together with colleague John Hatfield of California State Polytechnic University at Pomona, undertook in the spring of 1995 a survey of enormous significance to chart what effect the study of world religions has on the attitudes of college students both before and after exposure to traditions beyond their own. It is impossible to overestimate the significance of religious understanding for the future relations of American citizens.

Stephen Carter's *Culture of Disbelief* may be one of the most important books to have come along as America searches for ways of allowing religious values a meaningful place at the table. The book doesn't explore the search for transcendent spiritual values in a multiethnic society in any depth. What it does accomplish is to set the stage for a broader future consideration of spiritual values in our public discourse, in a way that highlights the frustrations many people feel with efforts to keep religion out of the public arena.

THE WISDOM OF THE EAST IS OURS NOW

In the future, we also should be open to the possibility that our Western understanding of prayer and contemplation may be enriched through exposure to the vast storehouse of spiritual knowledge brought to us from other cultures. This brings us to the fourth area where a new accommodation may be possible. The new religions in our midst provide us with fresh ways of looking at familiar issues or dilemmas.

The moment of silence question is a good starting place. It has been framed largely as a promotion of religion in the noisy public policy debate of contemporary American society. But for cultures where meditation and contemplation are standard fare, it is not so necessary to reconcile conflicting denominational views to agree on the psychological and spiritual value for anyone of a few calm moments.

Our Western certitude might benefit from a dose of openness in these areas. The wisdom of the East gently invites us to consider that the interior life is itself a field worthy of scientific and psychological exploration. It is one that has been thoroughly charted for thousands of years in Hinduism, Buddhism, and other rich traditions. Moreover, much of the activism of Christian fundamentalists arises from a perceived conflict over science and religion going back to the Scopes Trial. Such skirmishes as the Peloza case in Orange County, California, where religion and science are cast as adversaries, remind us of the old battle between creationism and evolution. In fact, one of the challenges of accommodation for the future will be to regard science and religion not as locked inevitably in conflict in a kind of CNN *Crossfire* debate, but as complementary, with the latter picking up in the realm of mind and spirit where scientific inquiry about matter and the physical universe leaves off.

Our new multiethnicity in fact makes available religious perspectives that regard nature as extending not only to the physical world outside, but also into the realm of humanity's inner life, areas of inquiry that are relatively young or in exploratory stages for Western psychology. For example, at the interfaith service in Hollywood discussed earlier, Dr. Maher Hathout, a physician who is president of the Islamic Center of Southern California, reminded his audience that science, for all its wonders and advances, was not in possession of all the answers about the human condition. He cautioned against the conceit that science alone could serve as humanity's lodestar and asserted that "absolute truth is not known to us."

Some of these ideas have been received and embraced by New Age practitioners in America, but mainstream appreciation of the potential of religion as a "science" exploring higher levels of consciousness has been slow in coming. These ideas have been seeping into the culture, but largely await a kind of translation and simplification that might make them more readily accessible in ways that do not turn people off.

This material in the future should not be considered solely the province of pop religionists and faddists. As early as 1945, Harvard University psychology professor Gordon Allport, who did seminal work on the nature of prejudice, wrote an introduction to a book on the psychological insights of Indian philosophy and religion and the contributions they might make to mental health in the United States. The book was *Hindu Psychology, Its Meaning for the West*, by Swami Akhilananda of the Ramakrishna Order of India. Allport wrote, "In some respects, I am convinced, American psychology will improve in richness and wisdom if it accommodated in some way the wise things that the author says about meditation and the necessity for an adequate philosophy of life."[25]

The implications of this kind of approach for teaching about religion are profound. If we can begin to see religion as a science of life, we may be able to move toward ground where there is less concern about giving offense over doctrine and dogma. There are admirable efforts underway to offer instruction in "character" by instituting "values" courses. Haynes has good ideas about teaching religion as an academic subject.

Maybe it is wise to begin this way in our pluralistic culture. However, we should not conclude in doing this that we have fully understood what religion is all about, or that we have to study religion only because it turns up in our art and literature. Philosophies that are relatively new to American shores have thousands of years of experience integrating the life of the spirit with that of the body, mind, and nature. The building of character through education and ethical training is seen as a building block that is a prelude to real religious understanding and even direct experience of the Ultimate Ground of Being, or God. And these approaches have been systematized in disciplines that are not contingent upon denominational affiliation. Nor in fact, to address the dilemma of the interfaith role of the Buddhists, are they the province only of those who make their religious understanding contingent upon belief in a personal creator.

Thomas Moore, in his popular look at sacredness in modern life, *Care of the Soul*, concludes that we have lost in modern times the integration of disciplines such as medicine, religion, and philosophy, and that while dealing with the same problems of the human condition, we have a new set of emotional problems even with the advent of technology.[26] We are a ways from the kind of accommodation that sees the panoply of religious content and ideas as a rich source of understanding our world alongside other disciplines. But we may not be as far from such reconciliation as some might think. In the next chapter, we shall consider how some of the new ideas imported to the United States have the capacity to enhance our understanding of what freedom and responsibility in American life are all about.

WHERE RELIGION AND DEMOCRACY INTERSECT

The traditional separation of church and state has been an important guiding principle in our history. However, today some Christian fundamentalists have no compunction about advancing their narrow views and, in some extreme cases, even trying to transform our political system into something other than a democracy. Will more mainstream Americans, who believe in the power of religious values to improve our lives and who are comfortable expressing them in ways that are accepting of the cultures and views of others, stand on the sidelines? We should hope that by identifying the areas where religious concerns intersect with the welfare of a diverse America, the nation will approach the future in a way that regards moral and spiritual values as energizing and creative forces in its national life and that does not relinquish these resources to those who are embracing an imagined past.

Chapter Thirteen

Freedom and Responsibility in a New America

One of the quiet but significant developments at the end of the twentieth century is that we now have available a top-to-bottom picture of what human freedom is all about. That statement may seem surprising. Since the United States has written the book on political freedom and to the extent that it has been a beacon for human rights around the world, it may appear that there is nothing much new to learn on these shores.

In fact, some of the religions that are thousands of years old but new to our continent have a lot to say about freedom in a spiritual sense, not just the freedom we are most accustomed to discussing—namely, political, social, and economic freedom. To all that the United States has stood for as a symbol of political freedom, we now have access to the world's library of understanding about a more elusive and intangible notion of freedom: freedom of the spirit, the intangible union of man's soul with the divine.

This is possible not because of any new home-grown intellectual, philosophical, or spiritual movement, but because of the importation of the treasures of the world's great religions as part of the twentieth century's tides of immigration. Some of these religions have thought in different ways about the human condition and, in their philosophical deliberations, have considered the soul as bound by nature. The effect is to give us more to work with

177

than ever before if we really want to talk about all that constitutes human freedom. Whatever wisdom Americans can glean from the "new" religious currents in our midst are there to supplement the prevailing Western notions of freedom in the political, social, and economic spheres. This has the potential to be a substantial development as we embark on a new millennium. We have a host of new religious ideas bubbling in our midst, and they are resources for a diverse nation.

FREEDOM AS WE HAVE COME TO KNOW IT

Freedom as a political, social, and economic ideal is central to the American experience. We see it expressed regularly in the campaign themes of our political elections. To this we can add some of the stirring of religious groups in local communities, which came in the lexicon of the 1990s to speak of "empowering" individuals to liberate themselves in some way or other. They seek emancipation from an environment filled with hopelessness, youth violence, racism, poverty, or whatever, so that they can participate more fully in the promise of American life and realize some spiritual fulfillment in the process. This effort is another way of describing the modern search for community, the twenty-first-century equivalent of the Puritans' "city set upon a hill," which, as history reminds us, was itself a quest for room to breathe.

Freedom, and how we handle it, are central not only for those who are worried about shoring up the society, but also for those who need shoring up. The degree to which our nation's moral health is at risk is manifest in the fact that we face the prospect of raising entire generations of people who, for whatever reasons, are not equipped for or committed to doing the work that is necessary to make a free society function. This was evident in a poll by *The Los Angeles Times* in the summer of 1994, which found concerns about personal responsibility to be a preoccupation of mainstream Americans. Individuals like "Father John" Lenihan in Anaheim, California, and his faith community and city, had identified personal responsibility as a cornerstone of their efforts to change a climate of despair.

Freedom as we have known and celebrated the ideal seems to be suffering from fatigue at the close of the twentieth century. The bicentennial of the Bill of Rights was observed in 1991, and the nation's achievement in proclaiming freedom and then reinforcing it brick by brick through judicial review and legislation stands as one of history's great accomplishments. We remain for the world the leading light, and our ideal of human rights gives hope and lends encouragement to the international community. A case in point was in 1993, when Secretary of State Warren Christopher spoke at a United Nations human rights conference in Vienna in the face of some Third World countries' opposition to international efforts to protect the rights of individuals and groups. He said that around the world no faith, no creed, and no culture that respected humanity would tolerate the disavowal of the United Nations Declaration of Human Rights. When these governments were trying to water down human rights by arguing that it was all relative, here was some real American insight on political and economic freedom. Hillary Rodham Clinton's meeting in Ahmadabad, India, in March 1995 with poor women who said they were no longer afraid to organize for better treatment was a symbolic statement of the support to be found for struggling peoples in the great American ideal.

But while freedom as a social, political, and economic framework retains its staying power, many people in the United States feel that they have fewer choices, not more, even with our espousal of freedom and with all that technology has made possible. The nineteenth-century romantic ideal of the frontier simply has run out of room. Everywhere, we see people trapped by life circumstance in poverty and hopelessness or limited somehow in their self-actualization by demons of their own creation. The wonders of our vaunted computer technology have been something of a mixed blessing; the value of human labor, which is central to participation of individuals in a free society, has been diminished in some cases through the elimination of jobs. Even our ideal of political freedom, the most advanced in the world, has been tempered by special interest politics, gridlock, rancor, and a flood of cynicism and money. In an interview with CBS News correspondent Mike Wallace, former Texas governor Ann Richards, offering insight and candor at the end of a political career, lamented after a lifetime of observing democracy at work that she was not sure the country even knew what it was all about any more.[1]

The customary antidote for burnout is rest and rejuvenation, but in one sense, much of this book has been about the search for how we go about taking our medicine. We have asked, for example, whether we should assign moral leadership to a band of well-meaning believers who in their zeal are easily manipulated by demagogues. Or, do we listen to those who are worried about the potency of religious ideas and decide that it is better to keep these ideas out of the public square entirely?

QUESTIONING FREEDOM AS LICENSE

John P. Sears, Ronald Reagan's campaign manager in 1976 and 1980, has articulated the peculiarly American dilemma of espousing individual liberty and handing the moral agenda for renewal over to a band of zealots who might restrict choices. He raised this point in an analysis of the relationship between the Christian Coalition and the Republican Party written for the *Los Angeles Times* in the spring of 1995, when the pot was beginning to stir for the 1996 presidential election.[2] Sears observed that in conversations with foreigners, he has come away sensing their astonishment at the status of individual freedom in America as the paramount virtue in the search for fulfillment, when by disposition others are inclined to seek happiness through more time-tested normative social and cultural behavior. That these questions are so pressing and that the options present themselves to us as polar opposites is evidence that we have only begun to wrestle with the problem.

Religion within the predominantly Christian and Jewish traditions has a significant role to play in helping Americans understand that their personal freedom has to be exercised in such a way as to assume some responsibility for the larger society. The Rev. Richard John Neuhaus, who argued with the Buckley team in the *Firing Line* debate that the wall of separation between church and state could be lowered safely, made this case when he said that a more prominent place for religion needed to be provided in "the public square." But actually mobilizing religion-based morality to reinforce freedom and democracy in a pluralistic society ends up being more complicated in practice. *U.S. News & World Report* identified the problem area when it found the nation conflicted over the role of religion in society, "uneasy with the perpetual tension between our religious impulses and our unwavering commitment to a secular society. We profess fidelity to traditional morality yet champion individual freedom and resist religious authoritarianism."[3]

Much of the debate about the deterioration of the social fabric, which has provided the religious right with ammunition, turns on the notion that we have responsibilities to go along with our freedoms and that things start falling apart if we abandon them. But in a sophisticated, multiethnic society, we need a more complex understanding of what the challenge of religious freedom is all about than can be gleaned from the political statements of any particular group pushing a narrow agenda. Such campaigns may be ignorant of or downright hostile to other moral and religious perspectives that in themselves are properly regarded as national assets.

The freedom of individuals in society is an old philosophical topic, and the original American commitment to democracy turned on some of the arguments. The rise of the Moral Majority in the 1970s and some of the larger complaints of Christian fundamentalists came about in part from frustrations and dissatisfaction tracing back to the theory of evolution in the nineteenth century and to the historic forces of reason and enlightenment that gave shape to the American Revolution. In acknowledging social and political freedom and in bowing to the altar of science, it seemed to some fundamentalists that the Western world was unleashing powerful forces that undermined authoritative teachings and value systems that kept destructive impulses in check.

In its current political context, the discussion really centers on a debate between liberals and conservatives over whether we are victims of our circumstances or whether people are entirely responsible for their own lives. Liberals tend to suggest that outcomes in people's lives are directly affected by conditions in their lives, such as poverty, racism, child abuse, human rights violations, and so forth. Conservatives claim that their view liberates society from the culture of victimization, holds individuals more responsible for their actions, and imposes a clearer sense of right and wrong.

MORAL EXCELLENCE AND SPIRITUAL FREEDOM

The significance of having all these "new" religions brought to our shores by waves of recent immigration is that their philosophies now are there to help us achieve fresh insight into our own established ideals, and also perhaps to help us blend the liberals' concern with decent and "compassionate" policy with the conservatives' yearning to hitch values to social programs. For example, the philosophies coming to us from India, for all their persistent association in the Western mind with such ills as caste and fatalism, tend at their core to think in broader terms than political and social contexts when they address the topic of freedom.

These "new" religions have charted the liberation of the spirit as their canvas. This pursuit of the individual soul's rendezvous with ultimate reality, or God, is seen as the goal of life and is achieved through precisely the moral and spiritual disciplines that make for a more harmonious social environment in a free society as well. The individual finds God within in part by behaving well in the society outside. There is an obvious benefit for community along the soul's journey, because character also turns out to be the building block for mature participation in the exercise of political freedom.

This is a less categorical view than that espoused by some

contemporary American conservatives. It recognizes the capacity for evil in the full play of human choices, but is much less likely to write off an individual as completely lost in the soul's evolutionary journey. It is less empirical and ultimately less willing to offer excuses than some of the liberal approaches, as it does not buy the notion that people are blank slates blown around like Forrest Gump's feather in the wind. Therefore, it acknowledges implicitly that expectations about behavior and responsibility are crucial to make a free society work.

Perhaps we are or should be at a point when we are ready for the maturation of our American notions of individual freedom and can be assisted in this evolution by the employment of the spiritual value systems of the new ethnic and religious groups, like the Hindus, the Buddhists, and the Muslims, who have come to our shores.

ARE WE READY TO THINK MORE BROADLY ABOUT FREEDOM?

This is not to suggest that everybody in America should abandon their political philosophy, quit their church or synagogue, and get themselves a mantra or join a mosque. What the imported religious philosophies can do is add important insights into the human condition to stand alongside whatever understanding more traditional groups of Americans already have gleaned both from the nation's rich political and religious experience and from science since the time of Charles Darwin.

In *The Disuniting of America*, a powerful complaint about balkanization, the historian Arthur M. Schlesinger, Jr., observed that a strength of the country historically was the ability of various groups and individuals to bring their contributions to the task of building the country while submerging particular claims. Schlesinger's concern in the book was with common democratic beliefs and assumptions, not religion. However, if a vision of a common national spirit is to prevail, it well might be facilitated through the mobilization of the spiritual ideas that this nation of immigrants now has available, especially to the degree that those ideas inspire people to look beyond themselves.

Of course, people would have to open themselves up to these ideas—in effect, make themselves vulnerable to them—and that, given the relatively narrow focus of much denominational activity at the present time, is a tall order. This will be discussed further in the final chapter, but whether or not we are willing to examine the new religious and spiritual resources for what they can do for us collectively, there is no denying that they are now very much in our midst and represent very powerful currents in the thinking of some of the newest Americans. The point is that we now have the capability of taking the best from our various traditions and of weighing how that exercise might contribute to restoring or shoring up a sense of national unity.

A good example of an individual absorbing these ideas and putting them into practice is the immigrant Indian priest, the Rev. Vivian Ben Lima in Los Angeles. It was he who reminded the interfaith audience in Hollywood that there was danger in comparing the best in our own traditions with the worst in somebody else's. The former president of the Interreligious Council of Southern California is a Christian and was very clear about not wanting to water down that perspective. However, he also has brought some of the universal perspective on the relationship between freedom and responsibility that resides in thousands of years of his country's religious thought to his ministry in the United States. For example, Lima focused on the relationship between religion and political freedom when he told a congregation of immigrants in a recent Fourth of July homily in Los Angeles that, "Liberty is not liberty unless it is tempered with morality."

Lima also recognizes pitfalls he has seen in his own country when religious aspirants disregard any obligations to their fellow human beings by selfishly pursuing their own spiritual liberation. Moreover, Mrs. Clinton's meeting in India and the wreath she laid at a monument to Mohandas K. Gandhi was testimony to how far that country still must go to translate its towering spiritual ideals into temporal reality. There is a good cautionary note in Lima's concern for Americans who are enamored of pop psychology, drawn to cults promising easy results, or unwilling to do the spiritual work that their own rich traditions require of them.

Vivekananda, the Indian monk who delivered the message of the harmony of religions at the Parliament of the World's Religions in 1893 and who was a brilliant expositor of his country's deep and ancient spiritual resources, spent a considerable amount of energy trying to get his own country in the latter stages of colonial rule to pay more attention to social conditions, education, and charitable work.

But the larger point of this reference to Indian philosophy and thought in particular is that the library of spiritual resources now available in America makes it possible for individual citizens to take what is useful and discard the rest, and to do this really for the first time. This has happened as the discussion of public policy in the United States seems to have been moving on both sides, liberal and conservative, toward a healthier recognition of the role of individual responsibility. With it comes an implied understanding that our task is to help people unlock their potential from within, to whatever extent we are able to understand that potential. Some of our new perspectives, such as Hinduism and Buddhism, suggest that the potential is unlimited.

A WIDER APPLICATION OF VALUES

These traditions add new voices to the religious perspectives to which the nation is more accustomed. Properly understood, they ask on a personal level the very things that a free society requests of its members collectively, that is, to live well, accept responsibility, care for one's neighbor, and strive for moral excellence. Those shared expectations are surfacing in interfaith conversation. It is precisely that recognition, for example, that drew together the Catholics and the Muslims in Los Angeles in the search for a stronger sense of community well-being.

If we begin to think in these terms, then there is a much wider application for moral and spiritual values than what the Christian Coalition's Ralph Reed had in mind when he said he wanted to "allow people of faith to enter the public square."[4] Neuhaus's vision suddenly becomes more expansive, too, and has less to do somehow with the imposition of a particular set of beliefs on others. Additional perspectives outside the exclusive orbit of conservative Christians and Jews are readily available now, and indeed much more so than they were to the Founding Fathers, who derived their religious inspiration and notions of political freedom chiefly from the best available thinking in England and on the continent.

As we study thousands of years of thought from other cultures, we are invited to consider a bigger picture than the social consequences of acting responsibly in a free society. Suddenly the canvas becomes the confluence of science and religion, the core values of modern Western democracy and how they might be reconciled with Eastern ideas about liberty and the inner life of man. These philosophies, properly understood, tend to be comfortable with scientific method and with the idea that man controls his destiny. Rather than being alarmed with science and with the implications of freedom as some of the religious conservatives are, Eastern philosophies embrace morality not as a way of keeping people in line but as a vehicle to liberation. Much is wrapped in cultures and traditions unfamiliar to Westerners, but Western science, psychology, and theology already are moving into some of these areas on their own. In fact, some of the groundwork for Western understanding of Eastern thought was laid as far back as the Transcendentalists in the nineteenth century and was picked up later in the West through intellectuals like Aldous Huxley and Christopher Isherwood, who acted as intermediaries.

What is different now is that our need to strengthen the basis for our understanding of freedom and responsibility is greater. And the need is pronounced at precisely the time that the resources are now available from other cultures, which are clamoring themselves for a fuller place in American life. The "new religions" such as Hinduism, Buddhism, Islam, and various offshoots may or may not appeal to individual Americans in and of themselves, but their core philosophical ideas are ripe for dissemination and integration in mainstream American thought. The question is whether we will accept them.

On our own as a society, we seem to have to keep relearning the hard way that freedom in a democratic setting cannot flourish without participants who are willing to restrain their own selfish impulses, cultivate civility, and, as the entire debate over "family values" has shown on all sides of the political spectrum, accept a certain amount of personal responsibility that government alone cannot furnish.

MORALITY AS PREPARATION FOR FULFILLMENT

What the Eastern philosophies bring is the idea that ethical conduct is the individual's first step in harmonious living with society, but that it doesn't end there. Accepting responsibility within the framework of political structure—in our case, democracy—is a prelude to a personal journey toward God that ultimately produces freedom of the spirit. For example, an Indian thinker who lived in the second century BC, Patanjali, addressed in his precepts on yoga, or union, the importance of self-control and moral excellence as preparatory to all religious experiences. Similar ideas are presented in various contexts throughout Indian thought as a framework for approaching religious activity of any kind in a systematic way. They link the ideas of moral conduct as a way of living and spiritual freedom as a goal. In the West, the idea of a relationship between personal conduct and the pursuit of Ultimate Truth, however we may define it, has been fractured in recent centuries by a false conclusion that religion and science are incompatible, a premise that is beginning to break down as theology and cosmology explore common terrain.

For the Buddhists, who share some common ground in the rich Indian philosophical tradition, there is what the philosophy professor and expert on world religions Huston Smith once termed "indifference to a personal creator."[5] But the ethical practices that lay the groundwork for the individual's spiritual destiny are preparatory in much the same way. It is no accident that the recent book by the Dalai Lama, one of the world's leading religious figures, is entitled *The Way to Freedom*.[6] Humanity's inner struggle is seen in these traditions not as a matter of blind faith or adherence to doctrine, but as a practical and orderly approach to life, accessible to one and all regardless of affiliation, built upon a unified philosophy of harmony with society outside and with the Godhead within.

Ethical training, then, is not merely necessary for a free society to work, but is a foundation for the approaches to a higher life of the spirit for the individual reached through prayer, meditation, and concentration, which are the venues to the inner realm of freedom. This idea is concisely presented with an image in the "Katha Upanishad" which belongs to the knowledge portion (as opposed to ritualistic portion) of an ancient body of writing in India called the *Vedas*. There is a parable where the individual soul is portrayed as riding in "a chariot," (the body) driven by the intellect and linked through by the mind. The way to achieve knowledge of God is by bringing under control the senses, which are compared to wild horses.[7]

This image, which is a kind of framework for viewing ethical conduct in a religious context, presents the human condition as a paradox. The idea seems to be that freedom is achievable in precisely the opposite way from what appears to be the case; that is, we get there through restraint, not through license, a lesson that seems to be coming home to us now almost daily in our somewhat weary democracy as we recognize the limits of a "me first" approach to modern life.

ARE WE READY TO LEARN FROM OTHERS?

In the century since the Parliament of the World's Religions in Chicago in 1893, it has become clearer that interfaith movement toward common precepts is a survival technique, not a luxury. In one sense, it can be seen as an evolving conversation about how to reconcile the ideal of freedom in the social and political realm with the ideal of freedom in its spiritual dimensions. It is being conducted at precisely the time that our exclusively political ideal of "freedom" seems to be suffering from battle fatigue.

The question of whether these ideas will really take root and whether people will see in an interfaith approach a way to resolve some of our differences is a serious one. Optimism is out of fashion in some quarters, tempered at the close of a century of war, nationalistic horrors, and spotty achievement for the "one worlders."

However, the best practical argument for taking the best of our new resources may be to consider what we will be left with as an alternative. If we don't take advantage of the spiritual insights of the imported cultures, we may be left to whatever conclusions politically active religious conservatives will draw for us and for others from their traditions about how to revitalize freedom and democracy in a time of moral crisis. Or, on the opposite spectrum among the best educated, we can have the product of self-centeredness and resignation, what the columnist John Leo of *U.S. News & World Report* called "the therapeutic ethic," that is, a preoccupation with private feelings and personal taste influenced by various self-help and self-esteem notions that began spreading in the 1960s, "some of them quasi religions based on the primacy of the self."[8]

RELIGION AS A MEDIATOR

In their book *Habits of the Heart*, an exploration of the relationship in America between private and public life, the sociologist of religion Robert Bellah and colleagues alluded to religion's role in the pursuit of temporal freedom. They suggested that there were separate trend lines within American religious life of individualistic or "internal" religion and collective or "external" practices, those imposed by organized church communities. They found, interestingly, that while these predictably have varying viewpoints on matters of authority and autonomy between organized institutions and individuals, both were very much interested ultimately in the advancement of freedom. It turns out that, in whatever form it is expressed in a nation as pluralistic as the United States, much of our religious activity has in common an attempt at mediation between the individual and the environment, the society, and "ultimate reality."[9] Alternatively, new ways of thinking about the array of traditional religious perspectives are crucially important to the support and sustenance of civic spirit in a multi-ethnic America.

The old ideas about responsibility and self-control go beyond the obvious social benefits to the functioning of a democracy, and we should find ways of stating them so that they are digestible for broader audiences of Americans. One source of misunderstanding in the West about religion in the East centers around the concepts of detachment and renunciation, which often are mistaken for otherworldliness. Smith, author of *The Religions of Man*, recognized this potential misreading when he wrote that: "... renunciation can also be a clearer sign of exhilaration and confidence in life's high calling than any amount of momentary indulgence. In this category falls discipline of every form, the sacrifice of the trivial now for a momentous then, the turning away from an easy this toward a beckoning yet-to-be."[10] Perhaps a succinct way of stating it is to say that anything worth becoming is worth sacrificing for.

Commentators on contemporary society like the columnist George F. Will and UCLA's professor of management and public policy James Q. Wilson have identified the resulting problems from our failure to incorporate this concept more fully into the fabric of American life. Will has written about how disastrous it has been for people who lack "internal restraints on good character"[11] to have a situation identified by Wilson where the individual has been emancipated from the restraints of tradition, community, and government.

How we deal with the surging egalitarian instincts in American life is a crucial challenge, one that we have not comfortably resolved in our quarrels over immigration, affirmative action, and the like. Essentially, we now have different strains in our thinking about freedom running along parallel tracks. These lie at the heart of the political confrontation between liberals and conservatives.

There is the idea on one side that we have to look out for the needy and promote economic fairness even if it means giving certain groups advantages for a time and the idea on the other that we can promote responsibility and empowerment best by removing crutches.

In the West, we historically have been accepting not only of the promise of freedom in the abstract but also of its burdens. Freedom's true meaning in social and political terms has been debated in the United States from our very colonial beginnings into the present. In its best moments, it has been approached not as something given to us, but as a basic right assumed to be ours, without the consent of government. So even if we are suffering a touch of burnout, we hold our ideal up for its staying power, and people around the world still are attracted to it.

The Los Angeles riots showed that freedom as a political idea has its limitations. We have seen that simply flocking to a place that purports to stand for freedom does not by itself guarantee much of anything. In recent times, even with our celebrated diversity, we find our multiethnic society suffering stress fractures of the kind that the Interfaith Coalition to Heal Los Angeles set out to address. In Orange County, religious communities dedicated to the transformation of personalities from within and those more traditionally concerned with social activism had begun to occupy some of the same ground through populist and grassroots activities designed to empower people and improve social conditions.

It will be difficult to do, but we ought to set as a goal having our diversity nourish our sense of unity as a people. Under this scenario, citizens would understand how there are many tributaries in our various ethnic and religious backgrounds that lead to a new common understanding of freedom and responsibility. Here we see the civilizing influence of religion in the social realm. Without it, the promise of secular freedom may deteriorate into little more than the pursuit of self-gratification.

In the world of politics, it may be reduced to the insistence by various interest groups that their individual agencies must take precedence over others. The author Don Eberly argues that social policy isn't enough to nourish and sustain a democracy without the cooperative efforts of individual Americans and that democracy is not "simply about the individual's franchise and having access to a responsive political process. It is about democratic disposition, habit and outlook, which is either nourished or starved."[12]

FREEDOM: EAST AND WEST

In the meeting ground of East and West, a marriage of concepts of freedom as both a way of organizing human affairs and a goal of life in the realm of religion may help us. Our constitution guarantees the exercise of enumerated and even implied freedoms in America. It turns out that we know a lot in the West about freedom as a secular article of faith, but in our American pluralism and separation of church and state, we often have tended to regard religion as an entirely private matter, quite separate from our common aspiration of political liberty.

The Western idea in America comes in part from the idea of Roger Williams that the individual conscience could not be prevailed upon, that there was a purity to religion that should not be corrupted by the state, and hence that there could be no establishment of religion.[13] In the West, we have built our commitment to political and social freedom over time, but these spiritual ideas brought to us by immigrant groups suggest likewise that there is a body of knowledge relating to a science of freedom of the soul that invites us to view religion in less contradictory or even confrontational terms. It has been refined and restated though many centuries in different scriptures, through different teachers, and even in different religious traditions.

To retain the American dream as a viable hope for future generations in our shrunken continent, our secular visions of freedom and unity alone may not be sufficient. There are signs that we are beginning to understand that religiosity has to do with the human condition as much as with particular belief systems and that we need to understand the complete human personality and its needs in a time of alienation. Thomas Moore, whose books on modern spirituality have made a mark in popular culture, has written that "spirituality is an aspect of any attempt to approach or attend to the invisible factors in life and to transcend the personal, concrete, finite particulars of this world."[14] Religion, understood in this context, is an extension of the concept of political and social freedom that we have developed in the West to include some deeper meaning and quest for freedom of spirit.

One of the most important ideas to come from the late twentieth century is that individual responsibility is paramount to civil society. The dismantling of central authority and the assertion of local control have a bureaucratic and political context, but they also have something to do with a reaffirmation of the power and place of character in American life. It is precisely this location of the wellspring of freedom as internal that makes the contributions of religion to the sustenance of democracy so worthy of our commitment. It is this phenomenon that we saw at work in Anaheim. It is this phenomenon that has prompted reconsideration of the role of religions in the amazingly diverse community life of Los Angeles in the period after the 1992 riots.

When we peel away the components of democracy, we find as the great Supreme Court justices Oliver Wendell Holmes, Jr., and Louis Brandeis did in their collaborations on free expression that our system is as much an act of courage and faith as anything else, a hardy crocus standing in the cold winds, one that must be prepared to tolerate and withstand dissent.[15] A central question in the experiment of democracy always will be whether or not we can afford to have it at all. The strains that personal freedom put on democracy have come into sharper focus as the social fabric has been tested and when we consider that "we live in an age of moral relativism" where rights have been emphasized over responsibility, as *Newsweek*'s religion writer Kenneth L. Woodward observed.[16]

What the East teaches us is that religion, freed of denominational claims and doctrines, is much more about the application of reason and scientific method to the inner realm of the human experience than we might otherwise have thought. What the West increasingly is discovering is that there is a good deal more faith and conviction in the rational ordering of our lives in a free society than we might have expected. Both religion and democracy are about separate but interconnected aspects of human freedom.

RELIGION AS "LIBERATING FACTOR"

As we stand on the verge of a new century, the religious traditions that have been brought in waves of immigration should not be regarded simply as New Age indulgences that belong only to a select group of spiritual seekers outside the mainstream religions. Rather, they should be seen as bringing a new dimension to our understanding of what it is to be an American.

Their association with freedom as an ideal is grounded in the acceptance of personal responsibility that many Americans now recognize as essential to make the wheels of democracy turn. The new religious cultures, which themselves may be based in very old ideas and teachings, have the capacity to supply new vigor to the traditional American virtues of hard work, unselfish behavior, and strong sense of personal ethics. These virtues have been the focus of Western "rehabilitation" efforts through the writing of Gertrude Himmelfarb and other prominent conservatives. As we have seen, some even bring a scientific approach to personal spiritual disciplines as a way to happiness and fulfillment.

All of these religious perspectives have the capacity to help us think in fresh ways about modern democracy. For example, Islam, which is growing rapidly, itself has been undergoing change internationally. There are progressive currents seeking to modernize the faith with new attention to the central idea of the dignity of the individual. These efforts have implications for American democracy that are yet to be fully understood, as Islam, like the Christian West, struggles with the tensions of fundamentalism and progressive modernism. But like the ideas about freedom from ancient India that are worth reconsidering in modern light, so too the Islamic attention to its compatibility with democratic ideals has profound implications for the approaches to shoring up our own society.

Dr. Maher Hathout, president of the Islamic Center of Southern California, in his talk at the centennial observance of the Parliament of the World's Religions held in Hollywood in 1993, stressed the idea of moral restraint in religion, that it provided humanity with what he called "a self-policing factor." He went on to suggest that this was not something that would restrict people, but in fact would do the opposite by helping them to live more fulfilling lives. "Religion is emerging as a liberating factor in the world," he said.[17]

In our modern multiethnic society, democracy and religious values ought to be complementary in this way. One deals with our collective civic and political experience; the other with a harmony at the individual level from which success in the former is possible. The exercise of freedom at every level of human experience is really very much about getting hold of ourselves. This is true as much in the spiritual area as in the temporal.

What separates the progressive currents in even the oldest religious ideas apart, and commands our attention, is that they tend to rely on the individual to exercise self-control as the primary vehicle for personal spiritual advancement. They do this rather than depending exclusively on scriptural law, official dogma, or in the worst cases, repressive measures to keep people in line with an enforced code of morality.

While religious ideas encased in ancient texts and brought to us by new immigrants may be unfamiliar, they are not necessarily alien or hostile to democratic ideals. Rather, they have the capacity to broaden our understanding of democracy, and these ideas belong to all of us.

Chapter Fourteen

How the "New" Religions Can Be Our Allies

America is bursting with new religions, testing our capacity to handle new diversity and inviting us at the same time to think in new ways. Religion is more a part of our lives than ever, as polling from *U.S. News & World Report* and other sources suggests.[1] Students working with Harvard University's Diana L. Eck, a professor of comparative religion, recently counted that Chicago alone had 70 mosques, Seattle–Tacoma had 62 Islamic, Buddhist, or Hindu centers, and Houston had 50 such centers. One of the great national questions before us is what we will make of this— whether we will do interesting and exciting things as a society, drift along in enclaves, or worse, slip into religious and ethnic conflict.

It is ironic that all of this is happening at a time when there is an uneasy feeling in the United States that the nation is facing a moral crisis. While we still hear much about the freedom we aspire to and stand for, there is much that is troubling around us. At a time when our ideals ought to cheer our spirits, we find ourselves casting about for light in the tunnel.

Self-interest, in its most enlightened forms, has been an engine of our national enterprise from the beginning. It fueled our break from England and to this day provides for immigrant groups who have come to escape pogroms and oppression a handle with which to pull themselves up and test the ideal of freedom in their own lives. Today, new arrivals and interest groups continue staking their claim. Even with all the gloom-and-doom talk, there is plenty of reason to put one's faith in America.

However, our travails have us groping for fresh answers, convinced if we were not before that we must find ways of shoring up our celebrated commitment to freedom with something more than a rousing fireworks display and the country singer Lee Greenwood's "God Bless the USA" on the Fourth of July. In the arena of public policy, our political leaders are well aware of our restlessness and have been debating legislative approaches to these problems, whether it be a crime bill, welfare reform, improved public education, or strategies aimed at using the power of government to strengthen something as uniquely outside its conventional province as the well-being of the family.

At the same time, while legislation, constitutional amendments, and court decisions have done much to shape in everyday reality some of the general promises that this country historically has made to its citizens, many Americans today have decided that government alone cannot cure what ails our spirit. In his 1994 State of the Union address, President Clinton, for one, rattled off a list of government initiatives, only to conclude as so many others have across the political spectrum that such things alone would fall short of renewing the nation's spirit. He said, "The American people have got to want to change from within if we're going to bring back work and family and community."[2] By the political conventions of 1996, the Democrats, through talk of modest government initiatives, were seeking openly to compete on the pro-family territory that the Republicans had claimed for decades.

There are similar expressions of concern all around us in various communities. One that caught the sentiment was a letter to the editor published in the *San Francisco Examiner* in response to an editorial the newspaper had published in 1993 about city projects awaiting attention. Elliot Hoffman, cofounder of the Just Desserts Bakery, wrote:

> To me there is a far more critical set of issues facing us and our children's future. It is the condition of the spirit and soul of our city, our community. We are a very divided city with

> nearly 700,000 special interests. We all have our pet interests,
> our pet projects, our own axes to grind. The common good
> gets short shrift nearly every time. We talk about our strength
> being our diversity, yet in reality we have made it our weak-
> ness.[3]

That, of course, was San Francisco, just one of our communities. Yet it easily could have been New York, or Boston, or Chicago, or others.

The spiritual restlessness that many people feel occurs at a time when society seems inclined to decentralize government. This political shift has a parallel in faith communities. Religious congregations that traditionally have been aligned as liberal or conservative are coming to very similar conclusions about the need to empower neighborhoods and individuals, and even to find common ground in the religious ideas themselves. Pragmatic concerns of community survival are forcing previously isolated denominations to go beyond the mere courtesies of interfaith conversation to a consideration of their fundamental spiritual assets as capital to be shared by a broader group of Americans.

Meanwhile, there is the factor of new religious perspectives. J. Gordon Melton, author of *The Encyclopedia of American Religions*, reports the greatest diversity of religious groups now in the United States in recorded history, some 1600 denominations, nearly half non-Christian.[4] *NBC Nightly News*, for example, notes that the Immigration Act of 1965 flooded the country with immigrants from Asia and the Middle East and with religious diversity.[5] *The Los Angeles Times* cited a study by the Islamic Resource Institute that found that Islam, at the current rate of growth, might overtake Judaism in the next century as the second largest religious group after Christianity in the United States and Canada.[6]

While the argument between liberals and the religious right has preoccupied national attention on the role of religion in American society, it potentially could be less consequential for the long term than the fact that we now have all these new points of view in our midst. If the contenders like Pat Robertson and the American Civil Liberties Union cling to their fixed ideas about religious values in our common life, they may find themselves arguing to a smaller audience in the next century as a tide of immigration and ideas casts the arguments about "family values" in a different light. The debates between right and left over tradition and values may actually be obsolete in their own time, because there is so much else going on out there. But whether the country can get beyond the ideological debates that it seems locked in is really a decision that has to be made by a broader group of Americans. Indeed, we appear to have a choice whether to remain stalled in the "culture wars" or to really broaden the canvas on which we consider the role of religion and values in modern American life.

WHAT WE DO ABOUT RELIGION IS AN OLD QUESTION

Freedom of religion in this country has much more to do historically with the inability of passionate believers to agree than it does with celebration of the diverse perspectives on God that we saw in Los Angeles during the centennial observance of the Parliament of the World's Religions. Today, our difficulty or unwillingness to get a better handle on our spiritual assets may be depriving us of valuable energies that could be transforming the discussion about "values" in the nation. It also may be ceding moral and spiritual high ground to extremists.

When we are confounded by profound religious mysteries and apparent discrepancies in various official teachings, the easy way out up until now has been to say simply that religion and moral certitude is a private matter, best left out of the public arena. The country now must decide whether we can afford any longer to keep the broad mobilization of religious values out of the public arena. The answer is unequivocally no.

Sometimes it helps to see ourselves as others do. In assessing the close of the twentieth century, Czech President Vaclav Havel told the Harvard graduating class of 1995 that the world seemed simultaneously to be on the verge of a single global civilization and perilously close to disaster from the threats of nationalism and fundamentalism or the misuse of technology.[7] If he is right, are we to stand by and let a flip of the coin determine our fate? Heads we all get along, tails we come undone? The fragility of our time is evident in Havel's suggestion that we are poised both on the verge of some significant period in human history and some awful one.

This is where religion can and must help. We already know that the misuse of religion within our own borders causes considerable angst and misunderstanding. *The New York Times*, for example, reported ominously on a surge in hate crimes against Muslims, noting in particular an incident in Springfield, Illinois, "where Abraham Lincoln alerted pre-Civil War America with a speech on 'A House Divided.'"[8] Yet we have seen examples of how the strength of religious resources at the grassroots level can inoculate the society from fragmentation and, more positively, nourish the entire experience of democracy. To date, the people who have identified the moral and spiritual crisis are not always reaching a broad audience with their messages of universality. It is worth imagining how the nation might strengthen its focus on the moral predicament if it could harness these resources in its public discourse to speak, in effect, more of a common spiritual language.

TOWARD A NEW SPIRITUAL STYLE

Religion is so basic to the American experience, and to our original statement of national purpose, that no satisfactory solution to our moral dilemma likely can exclude it and still be successful. At the time of the bicentennial observance of the Bill of Rights, Ronald C. White, Jr., a scholar at the Huntington Library in San Marino, California wrote that the United States' fundamentally religious underpinnings from its earlier days were based in a reality that still applies nowadays. That is, he wrote, "morality and ethics cannot endure without a religious foundation."[9]

In an essay written for the commemoration of the bicentennial in 1991, White described the relationship of religion and the First Amendment in our modern era as "an unsettled arena." He counted first among challenges that

> The United States in the 21st century will be infinitely more pluralistic than the new nation of the 18th century or even the

nation of the 20th century. This pluralism is of many dimensions. Women, African-Americans, and Native Americans enjoy rights today not imagined in 1791. ... The pluriformity of *Protestant-Catholic-Jew* [Will Herberg's 1955 book on the dimensions of religiosity in America] has been expanded to include all of the world's religions and many who claim no religion at all.[10]

Today, we need to fashion a flexible and accommodating way of mobilizing belief systems. This would allow for the full range of our diverse religious values and core teachings to be brought more directly into the currents of our national life. The idea would be to do this in ways that do not require conversions, adherence to dogma, or adoption of rituals. That would not entail the creation of a new religion, but rather the development of a new style of bringing available moral and spiritual values to bear on societal problems.

In fact, bringing everybody together in the realm of spirit surely will test the diplomatic skills of the American "family" as a society. During one of Los Angeles' many crises in the early 1990s, Kevin Starr, a professor at the University of Southern California, asked what it would take for that city to find a sense of unity and purpose in the aftermath of the Reginald O. Denny beating trial. Denny was beaten mercilessly in the L.A. riots of 1992, and yet, as Starr observed in an article in *The Los Angeles Times*, the victim later rose to an uncommon level of capacity for forgiveness. The author asked this penetrating question, which is as much for the nation as it is for his city: "In the silence that will come after the anger on both sides of the Denny verdicts has spent itself, let the question be asked: Where do we go from here? Who are we building this city for, if not for each other?"[11]

In one gesture, Denny did more to convey a central message of Christianity than would a thousand legal briefs on prayer in the public schools. It would seem to follow that if he could identify the restorative power of forgiveness within himself, going beyond the grievance of a lifetime to urge others to a higher sense of community, it would not be asking too much of the rest of us to at least aim high. That would meet the test of most any religion's ideal of going beyond the limited self to some larger identification with the rest. It also suggests one way of bridging diverse cultures, which White said would prove to be such a test. For example, in the public behavior of Denny, we witnessed in a modern setting the universal application of the central Christian idea of forgiveness.

In fact, there is plenty to push us in the direction of spiritual integration as a society. Faced with a growing sense of frustration while expectations go unfilled, we either can retreat in anger or resolve to be a mature people. Our national experience, and the uneasiness today in our cities and streets, suggest that the mere pursuit of self-interest, all the while we espouse the individual rights that our political system allows and protects, is not enough to make us well as a nation.

We did reasonably well as long as we had boundless horizons. What the Progressive-era public philosopher Herbert Croly described as "the promise of American life" brought people to the United States by the millions.[12] Now, however, the nation in its overcast moments seems to be so many races and ethnic groups, crowded along the coasts and inner cities, appallingly lacking in knowledge and understanding of each other.

Newton Minow, the former Federal Communications Commission (FCC) chairman who in 1961 called television a "vast wasteland," has written about one small corner of this problem, the excessive violence in our television programming, even as we search for ways to cut down on the slaughter in our streets and to arrest the deterioration of the social fabric. Writing with colleague Craig LaMay in an op-ed article in *The Los Angeles Times*, he said that even Adam Smith, the high priest of laissez-faire who provided some of the intellectual justification for our getting to where we are as a society, warned that the entire experiment might collapse if self-interest wasn't also informed by morality and responsibility. Minow and LaMay said that freedom of expression, a fundamental component of American democracy, would come undone if those who championed its use did not also exercise greater moral responsibility.[13]

This theme found repeated expression in the "family values" debate in the period leading up to the 1996 presidential election. It turned up at various points in the comments of public officials as varied as former Vice President Dan Quayle and Senator Robert Dole of Kansas on the Republican side and President Clinton and Attorney General Janet Reno on the Democratic side.

Political or not, many of these sentiments about threats to our national cohesion are on the mark. Still, they do not go far enough. Attempting to rehabilitate a shared secular vision of America as a unique social and political experiment—the coming together of diverse peoples—is important and well-intentioned, but it may fall short if it does not include some kind of broad-based spiritual component to sustain it. The religious right seems to understand the power of specifically religion-based values, but its vision too often ends up being a narrow one.

WHAT WE DON'T KNOW CAN HURT US

The religious dimension to American life, and the constitutional principle of "free exercise," have been so central to our national experience that they are intrinsic to democracy. The great religions by nature are society's custodians of values; they remind us not only that we should be good, or compassionate, or just, but also that such virtues link us to something transcending in life beyond our natural impulses to seek self-satisfaction.

As suggested, there is some irony in the quest. Even with the glum assessments of our moral condition, even with the hate crimes reported at record levels, and even with firearms in line to become the leading cause of death by injury, Americans are thought to be as or more religious, or at least "churched," than ever. We are a country where slaughter by gunfire is chronicled appropriately enough under the watchful eye of the Centers for Disease Control and Prevention, yet the pollster George H. Gallup, Jr., said there was so much interest in religion these days that "It's the new frontier of the social sciences."[14] *The New York Times* reports that the baby boom generation, swaddled in middle-age guilt and skepticism, has been returning to organized religion in search of moral bearings in a troubling world, seeking a sense of religious community for itself and its children.[15]

And still there is uneasiness, even with the religious stirring. Gallup, for one, has identified some spiritual ambivalence on the part of Americans. He told The Associated Press that most people affirm religious faith but are not all that informed about its underlying premises. And perhaps more important, but not surprising, he found that they were not very informed about the faiths of others, either. He worried that "A climate of pluralism has stifled them, stifled their religious convictions."[16]

One would think that pluralism would be an asset, not a liability or a hinderance to a fully informed populace in a spiritual sense. But it may be, as Gallup seems to suggest, that ignorance prevents Americans from realizing not only the value of other religious ideas for ourselves, but also the full power of their own traditions. Somehow, we have to get beyond that.

White sees in "the privatization of religion" a second significant trend in the future, in addition to the increasingly multiethnic religious base. Perceptively, he contrasts the eighteenth century, when religion was considered both a private and public condition of the collective life of an aspiring nation, with recent Supreme Court decisions that have tended to define religion as a private matter.[17] What is troublesome about this phenomenon of privatizing or trivializing religion is that it effectively cedes the power of religion-driven values in the public arena to whomever will climb on a soap box.

This phenomenon is evident in the exclusive moral claims made by religious conservatives in our politics and cultural life. We also can see even more harm in the menacing fundamentalist political movements around the world alluded to by Havel. Moreover, ignorance about others has led to unfair and potentially dangerous stereotyping. Muslim leaders, for example, found themselves throughout the 1990s having to explain after incidents such as the bombings of the World Trade Center in New York and the federal building in Oklahoma City that terrorism has nothing to do with their religion.

It is difficult to imagine how we are going to get anywhere in the great search for transcendent values unless we advance beyond the notion that religion is something that Americans do off on their own, outside the public arena, and without much interconnectedness. People of good intention will have to find meaningful ways of identifying common ground and living by their moral and spiritual codes in a way that is public without imposing on others.

This is very hard to do, but there are hopeful signs. We have come some of the way with the ecumenical movements and interfaith dialogue initiated in recent years. Also, the practical search for commonality has been given a mighty push by some of the great moral and social concerns of post-war America, where people of various faiths joined hands in the struggles for civil rights and nuclear sanity.

However, we should not kid ourselves, either, about the state of the dialogue. We remain at a relatively primitive stage in the evolution of a moral and spiritual discourse that incorporates and reflects the diverse society we are today.

THE "FREE EXERCISE" IN THE TWENTY-FIRST CENTURY

To flourish as a nation, we need to find new relevance and inspiration in what the "free exercise" of religion clause of the First Amendment will mean in the America of the coming century. This we can and must do without any new constitutional amendment designed to further the agenda of any particular group.

Freedom of religion in the past has meant freedom to worship as we choose; in the future it may carry an additional obligation of citizenship that Americans actively seek out and promote the core moral and spiritual messages of all these religions.

The constitutional language that we have already is broad and wise enough to enable us to do that. What we need is understanding and resolve. Americans also ought to be inspired by having managed over several centuries to develop a national identity that recognizes the uniqueness and diversity of backgrounds and ideas. But there also are obstacles that go to the heart of our tradition of free exercise.

Agreeing to disagree is part of our unique American culture that is manifest in the commitment to the toleration of dissent. It's what the nation did in the very beginning when its approach to religious diversity was toleration in the most neutral sense. Today, many well-intentioned Americans seem to believe that their belief system is the only way, even if, as Gallup suggests, they don't know very much about everybody else.

But while the separatist impulse, protected by the First Amendment, has left Americans relatively free to pursue their own individual inclinations, they are not now as well off collectively for having gone their own way as some might think. Essentially, the founders deferred to future generations the question of what to do with our different belief systems if ever the nation ran out of sufficient room to keep them from crowding each other.

That day of reckoning is upon us. Making it all work should be regarded as some urgent unfinished business of the American Revolution.

The author Garry Wills has pointed out that Roger Williams, one of the charter thinkers on separation of church and state, was evenhanded "only in the impartiality of attack" in his tolerance of other less enlightened souls all around him.[18] That is, in a world where people were tried for their beliefs and where nuances of theological correctness were tests of fitness to remain in town, Williams saw no practical alternative but to put up with all of the "error" that he saw around him.

As Wills suggests, a primary motivation for the doctrine of separation throughout our history to the present day, not just with Williams in Rhode Island, seems to have been to regard disestablishment as a vehicle for protecting "orthodoxy" from the poisonous currents of heretics who might seek to enlist the government in their cause. There is a measure of "live and let live" in that approach, and there certainly was some broad spiritual thinking among the Founding Fathers. However, in a sense we also have backed ourselves into the lofty principle of freedom of religion. It's been a pragmatic way of dealing with what are perceived essentially as deep and irreconcilable differences.

Accordingly, we ought to understand our society to be dynamic, a place where we should be respectful of yesterday's conventional wisdom, but not paralyzed by it. The fact is that we know a lot more about the religious traditions of the world today, and we have run out of excuses for saying that it is best that we all just keep to ourselves.

Americans today are living side by side with people who may be quite different culturally and historically—not just Protestant, Catholic, and Jew, but Muslim, Hindu, Buddhist, and other; not just Anglo, but Latino, Asian-American, and Native American. Several centuries into the experiment with democracy, the scope of our diversity may compel individual groups to reexamine dogmatic assumptions, free as they are and ought to be to hold them. This must be so if we are to have any hope of making accommodation with moral and spiritual truths as discovered and understood by religious or ethnic groups different from our own.

The nation until now has gone about its spiritual business with the assumption that we all should go our own way and hope that it will work out. That is, we have trusted that the freedom to pursue our own denominational inclinations somehow will prove to be the invigorating ingredient for democracy that the nineteenth-century French visitor Alexis de Tocqueville envisioned.[19] Whenever there is a fundamental conflict, we have relied on the courts to sort it out, to serve as our traffic cops in the intersection of competing values.

If we have made it to this point intact, the journey has not left us well poised to bring resources from our library of spiritual values to bear on what ails us in a vastly different world. It is good first to recommit to the concept of freedom of religion, something that actually was done when nearly 200 national leaders signed the Williamsburg Charter in 1988, a celebration of the religious liberty clauses of the First Amendment.

Obviously, we should not be tampering with anybody's religious freedom or their ideas; we should encourage the fullest range and diversity of spiritual resources, which is what the celebrants of religious liberty want. However, it is now clear that we will be a better society, and better human beings, if we can manage to go a bit further. Now we must look beyond mere toleration to seek and promote all that is good and true that religions have in common.

The First Amendment as it currently exists is broad enough to handle any exigencies. It is also true, however, that the United States at this point in its history will have to do better than merely offering statements of intended toleration.

Accordingly, an assignment for ourselves at the end of the twentieth century will be to enrich the nation's public life and discourse with the best of the values and traditions available.

Those who look with nostalgia to an earlier America may have a point if they wish that it were easier now to be openly "religious" in modern culture. But there was a broader set of shared assumptions about religion at a time in our history when it was more possible to wear a particular set of values on one's sleeve. It was easier for Williams, Thomas Jefferson, and others, who had relatively nuanced theological differences. That consensus played a nourishing role in our break from the mother country, in the self-confident, self-reliant formation of the colonies and in the fervor of revolutionary sentiment.

Robert Bellah and colleagues note, "Today religion in America is as private and diverse as New England colonial religion was public and unified."[20] America can draw inspiration from the knowledge that it has realized some of what it aspired to, beyond declarations of intention. Had it just talked about freedom and not actually made some of it happen, its ideas would not stand for much today.

The challenge of making freedom meaningful for new generations is more daunting. There is less room to roam, and not every misfit or free spirit can pick up and move on to a limitless frontier. Today, the free exercise clause must inspire something more in us than simply the license to worship however we choose in pursuit of what Bellah calls the tradition of "expressive individualism" in American life.

DIVERSITY AS A RESOURCE

How do we get everybody, or as many people as possible, on the same page? The ability to pay more than lip service to democratic ideals lies as the basis for the great movements of abolition, civil rights, women's rights, and the general enfranchisement of minorities against the threat of tyranny or repression by empowered majorities. The Bill of Rights, in not merely assuming that Americans had rights but in enumerating and adding to them, has effectively held the country together for more than two centuries and defined for the world what it was to be an American.

But to the idea of national unity based on a consensus about political values we might now add that the United States also must develop a facility with the language of different spiritual ideas. Its citizens should come to regard religious diversity not as a threat but as a great national resource.

The noise over religion in politics that has attended the activism of Christian fundamentalists has showed us something about "arm's length" as an operative guideline for the mainstream. The religious right has gone ahead and taken up its agenda anyway, citing the amorality and bankruptcy of traditional liberal approaches. This has hardened the resolve of well-meaning liberals in the process and has made them suspicious of religious ideas in the marketplace and justifiably worried about what fanatics will do.

The separation of church and state in America is a cherished article of faith, and freedom of worship has been a source of strength and inspiration in the currents of national life. It also has protected the rights of varieties of believers and nonbelievers alike from tyranny by majority. But the nation still is sorting all of that out, as its shrunken borders have created a new playing field where rights and expectations of various groups at times are in collision.

Fundamentally, there is a paradox: The United States is a deeply religious country wrestling uncomfortably with diversity. Some of the country's new immigrants are bringing with them the idea that religious toleration is broader; it involves active acceptance of other ideas on merits.

To fulfill the promise of freedom of religion in America in the next century, the country somehow needs to bottle and distribute the sentiment of the Parliament of the World's Religions session in Hollywood in 1993. That means recognizing that diversity of viewpoint is not merely something to be put up with in an unruly democracy. It is actually an asset for the society and a demonstration, as the rabbi said, of "God's inordinate fondness for beetles."

There is an old saying that you can't feed a hungry person religion, and many of our nation's most pressing problems have to do with basic necessities: housing, food, jobs, healthcare, and the like. However, there is no denying either what was identified by the MacNeil–Lehrer panelists on the eve of the 1994 election—the underlying sense of a crisis of the spirit in America and a need to frame a more positive view of national purpose for the future.

Our new religious diversity offers us the way to have more active involvement of faith in our common life, if only we are willing to do the work. A failure to follow through may mean that we just drift or, given the fraying of our nerves and our society, that we endure more serious crises. The same diversity that offers us great hope as a nation can be our undoing if mishandled. It is time to wake up, as the citizen activists in southern California and elsewhere have. We have work to do, and thankfully, some people have thrown themselves into the fray to point the way.

The future belongs to those who regard our various spiritual traditions as resources to build a nation that, for all the inevitable problems of modern life, lives in tune with its ideals. We should proceed with the confidence that it is entirely possible for us to succeed in this great adventure.

Chapter Fifteen

Conclusion

*Religious Literacy and the Beginning
of a New Awareness*

We have witnessed the fractious national debate over the role of religion in public policy. We have seen the unsung glory of people working in neighborhoods to sow the seeds of a new accommodation and have considered how the new ethnic religious diversity can supplement our vision of what America is all about. So where are we? The answer: We are doing some things well, but still are a very long way from incorporating a spiritual style in our national life that can help see us through our future problems as a multi-ethnic society.

This book began by asking why we can't have a society that freely expresses religious values in "the public square" without driving people of good will into opposing camps. This question has new meaning and urgency now that we have so many different religions and ethnic groups in our midst. Somehow we have it backward when the prevailing public religiosity gives us the religious right out front, in some instances willing to bend the Constitution for political aims, while people doing the important work of community building are relegated to the background.

Points raised in Chapter Fourteen ought to offer some encouragement. We do have all these new religions in our midst. There is a sense of moral crisis that people say they want to address. The broad First Amendment provides plenty of room to give new and fresh meaning to the concept of the free exercise of religion.

Religious conservatives have proven to be a potent force in contemporary American life and are not likely to go away. To date, the response of liberal and mainline religious leaders to attempts by the religious right's most extreme voices to preempt the spiritual agenda has been to produce their own separate moral perspectives on public policy issues. This approach is helpful to the extent that it educates the nation about the complexity of moral issues in policy choices and demonstrates that there are important spiritual values related to the welfare of America not always adequately addressed by religious conservatives. It also serves as a peer review so that extremists cannot lead the country off track without being called into question.

However, there also is a risk in remaining bogged down in the same "battle over language" that has characterized the discussion of values on the national stage. This is the challenge facing groups like the Call to Renewal, a coalition of Christians who organized as an alternative to the political activism of religious conservatives. The public, impatient for progress on the moral front, has become skilled at tuning out what it perceives to be "noise." Those claiming to speak with moral authority, whether from the left or right, will find that what they have to say does not resonate well or for long if it has an ideological or partisan cast.

OUR NEW DIVERSITY CHANGES THE DEBATE

So what will it take for the nation to have a better comfort level with the expression of religious values in our common life? How do we make people more aware? Is it only when they reckon personally with concerns about mortality and the meaning of life? Are we locked into recurring patterns of misunderstanding because we have so many different belief systems in our midst?

There is a general answer to all these questions: Just as we have to prepare people for informed participation in our civic life by educating them about democracy, we also must raise the level of our societal understanding about religion itself; in effect, we must become more "literate."

Unless we work from a basis of broad understanding, it is unlikely that we will achieve a workable manner of expressing religious values to inform public policy choices. If ignorance informs our approaches to faith in the public square, activism continually will be reduced to merely another competing political point of view. The same players will continue to argue about the role of church and state, with those on the right saying that people of faith are being marginalized in favor of secularization and those on the left worrying that non-Christians, agnostics, and atheists will be made uncomfortable, or worse, persecuted.

Alternatively, the introduction of diverse religious perspectives changes the playing field of the debate for everybody. The voices arguing from narrow religious perspectives will be understood more easily in their proper context if the population in general is better informed about the truly broad spiritual foundation of modern society, with its many varieties of faith and culture.

WHERE WE'RE GETTING BOGGED DOWN

In the political realm of public policy, our leaders' failure to provide an overarching vision for what the country should aspire to be has left the nation caught between two caricatures of government, one entirely absent from the welfare of its citizens and leaving them to the wolves, and the other a monolithic obstacle to free enterprise and the exercise of personal choice and responsibility. Moreover, the difficulty we are having with a comfortable expression of specifically religious values in the conduct of our common business in a democracy suggests that mere expressions and hopes for "tolerance" are insufficient to our task.

There are too many contenders who either are trying to advance their own religious agendas or, on the opposing side, arguing in effect for a society in which secularism (not merely a secular government) is the highest ideal.

This brings us full circle to the concept that arose from the discussion of the new civic spirituality in southern California, the idea of a "moral middle," a large group of Americans who share the concern of religious conservatives about a crisis of values, but who are put off by what they perceive as intolerance or even bigotry.

We need a long-term approach that cultivates and makes better use of this group as a national resource. Religious literacy for these citizens will not cut off the debate between the left and right, and it will not solve our long-term questions about what government can and cannot do. But it arguably will inoculate a crucial segment of the population and electorate against the manipulation of extremists, and it likely will reduce some of the anxiety that has been generated by the political activism of select groups of religious conservatives.

Accordingly, success in maximizing the participation of public-spirited moderates, who are open about the religious motivation that their base of faith provides, well may lie at a deeper level than trying to get partisans to moderate their language or to sign on to affirmations of toleration. These things are important, but we need also to develop this citizenry's broad-based understanding of world religious traditions. This will not only empower them with the knowledge of their own tradition, but also ground them in the concepts of others.

This book has explored and sought to clarify some of the issues raised by the presence of religious values in "the public square." Now, it seems appropriate to try to draw some conclusions about how we might go about constructing an accommodation that transcends "liberal versus conservative" in the expression of religious values in our common life and, at the same time, provides building blocks for the approaches to these questions in the future. This important task should be taken up by a broad group of citizens, not relegated only to national leaders.

The inability of those leaders to inspire confidence as a frustrated electorate chooses to distribute power between competing ideologies in fact suggests that ordinary Americans already may have to be reconciled to supplying the moral vision for themselves. It is in this vacuum that a citizenry schooled in religious values can be most effective as the nation experiments with solutions to particular policy dilemmas. If the language of "values" that now has entered the mainstream political discourse is to be anything more than platitudes, citizens and those entering public life in the future will have to bring to our national problems their own strength of character to give phrases like "personal responsibility" real power and meaning. This suggests that religious values themselves can and must play a bigger role in preparing a wider group for participation in democratic processes.

AN APPROACH TO SPIRITUAL RENEWAL

In previous chapters, we have explored some of the territory where the nation is engaged in a quest for its spiritual bearings. The country does not need yet another political platform, or a new religion. But it might benefit from identifying by consensus a broad but informal "program" for overcoming spiritual, racial, and cultural differences to reach common ground.

The operative concept in the final part of this book has been "style," which suggests not so much a concrete plan to be voted on or adopted, but rather a way of approaching the practical dynamics of spiritual values in American life. I present here some conclusions based on the foundations of interfaith community-building and dialogue that are taking place in the United States and discussed in the case studies earlier in this book. These experiments provide real-world data from which a model can be constructed. The following objectives, therefore, are not mere wishful thinking. Rather, they seem to arise as logical conclusions to be drawn from things that already are happening today in the real world.

Develop a new concept of spiritual citizenship. Americans ought to be able to feel at home in any church, synagogue, mosque, or temple, just as they may be residents of one state but are free to drive anywhere. We should explore new ways of thinking about how the content of different religions might apply to all. To extend the driving analogy, it might be possible to extend the "dialogues" that now exist between individual faith communities and to construct the equivalent of "reciprocal agreements," wherein people are committed to one particular tradition but assimilate the spirit of the others. Some will complain that this goes against their dogmatic convictions and may take offense or stand in the way, but the nation as a whole should press forward. In Orange County, California, the National Conference began conducting a wonderfully successful tour of local houses of worship in the latter part of 1995. This kind of deliberate exposure to the faith resources around us is a foundation upon which societal harmony can be built.

Today, communication, technology, and immigration have made it a smaller world. People now can see for themselves a contradiction that religion must explain even as it searches for ways to bolster its credentials as a solver of problems. Claims that any one denomination holds the exclusive franchise on God will not stand up under scrutiny. Rather than continuing to see this as a problem, we should see it as an opportunity to explore the world's religious thought in the search for universal spiritual principles to supplement the nation's broad-based commitment to democracy.

Americans eventually might come to regard all, not some, of the world's great religions and their teachings as guides and resources for living. Vivekananda's message to the Parliament of the World's Religions in Chicago more than a century ago was a challenge to begin thinking globally in spiritual terms. For religion to have credibility as a provider of solutions, it may be essential that future generations become comfortable with that idea.

Literacy in world religious thought can provide a tool for narrowing the gap between the private lives of religious Americans and the need to have their values put to work for the resolution of our common problems. Without such broad areas of understanding, some good things still will get done by people of good will, but there will be no consensus to empower everybody at the same time toward the same objectives. Those who make exclusive claims, on the other hand, still will deliver their messages to a narrow group of followers. Absent a countervailing broad view, that can only deepen racial and ethnic divisions.

Some ideas for bringing about a new concept of spiritual citizenship follow.

Affirm that the highest ideals lie not within race, ethnicity, or any form of group solidarity, but within those of broadly based religious values. The issue here may be nothing less than how we make democracy work for the long term. Realizing the dream of making the country a canvas on which we paint the bright colors of our diversity well could depend on our success in bonding at the very deepest level of human experience, that of our belief systems. A connection on any lesser ground is precarious at best.

If we learn nothing else from our episodic crises, we will come away wiser as a nation if we understand that the quality of our relationships is related directly to the ideals to which we aspire. If the best we come up with is to advance some limited group identification, that will be our highest ideal, and the standard by which we try to solve our problems.

Our understanding of and respect for others will be limited without understanding and full acceptance of the validity of the beliefs from which attitudes and behavior spring. Americans seem to know little about other religions, and there is not much substantial movement right now in the opposite direction. The observation was made earlier by one of the pioneers in interfaith dialogue in Los Angeles that decades of work still had yet to produce a broad-based interreligious awareness in his city. If that is so among those who are "churched" and presumably motivated, it is not a promising prognosis for much of the nation.

In the aftermath of the O. J. Simpson verdict, the Million Man March, and at other times, we are reminded of vastly different perspectives that people bring to democracy's table. It will be difficult for people in the United States to make meaningful and lasting connections unless they do so on their most cherished territory. This does not mean only in the area of a shared commitment to a system of government. It means doing it at the core of the religious beliefs and attitudes that inform our deepest approaches to living.

One way to think about this is to consider life as a circle; we will be closer together if we orbit near the center rather than at various locations on the perimeter. It is well to talk about getting beyond race, economic class, and gender, but to unite people it may be necessary to give them ideals that speak not only to their political aspirations but also to their souls. In times of strife, the temptation will be strong to return to identification by group or class. If what we aim at and speak to in others is anything other than a common spiritual essence, we will miss the one reliable target and remain vulnerable to misunderstanding.

In interfaith conversation, go beyond preclaiming a commitment to religious liberty. Begin doing the extra work to make better and more lasting connections. An example is the Williamsburg Charter, drafted in 1988 by a group of religious leaders and signed by many national leaders, which articulated a vision of religious liberty under the First Amendment in modern times. It was a wonderful document, reflecting commitment and dedication, and was a substantial achievement given the diversity of the participants. Issued in conjunction with the observation of the 200th anniversary of Virginia's call for the Bill of Rights, it had many shining moments, one of which anticipated a central theme of Stephen L. Carter's popular 1993 book, *The Culture of Disbelief*. It asserted that "The role of religion in American public life is too often devalued or dismissed in public debate, as though the American people's historically vital religious traditions were at best a purely private matter and at worst essentially sectarian."[1]

It is also mentioned as an illustration of what can happen in interfaith discussions. That is, it contains what might be termed in its various forms of expression the "we have our differences" clause. This, in the summary of principles, says, "We acknowledge our deep and continuing differences over religious beliefs, political policies and constitutional interpretations."[2]

There is, of course, a measure of truth in such an acknowledgment. However, interfaith efforts, in their eagerness for a statement that everybody can sign on to, seem almost to anticipate slow progress by providing a disclaimer. It is possible then to say that at least we tried before returning to our various corners.

However, it is one thing to have differences over "policies and constitutional interpretations," many of which have been discussed in this book, and quite another to keep coming up short on "religious beliefs." One of the challenges for the future is to reckon more fully with the question of whether all religions are in fact true, with each providing a separate window on the same divine ground.

A "we have our differences" preamble can be a hint of good intentions about to gather dust. It suggests that the undertaking is merely an exercise in good will, with participants intending to return to whatever they were doing after the salutary words and joint statements. Many will do so unconvinced of the merit of others' beliefs or, worse, resigned to awaiting their conversion.

The point is that it may not be enough any more for the nation simply to salute the achievement of religious liberty. Rather, we may need to shift the discussion of religion in American life away from doctrines and institutions, which indeed are the things over which we have "deep differences" in the beliefs area, and toward the core ideals and messages.

Such a change would represent a significant step forward from the posture of general resignation about our inability to reach agreement. The prevailing assumption is: "The best we can do is affirm human dignity, rather than trying to make sense of the actual content of the religions themselves." That can change if people are willing to do the work.

State clearly that the individual religions have their place and that no attempt will be made to supplant them with some watered-down replacement. This should be understood not as a contradiction of what has preceded, but as an affirmation of the principle that "the more the merrier" applies in the religious life of the nation. Retain what is good and enduring within individual faiths, and recognize the continuing value of custom and tradition. Keep in mind the visions of one nation and one reality behind the faiths.

If this is possible, and it ought to be if the participants in the Hollywood meeting described earlier in the book were correct, then an important observation can be made. Religious understanding really comes down to a statement of confidence that more than one expression of truth can be right and that one's own religious traditions and values will not be shaken loose by exposure to others. At the same time, those who wish to stay exclusively within their own belief systems can be left undisturbed, but invited to learn of the common points to be found in other faiths.

Religious leaders and the congregations that support them will need the maturity and courage to recognize that opening up religious education programs and pulpits to let in the light of the world's religions will not diminish the power and majesty of their own traditions. The idea is not to throw out everything and start over. Customs, rituals, and the teachings of the founding saints provide tangible meaning and context for people trying to come to grips with profound and subtle mysteries. These still can be featured as the main event for the faithful, but presented alongside a broader spectrum of religious thought.

In this era when people already are adapting New Age thinking to their own more established traditions, it ought to be possible on a wide scale to incorporate useful ideas from other religions in one's own basic religious curriculum.

If this seems abstract, consider that the Council on American–Islamic Relations issued a news release to mark the beginning of the monthlong fast of Ramadan in early 1996 that described for a broader audience the activities of Muslims. The goals, it said, were "to learn discipline, self-restraint and generosity while obeying God's commandments." Spiritually inclined people of any faith can identify with those practices and also with the obstacles faced and the benefits received along the journey to personal growth. Indeed, those who capture the true spirit of the world religions' call to a life of self-examination often learn that they share a commonality, in some cases more than with those who do not practice the teachings of their own traditions.

Modern observers may be interested to discover some similarities in the inner life between various faiths. In fact, the rich philosophical tradition of India long has understood there to be a "science" of religion, in which paths of self-examination and personal development can be tailored to meet the personalities, inclinations, and belief systems of any individual. Those approaches can be adaptable to modern life. It is at this level of understanding that benefits for family, community, and nation may be realized most effectively.

Write off everybody over 25. This is an overstatement for dramatic effect, but there's a method in this madness. Wisdom comes with experience, and religiously inclined Americans develop their perspectives and understanding over a lifetime. However, there is no substitute for working on a clean slate. The one sure place we can bring about change in attitude on a broad national scale and for the long term is in the spiritual education of future generations.

We already have examined how the fresh thinking about the discussion of religious topics in the schools offers a new route to accommodation in the struggle to find a balance between separation of church and state. Anybody familiar with the day's news is aware of the tension inherent in introducing worship in the public education area. But we also have seen earlier in the book how some progressive thinking on learning about religion in the schools can promote better understanding and awareness.

The most important arenas in this era of privatizing and localizing approaches to our problems actually may not be in the public schools, but rather in the home and in the religious training that takes place in houses of worship.

Can parents and religious educators see beyond their own backgrounds to learn and also teach about Buddha, Krishna, and St. Francis, for example? This is not so much a question as a challenge. How we respond could have profound consequences for promoting better understanding.

It ought to be easy enough to do, but we know in fact how tricky it will be. In early 1995, Pope John Paul II spoke of his respect and esteem for Buddhism, but not before there was controversy over observations he had made in a book with respect to a perceived indifference in that faith about the world. Some progress is being made at the grassroots level; for example, Americans have had since the late nineteenth century wave after wave of spiritual ambassadors from abroad living in their midst, explaining to people in mostly small groups that the concept of "detachment" in the religions of the East is not at all the same thing as a lack of concern for the affairs of the world. However, if there is confusion among religious leaders, getting teachers to convey such concepts accurately to people learning about religion for the first time poses an extra challenge.

If understanding world religions was previously the province of scholars and browsers in New Age bookstores, we risk misunderstanding in this melting pot of a nation in the future if we do not make the effort to at least expose everybody to others' belief systems. The bedrock American settings of home and Sunday school can be helpful in preparing future generations for meaningful spiritual citizenship.

Young people do not come into the world believing that the particular tradition into which they are born is the sole custodian of ultimate truth. Parochialism is something passed along by elders, who as time goes on, may be inclined themselves to be more fixed, and even inflexible, in their ideas about religion. Having a broad outlook takes work, and doing spiritual work is something that takes personal commitment in adulthood.

In a sense, society's stake in early intervention on religious education parallels the need for early intervention in other areas where young people may be at risk. It's not the same kind of problem as exposure to drugs or gang life, but we should understand that any youngster starting out without some early and broad moral and religious training is to be considered disadvantaged.

Getting any at all will be a start in life. It may be that the home is the best place for training and growth within a particular religious tradition. The area of real innovation for now, however, is more likely to be in the religious education offered in houses of worship. There, with parental support and the leadership of an enlightened clergy, youngsters can be introduced slowly to the wisdom of other faiths. Learning about other religions in the schools can help. It may take several generations to produce a population that is literate in the world's religious traditions, but this will be a formidable achievement if accomplished.

For youngsters with guardians who care enough to provide exposure to religious ideas, obviously, the "risk" of going through life believing that one's religion is the only right one is not anything like losing a generation in a neighborhood to gang life. But centuries of religious strife should caution us against underestimating the misunderstanding that can arise in a nation living at close quarters where opportunities to educate the young are missed.

Don't demean organized "dialogue." Encourage it as the best small-group device available to break the ice. We find from our national experience that there are those only too willing to criticize as cosmetic any efforts to bridge social and cultural differences through such initiatives as the "Hands Across L.A." after the 1992 riots and the "Day of Dialogue" that followed the verdict in the O. J. Simpson murder case in 1995. In the case of the former, there were some liberals who thought that it was at best a media event, and in the case of the latter there were conservatives who proclaimed it a waste of time.

Symbolic events and conversations should not be expected alone to produce solutions, but can be regarded as one aspect of the larger work of identifying common ground. Various denominations in major cities have taken the idea of "dialogue" seriously enough to engage in faith-to-faith conversations. The National Conference has done important work in this area. The authors Cornel West and Michael Lerner report from their public dialogues between blacks and Jews that many young people seemed enthusiastic about improving relations between the two communities.

This work is but a small component of what it could be considering the melting pot of religions we now have. However, the alternative to something is always nothing or, worse, in the case of relations between ethnic and religious groups, the suspicion and misunderstanding that arise from silence. Moreover, we learned from a tragedy in Israel about the power of words when extreme rhetoric found expression in the assassination of a leader committed to making peace, Prime Minister Yitzhak Rabin. If words can lead to terrible outcomes, they also must be understood to possess the power to build bridges.

Reaching out must be not only for the mainstream groups.

Some of the custodians of the religious perspectives newer to the American landscape have kept to themselves for reasons such as preserving community identity or even fear of persecution. Immigrant followers need no help in understanding the cultural and spiritual depths of their own traditions, but many Americans regard them as curiosities, if they pay any attention to them at all.

It is time to move these faiths out of the categories of self-help and New Age experimentation and into the mainstream of national resources. The country never will benefit fully from the wealth of spiritual knowledge contained in Islam, Hinduism, and Buddhism, for example, if the great messages of these groups are not exposed to broader audiences and, in the cases of certain counterculture groups, if followers in the United States are left to alter their cultural identities.

Reject any plan to change the Constitution with a "Religious Equality Amendment," or something like it. There is enough room for the free exercise of religion in what we have now. Professor Benjamin J. Hubbard, professor and chair of the Department of Religious Studies at California State University, Fullerton, is among those who have written eloquently about the sturdy serviceability of the First Amendment. As he notes, for example, proposed guidelines of the Equal Employment Opportunity Commission that would have said having a Bible on one's desk at work created a hostile work environment were squelched in a Senate hearing in 1994. He also observes that it is easy enough for teachers to offer explanations of various religious holidays and festivals during the school year or to show respect for the beliefs of evangelical Christians, Orthodox Jews, Muslims, and Jehovah's Witnesses who are uncomfortable with Halloween and leave the observance to parents.[3] We don't need to change the Constitution.

Find innovative ways of having government and religion work toward common objectives. The strict separationists may resist, but this book has reported on some trends that suggest it can happen without threatening the cherished principle of separation of church and state. These include the evolving concept of "civil religion" and the collaborative work of local government and community groups.

Meanwhile, the nation is in need of striking a balance between powerful political ideas. The first is the notion ascendant in the Republican landslide of 1994 that less government is better and that decision-making should be returned to localities. The second is the longstanding "value" of the Democrats that government must provide a safety net and be an advocate for social justice. Religion can help pave the way for responsible, moderate strategies that incorporate the best ideas of contending groups.

Collaborations between government and religion that help society address its problems without being constitutionally problematic should be facilitated. The experience in Anaheim, California, is a case in point. There, a motivated faith community, the presence of church infrastructure, and a receptive city government combined to make sufficient progress over a 10-year period that the community began to move from basic safety and survival concerns to take up its next priorities, job training and education.

Almost nobody there was talking about political philosophy. The Williamsburg Charter's summary of principles got it right: "The No Establishment clause separates Church from State but not religion from politics or public life. It prevents the confusion of religion and government which has been a leading source of repression and coercion throughout history."[4]

Educate current and future business leaders to recognize that they too must be involved in sustaining community life. Corporate profits and strategies are in the province of business and public policy experts, but they have significance for the spiritual health and well-being of the nation. The growing income gap, the stirring of economic populism brought on by the disruptiveness of new technology, mergers and corporate restructuring, the decline in real wages are signs of a toll being taken on the morale and psyche of the nation. Leading economic thinkers like Rosabeth Moss Kanter have said that enlightened companies recognize the benefit for themselves of sharing the benefits of their prosperity with workers. Interestingly, there is a kind of parallel between having a forward-looking global economic culture planted in American localities and having the core values that inform people's daily lives anchored in world religious thought. What the two have in common is the infusion of global thinking into what happens locally.

These concerns are a reminder that with all the attention given to social and cultural issues in the debate over "family values," there are still bread-and-butter economic issues of abiding importance. Those who bring spiritual perspectives to the public policy arena have fertile ground and much work to do in advancing the notion of the value and dignity of labor.

Having made provisions for the diversity of religious views in the lifeblood of the nation, having resolved to leave the Constitution alone, the nation should be confident about broadening the intersection of religion and moral values in the public square. For all its excesses, the religious right, which prefers to think of itself as a family values movement, deserves acknowledgment for its contribution to a national awareness of a pervasive moral crisis. The conservative ascendancy in politics with which it has been allied had its roots in significant historical trends: the demise of confidence in big government and the social upheaval of the 1960s. To this, however, the social and cultural conservatives have added a powerful set of national concerns about family structure and moral well-being.

The policy issues with which the religious right is allied are by nature topics on which reasonable and moral people can disagree. However, the larger notion of moving the country in the direction of a new spiritual style, specifically, toward an environment in which it is desirable and possible to bring religious values openly into the public square, may be a more enduring legacy. The activism of church-based liberals in the civil rights and anti-war movements has been enormously significant, of course, but those efforts did not also leave the nation with an enduring preoccupation with values in every corner of our national life.

What is new today is that, increasingly, people across the political spectrum are becoming convinced that there is a moral component to the deterioration of the social fabric. While this ground was charted by social and cultural conservatives, it is in fact work that must be picked up by people in the middle.

The activist moderates the country needs are in short supply, but the best way of producing them may be to cultivate a core of citizens whose guiding principles arise from a wide religious base, so that nobody is made to feel excluded or persecuted. The conflict between the religious right and liberals explored earlier in the book has its own dynamics and may not be entirely resolvable by a broad-based accommodation that regards all the faiths as common resources. However, there is unlikely to be any common ground established between these contending parties over the perceived "moral crisis" without also expanding our sense of what we mean when we talk about allowing the full play of religious values "in the public square." Moderates grounded in broad religious understanding will be the pragmatists in future generations with the best hope of seeing the moral dimensions in the whole of life. This is why getting the diversity of religious perspectives now available into mainstream American life is so important.

Today, we find ourselves living with a kind of paradox. The nation is light years away from having in place the kind of serviceable interfaith understanding that can support it in times of trauma. At the same time, this gap could be bridged very quickly if enough citizens were willing to modify deep-seated attitudes or simply to begin thinking in broader terms about "religious values."

It is fair to ask whether the public is ready to make these adjustments. The existence of a tolerant "moral middle" that shares with religious conservatives a set of concerns about a crisis of values suggests that the foundation for such a new accommodation is there. But in any case, our new diversity is a powerful engine that is moving us in this direction on its own.

The best investment well may lie in a generational strategy. The nation should try to incorporate some of these ideas by the middle of the twenty-first century and all of them by its end. There are a number of groups exploring this area now, but as a society, we remain very much in the early stages of work. Enthusiasm even among the committed can be affected by such changeable factors as the commitment at any particular time of top church leadership, the distractions of daily institutional operations, and the importance or lack thereof assigned to this work by congregations.

We can get in the express lane or we can take the slow boat. Either way, this work likely will not be optional in the future. At least, it will not be so if religion is to play a truly meaningful role in sustaining a healthy democracy in the centuries to come.

Notes

CHAPTER ONE

1. The poll results were reported in Jeffery L. Sheler, "Spiritual America: This Nation 'Under God' Is Deeply Conflicted Over the Role of Society in Religion," *U.S. News & World Report*, April 4, 1994.
2. Christopher John Farley, "Prodding Voters to the Right," *Time*, November 21, 1994.
3. "Washington Wire," *Wall Street Journal*, November 11, 1994.
4. Gustav Niebuhr, "Full G.O.P. Menu Splits the Religious Right," *New York Times*, January 19, 1996.
5. Religion News Service, "Religious Right Yields Limelight in GOP—for Now," *Los Angeles Times*, August 17, 1996.
6. Ronald Brownstein, "Christian Coalition Attacks Clinton," *Los Angeles Times*, September 14, 1996.
7. Irving Kristol, "Conservative Christians: Into the Fray," *Wall Street Journal*, December 22, 1995.
8. Author's interview with the Rev. Stephen J. Mather, Anaheim, CA, July 6, 1994.
9. Gustav Niebuhr, "Church Group Seeks Political Middle Ground," *New York Times*, May 23, 1995.
10. Mather interview, July 6, 1994.
11. Ralph Reed, "Conservative Coalition Holds Firm," *Wall Street Journal*, February 13, 1995.
12. Reed, *Wall Street Journal*, February 13, 1995.
13. Laurie Goodstein, "Alternative Is Offered to Religious Right Plan," *Washington Post*. Reprinted in *Boston Globe*, May 24, 1995.
14. Brownstein, *Los Angeles Times*, September 14, 1996.
15. Elyce Wakerman, "Alliance Seeks to Counter Religious Right," *Los Angeles Times*, June 29, 1996.

16. John Balzar, "Women of Influence Feel Estranged from the GOP," *Los Angeles Times*, June 2, 1996.

17. Kim Hubbard and Linda Kramer, "Bio: Ralph Reed," *People*, February 27, 1995, pp. 60–64.

18. Gustav Niebuhr, "Olive Branch to Jews from Conservative Christian," *New York Times*, April 4, 1995.

19. Ralph Reed, "We Stand at a Crossroads," *Newsweek*, May 13, 1996, pp. 28–29; the article is an excerpt from *Active Faith*, New York: Free Press, 1996.

20. Ralph Reed, *Politically Incorrect, The Emerging Faith Factor in American Politics*, Dallas, TX: Word Publishing, 1994, p. 242.

21. Anti-Defamation League, *The Religious Right: The Assault on Tolerance & Pluralism in America*, New York: ADL, 1990, pp. 11–26.

22. Frank Rich, "Bait and Switch," *New York Times*, March 2, 1995.

23. "Two Letters and Excerpts from Book," *New York Times*, March 4, 1995.

24. Lisa Richardson, "This Gingrich a Proponent of Gay Pride," *Los Angeles Times*, July 13, 1995.

25. Reed, *Wall Street Journal*, February 13, 1995.

26. Richard L. Berke, "Is Suffering in Silence the Democrats' Cross?" *New York Times*, August 21, 1994.

27. Ronald Brownstein, "Failure of Both Parties to Deliver Could Spawn a Third," *Los Angeles Times*, January 2, 1995.

28. "The People, the Press & Politics: The New Political Landscape," Times Mirror Center for the People and the Press, September 21, 1994.

29. "America's Challenge: Revitalizing Our National Community," Senator Bill Bradley (D-New Jersey), in an address to The National Press Club, Washington, February 9, 1995.

CHAPTER TWO

1. Ronald Brownstein, "Polarization Politics Seen as Key Obstacle to Welfare Proposal," *Los Angeles Times*, June 15, 1994.

2. An excellent analysis of the evolution of the Christian right can be found in Nancy T. Ammerman, "North American Protestant Fundamentalism," in *Fundamentalism Observed*, Martin E. Marty and R. Scott Appelby (Eds.), Chicago: University of Chicago, 1991, pp. 42–56.

3. James Davison Hunter, "Before the Shooting Begins," *Columbia Journalism Review*, July/August 1993, pp. 29–32.

4. John M. Pitney, Jr., "Left's Muddled Assault on the Religious Right," *Los Angeles Times*, June 30, 1994.

5. Ronald Brownstein, "Is the GOP Too Timid to Say No to the Religious Right?" Washington Outlook, *Los Angeles Times*, July 11, 1994.

6. Bob Sipchen, "The Worried Women Bloc Prefers Clinton," *Los Angeles Times*, April 29, 1996.

7. Michael Kinsley, "Casting Stones," *New York Times*, July 5, 1994.

8. Robert Shogan, "GOP Has Pulpit at Meeting of Religious Right," *Los Angeles Times*, September 18, 1994.

9. E. J. Dionne, Jr., "Bill & Dan & Murphy Brown," *Washington Post*, September 13, 1994.

10. James Wolcott, "Beyond the Values of the Supervixens," *The New Yorker*, February 13, 1995, pp. 89–91.

11. David R. Carlin, Jr., "It's the Culture, Stupid," *Commonweal*, September 23, 1994, pp. 9–10.

12. Heather R. Higgins, "The Principles behind the Policies," *Wall Street Journal*, February 16, 1995.

13. Paul Lewis, "Column Left: Let Someone Else Try on the '96 Ticket," *Los Angeles Times*, February 21, 1995.

14. Laurie Goodstein, "Mixing God and Politics Concerns Evangelical Leaders," *Los Angeles Times–Washington Post* News Service, March 27, 1995.

CHAPTER THREE

1. Religious News Service, "Conflicts between Church, State on Rise," *Los Angeles Times*, September 25, 1993.

2. David G. Savage, "The Duel Over Prayer in Schools," *Los Angeles Times*, April 13, 1994.

3. American Jewish Congress, "Religion in the Public Schools: A Joint Statement of Current Law," Washington, DC: AJC. April 1995.

4. Anthony Lewis, "On Madison's Grave," *New York Times*, November 7, 1994.

5. This argument was made forcefully by James M. Wall, editor of *The Christian Century*, in an article written for *Newsday* in January 1995 and distributed by the *Los Angeles Times–Washington Post* News Service.

6. James Davison Hunter, "Before the Shooting Begins," *Columbia Journalism Review*, July/August 1993, p. 30.

7. Cornel West, *Race Matters*, Boston: Beacon Press, 1992, p. 49.

8. Transcript, "A *Firing Line* Debate, Resolved: We Need Not Fear the Religious Right." *National Review*, 1993, pp. 3–5.

9. Transcript, "A *Firing Line* Debate, Resolved ...," p. 3.

10. Transcript, "A *Firing Line* Debate, Resolved ...," p. 4.
11. Transcript, "A *Firing Line* Debate, Resolved ...," p. 9.
12. Transcript, "A *Firing Line* Debate, Resolved ...," p. 9.
13. Transcript, "A *Firing Line* Debate, Resolved ...," p. 9.
14. "A *Firing Line* Debate: Resolved: The Wall of Separation between Church and State Should Be Lowered," aired on public television station KCET Los Angeles, September 16, 1994. All quotes from this show are from a recording made by the author.
15. Robert N. Bellah, "Civil Religion in America," in *Religion in America*, William G. McLoughlin and Robert N. Bellah (Eds.), Boston: Beacon Press, 1968, p. 21.
16. "Orange County Newswatch," *Los Angeles Times*, Orange County edition, November 27, 1994.
17. *A Public Voice '94: Politicians & Journalists Address the Federal Deficit, Poverty & Health Care Costs*, a PBS program that aired on KOCE, Huntington Beach, California, October 5, 1994. Quoted from a recording made by the author.

CHAPTER FOUR

1. Richard L. Berke, "White House Tries to Clarify Stand on School Prayer," *New York Times*, November 18, 1994.
2. Kenneth L. Woodward, "Soulful Matters," *Newsweek*, October 31, 1994, p. 23.
3. Robert N. Bellah, "Civil Religion in America," in *Religion in America*, William G. McLoughlin and Robert N. Bellah (Eds.), Boston: Beacon Press, 1968, pp. 3–23.
4. Bellah, p. 5.
5. Bellah, p. 21.
6. Religious News Service, "Clinton Attempting to Combine Moral Vision with Political Message," *Los Angeles Times*, May 21, 1994.
7. Gustav Niebuhr, "Books on Faith Are a Comfort, President Says," *New York Times*, October 4, 1994.
8. The White House, Office of the Press Secretary, "Remarks by the President in Photo Opportunity during White House Interfaith Breakfast," August 30, 1993.
9. John M. Broder, "Clinton Vows to Battle National 'Crisis of Spirit,'" *Los Angeles Times*, November 14, 1993.
10. Paul Richter, "Clinton Appeals to Hollywood on Film, TV Violence," *Los Angeles Times*, December 5, 1993.

11. Ronald Brownstein, "Democrats to Spotlight Pro-Family Agenda," *Los Angeles Times*, August 27, 1996.
12. Bernard Weinraub, "Despite Clinton, Hollywood Is Still Trading in Violence," *New York Times*, December 28, 1993.
13. Ellen Goodman, syndicated column released January 28, 1994; copyright, The Boston Globe Newspaper Co.
14. Paul Richter, "Clinton Tells Students Sex Is 'Solemn Responsibility,'" *Los Angeles Times*, February 4, 1994.
15. Douglas Jehl, "Echoing a Kennedy, Clinton Calls for Peace," *New York Times*, May 15, 1994.
16. Michael Wines, "Lamenting Petty Politics, Clinton Pushes Crime Bill," *New York Times*, August 15, 1994.
17. The White House, Office of the Press Secretary, "Remarks of the First Lady at Liz Carpenter's Lectureship Series," University of Texas, April 6, 1993.
18. Michael Kelly, "Saint Hillary," *New York Times Magazine*, May 23, 1993.
19. Nancy Benac, "In Thirst for Input, Clinton Consults Friends, CEOs, Academics, Gurus," The Associated Press, March 7, 1995.
20. Howard Fineman, "The Virtuecrats," *Newsweek*, June 13, 1994, p. 31.
21. Gerald F. Seib, "The Federalist: Alexander Would Send Chunks of Government Back to the States," *Wall Street Journal*, February 24, 1995.
22. John Harwood, "Candidate Phil Gramm Rarely Skips a Chance to Raise More Money," *Wall Street Journal*, February 17, 1995.
23. Michael Kelly, "Bill Clinton's Climb," *New York Times Magazine*, July 31, 1994.
24. "Polls Show More Than Economy Dogs Clinton's Appeal Ratings," *Los Angeles Times*, September 18, 1994.
25. David Lauter, "Times Poll: Clinton Image Hurts Him, Not His Ideas," *Los Angeles Times*, January 28, 1995.
26. David S. Broder, "Clinton's One-Year Report Card: C," *Los Angeles Times*, January 16, 1994.
27. John M. Broder, "Administration Ethics: What Went Wrong?" *Los Angeles Times*, February 25, 1995.
28. Charles Krauthammer, "Why Whitewater Matters," *Time*, March 28, 1994, p. 76.
29. Eleanor Clift and Mark Miller, "Saint or Sinner?" *Newsweek*, April 11, 1994, pp. 24–26.
30. Ronald Brownstein, "Administration Tackles 'Great Crisis of the Spirit,' in America," *Los Angeles Times*, December 22, 1993.
31. Ronald Brownstein, "The Times Poll: Good Feelings Carry Clinton to Solid Lead," *Los Angeles Times*, September 12, 1996.

32. Letters to the Editor, "Don't Trust God to the Politicians," *Wall Street Journal*, March 29, 1995.
33. William Safire, "Blizzard of Lies," *New York Times*, January 8, 1996.
34. William Safire, "Clinton at His Best," *New York Times*, May 16, 1994.

CHAPTER FIVE

1. MacNeil–Lehrer News Hour, November 7, 1994.
2. Michael Barone and Grant Ujifusa, *Almanac of American Politics 1996*, Washington, DC: National Journal Inc., 1995, p. 763.
3. "Ten-Point Coalition Hopes to Counter Religious Right," transcript, National Public Radio, May 20, 1995. Segment reported by Tovia Smith, member station WBUR in Boston.
4. James L. Franklin, "Housing Pact Shows Coalition's Clout," *Boston Globe*, October 3, 1994.

CHAPTER SIX

1. Orange County Congregation Community Organization (OCCCO), Convention 1992 booklet, p. 5.
2. OCCCO, p. 5.
3. The *Times* poll, taken July 23–26, 1994, surveyed 1515 adults nationally; results were reported in *The Los Angeles Times*, July 28, 1994. The margin of sampling error was ± 3 percentage points.
4. Dianne Horn. Telephone interview by author, Orange County, CA, fall 1994.
5. Greg Hernandez, "Church Alliance Gains Support by Offering Solutions," *Los Angeles Times*, Orange County edition, January 8, 1995.
6. The attendance estimate of 350 is from Leslie Berkman, "Residents Plead for More Youth Programs," *Los Angeles Times*, Orange County edition, June 21, 1994.
7. Jaime Soto, "Orange County Voices: Santa Ana Shows Unity in Divided Times," *Los Angeles Times*, Orange County edition, June 7, 1994.
8. Author's notes, Orange County Congregation, Community Organization meeting at St. Boniface Church, Anaheim, CA, June 20, 1994.
9. Meeting notes, June 20, 1994.
10. Michael Barone and Grand Ujifusa, *Almanac of American Politics 1994*, Washington, DC: National Journal Inc., 1994, p. 196.
11. Robert Scheer, "Celebrating Its 100th Year; A Frontier Dream Comes of Age for Orange County," *Los Angeles Times*, June 4, 1989.

12. Robert Scheer, "Residents Complex, Polls Show: Orange County, Home of the Happy and Optimistic," *Los Angeles Times*, June 5, 1989. The article reported on polling conducted for the newspaper by Mark Baldassare & Associates.

13. Matt Lait, "Bloody O.C. Weekend: 6 Slain and 8 Wounded," and Len Hall and Anna Cekola, "O.C. Teen Remains in Deep Coma," *Los Angeles Times*, Orange County edition, March 18, 1993.

14. Rene Lynch and Ching-Ching Ni, "Long Prison Term in Woods Slaying Stirs Emotions," *Los Angeles Times*, Orange County edition, January 28, 1995.

15. Mark Baldassare and Cheryl Katz, *Orange County Annual Survey: 1993 Final Report*, Irvine: University of California, Irvine.

16. "Southern California's Problems Are O.C.'s Problems, Says 1993 Survey," *UCI News*, November 30, 1993.

17. Eric Lichtblau, "We're Not All Getting Along," *Los Angeles Times*, Orange County edition, October 24, 1993. The article reported on a *Times* poll of 943 adults in Orange County conducted by telephone.

18. Lynn Smith and Dave Lesher, "Christian Activists Assume Large Role in O.C. Politics," *Los Angeles Times*, Orange County edition, December 20, 1991.

CHAPTER SEVEN

1. Author's interview with Steve Swaim, Anaheim, CA, July 6, 1994.

2. Matt Lait, "Anti-Abortion Rally Targets Pastor's Role," *Los Angeles Times*, Orange County edition, June 27, 1994.

3. Author's interview with the Rev. John Lenihan, Anaheim, CA, June 24, 1994.

4. City of Anaheim, *Gang/Drug Citizens Task Force Report*, June 1992.

5. City of Anaheim, *Gang/Drug Citizens Task Force Report*.

6. Swaim interview, July 6, 1994.

7. Author's interview with the Rev. Stephen J. Mather, Anaheim, CA, July 6, 1994.

8. Swaim interview, July 6, 1994.

9. Swaim interview, July 6, 1994.

10. Author's telephone interview with John Gaudette, Orange County, CA, 1996.

11. Swaim interview, July 6, 1994.

12. Elizabeth Shogan, "Traditional Family Nearly the Exception, Census Finds," *Los Angeles Times*, August 30, 1994.

13. Mark I. Pinsky, "Houses of Worship Return to a Full-Service Concept," *Los Angeles Times*, Orange County edition, December 16, 1991.

14. Lenihan interview, June 24, 1994.
15. Horn interview, fall 1994.
16. Mather interview, July 6, 1994.

CHAPTER EIGHT

1. Ronald Brownstein, "The Times Poll: Dissatisfied Americans May Spell Democrat Losses," *Los Angeles Times*, July 28, 1994.
2. PBS's *Washington Week in Review*, September 16, 1994.
3. Steven V. Roberts, "The Religious Right: Church Meets State," *U.S. News & World Report*, April 24, 1994, p. 26.
4. Melissa Healy, "Fighting to Fill the Values Gap," *Los Angeles Times*, May 26, 1996.
5. Liz McCloskey. Telephone interview with author, spring 1995.
6. John Gaudette. Telephone interview with author, summer 1996.
7. Mario M. Cuomo, "Religous Belief and Public Morality: A Catholic Governor's Perspective," September 13, 1984, speech delivered to the Department of Theology at the University of Notre Dame.
8. Seth Mydans, "A City Pulls Its School Board Back toward the Center," *New York Times*, November 28, 1994.
9. Mather interview, July 6, 1994.

CHAPTER NINE

1. John Dart, "Riordan Is a Catholic, but He'll Be Judged On His Acts as Mayor," *Los Angeles Times*, July 17, 1993.
2. Dart, *Los Angeles Times*, July 17, 1993.
3. Larry B. Stammer, "Massive Post-Riot Efforts Have Fallen Short, Clergy Say," *Los Angeles Times*, June 9, 1993.
4. Author's interview with the Rev. Vivian Ben Lima, Los Angeles, October 24, 1994.
5. The Religion and Civil Order Project, *Politics of the Spirit, Religion and Multiethnicity in Los Angeles*, Los Angeles: University of Southern California, 1994.
6. Stammer, *Los Angeles Times*, June 9, 1993.
7. Author's telephone interview with Rabbi Harvey J. Fields, Los Angeles, fall 1994 and summer 1996.
8. Author's interview with Dr. Maher Hathout, Duarte, CA, fall 1994.
9. The Religion and Civil Order Project, p. 8.
10. Fields interview, fall 1994.

11. Author's telephone interview with Rabbi Alfred Wolf, fall 1994.
12. Wolf interview, fall 1994.
13. Lima interview, October 24, 1994.
14. Hathout interview, fall 1994.
15. Hathout interview, fall 1994.
16. Fields interview, fall 1994.
17. The Religion and Civil Order Project, p. 1.
18. The Religion and Civil Order Project, p. 2.
19. The Religion and Civil Order Project, p. 36.
20. The Religion and Civil Order Project, p. 12.
21. John Orr, "Empower Communities to Stay Healthy," *Los Angeles Times*, September 17, 1996.
22. Rosanne Keynan, "Southern California File," *Los Angeles Times*, June 26, 1993.

CHAPTER TEN

1. Author's interview with Dr. Maher Hathout, Duarte, CA, fall 1994.
2. Hathout interview, fall 1994.
3. Hathout interview, fall 1994.
4. Dennis Prager, KABC Radio, Los Angeles, January 6, 1995.
5. Peter Steinfels, "Religious Leaders Hold a 2d World Parliament," *New York Times*, August 30, 1993.
6. Audiotape, Vivekananda Centenary Service, Vedanta Society of Southern California, Hollywood, May 2, 1993.
7. Vivekananda Centenary Service, May 2, 1993.
8. Vivekananda Centenary Service, May 2, 1993.
9. Koran quotation from Huston Smith, "Islam," in *The Religions of Man*, New York: Perennial Library, 1965, p. 249.
10. Vivekananada Centenary Service, May 2, 1993.
11. The view of other religions is in the pamphlet *Introduction to Science of Spirituality*, published by Science of Spirituality, Naperville, IL.
12. Author's notes, Interfaith Spiritual Dialogue, Airport Hilton, Los Angeles, CA, August 1, 1994.

CHAPTER ELEVEN

1. George W. Cornell, "The Evolution of the Religion Beat," in Benjamin J. Hubbard (ed.), *Reporting Religion: Facts & Faith*, Sonoma, CA: Polebridge Press, 1990, pp. 26–30.

2. Remarks by the Rev. Vivian Ben Lima at Vivekananada Centenary Service, Hollywood, CA, May 2, 1993.
3. Remarks by Dr. Fred Register at Vivekananada Centenary Service, Hollywood, CA, May 2, 1993.
4. Fields interview, fall 1994.

CHAPTER TWELVE

1. "On Values: Talking with Peggy Noonan," produced by WNET, aired on KCET, Los Angeles, February 10, 1995.
2. Viveca Kovak, "Clinton Wants a Religion-Friendly White House, but Acting on His Strong Views Will Be Tricky," *Wall Street Journal*, February 6, 1995.
3. Linda Greenhouse, "Justices Hear Campus Religion Case," *New York Times*, March 2, 1995.
4. Anti-Defamation League, *The Relgious Right: The Assault on Tolerance & Pluralism in America*, New York: ADL, 1994, p. 7.
5. Jonathan Kaufman, "Religious Fervor: Some Liberal Jews, to Their Own Surprise, See a Rise in Bigotry," *Wall Street Journal*, March 8, 1995.
6. Anti-Defamation League, p. iv.
7. Anti-Defamation League, pp. 71–72.
8. Religious News Service, "Jews, Conservative Christians Defuse War of Words," *Los Angeles Times*, December 3, 1994.
9. "Los Angeles Times Poll: Mood of the Nation," *Los Angeles Times*, January 24, 1995. The poll interviewed 1353 adults nationwide by telephone January 19–22. The margin of sampling error was ± 3 percentage points.
10. Paul A. Gigot, "What the Christian Right Was Really Trying to Say," Potomac Watch, *Wall Street Journal*, February 17, 1995.
11. "Spiritual America," *U.S. News & World Report*, April 4, 1994, p. 54.
12. C-SPAN, National Rainbow Coalition coverage, January 7, 1995.
13. Kimberly J. McLarin, "Curriculum or Not, Teachers Teach Values," *New York Times*, February 1, 1995.
14. Charles C. Haynes (Ed.), *Finding Common Ground: A First Amendment Guide to Religion and Public Education*, Nashville, TN: The Freedom Forum First Amendment Center, 1994.
15. Haynes, Chapter 1, p. 3.
16. Remarks during panel discussion on November 28, 1994 at The Freedom Forum World Center in Arlington, Virginia. News release by The Freedom Forum.
17. Haynes, Chapter 5, p. 1.

18. *60 Minutes*, aired on KCBS, Los Angeles, March 26, 1995.
19. Benjamin J. Hubbard, "Cautionary Tales about Religious Agendas," *Los Angeles Times*, Orange County edition, November 14, 1994.
20. Letters to the Editor, "Don't Entrust God to the Politicians," *Wall Street Journal*, March 29, 1995.
21. Gertrude Himmelfarb, "Beyond Social Policy: Re-Moralizing America," *Wall Street Journal*, February 7, 1995.
22. John Leo, "Praying for Sanity in Schools," *U.S. News & World Report*, November 28, 1994.
23. McLarin, *New York Times*, February 1, 1995.
24. Maureen Dowd, "Americans Like G.O.P. Agenda but Split on How to Reach Goals," *New York Times*, December 15, 1994.
25. Swami Akhilananda, *Hindu Psychology, Its Meaning for the West*, London: Routledge & Kegan Paul Ltd., 1948, introduction, p. x.
26. Thomas Moore, *Care of the Soul*, New York: HarperCollins, 1994, p. xvi.

CHAPTER THIRTEEN

1. Mike Wallace's interview with Ann Richards and former New York governor Mario M. Cuomo appeared on CBS's *60 Minutes* in a segment aired March 12, 1995.
2. John P. Sears, "The GOP Weighs Support from Christian Coalition," *Los Angeles Times*, May 21, 1995.
3. Jeffery L. Sheler, "Spiritual America," *U.S. News & World Report*, April 4, 1994, p. 49.
4. Ralph Reed, *Politically Incorrect, The Emerging Faith Factor in American Politics*, Dallas, TX: Word Publishing, 1994, p. 141.
5. Huston Smith, *The Religions of Man*, New York: Perennial Library, 1965, p. 126.
6. The Dalai Lama, "The Way to Freedom: Core Teachings of Tibetan Buddhism," San Francisco: Harper San Francisco, 1994.
7. Katha Upanishad, "The Parable of the Individual Soul in a Chariot," in *The Thirteen Prinicipal Upanishads* (2nd ed., rev.), Robert Ernest Hume (Ed.), Oxford: Oxford University Press, 1965, p. 351.
8. John Leo, "On Society: The Unmaking of Civic Culture," *U.S. News & World Report*, February 13, 1995.
9. Robert N. Bellah, Richard Madsen, William M. Sullivan, Ann Swidler, and Steven M. Tipton, *Habits of the Heart, Individualism and Commitment in American Life*, New York: Perennial Library, 1986, pp. 235–237.
10. Smith, p. 22.
11. George F. Will, "About Those 'Orphanages,'" *Newsweek*, December 12, 1994, p. 88.

12. Don Eberly, "Beyond Social Policy: Even Newt Can't Save Us," *Wall Street Journal*, February 3, 1995.
13. Gary Wills, *Under God: Religion and American Politics*, New York: Touchstone, 1990, p. 371.
14. Thomas Moore, *Care of the Soul*, New York: HarperCollins, 1994, p. 232.
15. A superb discussion on Holmes and Brandeis is contained in Anthony Lewis, *Make No Law: The Sullivan Case and the First Amendment*, New York: Random House, 1991, pp. 80–89.
16. Kenneth L. Woodward, "What Is Virtue?" *Newsweek*, June 13, 1994.
17. Dr. Maher Hathout's remarks, Vivekananda Centenary Service, Hollywood, CA, May 2, 1993.

CHAPTER FOURTEEN

1. Transcript, Bob Abernethy's report on religious diversity on *NBC Nightly News*, March 12, 1995, National Broadcasting Co., Inc.
2. "Speech: Clinton Pushes Health Plan," *Los Angeles Times*, January 26, 1994.
3. Letters to the Editor, "Healing San Francisco Is Not a Job for Bricks and Mortar," *San Francisco Examiner*, December 19, 1993.
4. Richard N. Ostling, "In So Many Gods We Trust," *Time*, January 30, 1995.
5. Transcript, *NBC Nightly News*, March 12, 1995.
6. John Dart, "A Closer Look at Islam in the West," *Los Angeles Times*, December 10, 1995.
7. Christopher Wilson, "Havel Urges U.S. to Take Global Responsibility," *Reuter*, June 8, 1995.
8. James Brooke, "Amid Islam's Growth in the U.S., Muslims Face a Surge in Attacks," *New York Times*, August 28, 1995.
9. Ronald C. White, Jr., "An Unsettled Arena: Religion and the First Amendment," in *A Time for Choices*, Claudia A. Haskel and Jean H. Otto (Eds.), Denver, CO: First Amendment Congress, 1991, p. 15.
10. White, pp. 17–18.
11. Kevin Starr, "For L.A., There Is No Destiny without Unity," *Los Angeles Times*, October 24, 1993.
12. Herbert Croly, *The Promise of American Life*, New Brunswick, NJ: Transaction, 1992.
13. Newton N. Minow and Craig L. LaMay, "From Wasteland to Land of the Wasted," *Los Angeles Times*, July 9, 1993.
14. The Associated Press, "Gallup Says Media Should Focus on Religion, the 'New Frontier,'" *Los Angeles Times*, March 14, 1992.

15. Susan Chira, "Generation That Left Church Goes Back with Its Children," *New York Times*, December 26, 1993.
16. The Associated Press, *Los Angeles Times*, March 14, 1992.
17. White, p. 18.
18. Garry Wills, *Under God: Religion and American Politics*, New York: Touchstone, 1990, p. 347.
19. Alexis de Tocqueville, *Democracy in America*, New York: The New American Library, 1956.
20. Robert N. Bellah, Richard Madsen, William M. Sullivan, Ann Swidler, and Steven M. Tipton, *Habits of the Heart, Individualism and Commitment in American Life*, New York: Perennial Library, 1986, p. 220.

CHAPTER FIFTEEN

1. "The Williamsburg Charter," reprinted as an appendix in Charles C. Haynes (Ed.), *Finding Common Ground, A First Amendment Guide to Religion and Public Education*, Nashville, TN: The Freedom Forum First Amendment Center, 1994, appendix A, p. 7.
2. "The Williamsburg Charter," Chapter 2, p. 2.
3. Benjamin J. Hubbard, "More Awareness, Not an Equality Amendment, Is Needed," *Los Angeles Times*, Orange County edition, October 1, 1995.
4. "Williamsburg Charter," Chapter 2, p. 3.

Index